THE BIG BANKROLL

THE BIG

BANKROLL

The Life and Times of Arnold Rothstein

LEO KATCHER

DA CAPO PRESS

Library of Congress Cataloging in Publication Data

Katcher, Leo.
  The big bankroll: the life and times of Arnold Rothstein /
Leo Katcher.—1st Da Capo Press ed.
     p.   cm.
  Originally published: New York: Harper, 1959.
  Includes bibliographical references and index.
  ISBN 0-306-80565-0
  1. Rothstein, Arnold, 1882-1928. 2. Criminals—United
States—Biography. I. Title.
HV6248.R7K3—1994
364.1′092—dc20   93-38956
[B]   CIP

Da Capo Press books are abailable at special discounts for bulk
purchases in the U.S. by corporations, institutions, and other
organizatons. For more information, please contact the Special
Markets Department at the Perseus Books Group, 11 Cambridge
Center, Cambridge, MA 02142, or call (617) 252-5298

First Da Capo Press edition 1994

This Da Capo Press paperback edition of *The Big Bankroll*
is an unabridged republication of the edition published
in New York in 1959.

Published by Da Capo Press,
A Member of the Perseus Books Group
http://www.dacapopress.com

Manufactured in the United States of America

10 9 8 7 6 5 4 3

Contents

For Dee

THE BIG BANKROLL

Preface and Acknowledgment

It is now some twenty-five years since I first interested myself in the life and career of Arnold Rothstein. I had known of him earlier, of course.

It was when I went to work as a reporter on the New York *Post* that I began to wonder about what manner of man he was. In Center Market Place, behind police headquarters, I heard tales of Rothstein's influence and power from reporters who had known him, covered stories in which he was a central figure, observed him as a contemporary.

To these men, the real professionals among reporters, Arnold Rothstein was already a symbol, a legend, in the early 1930's. Joe Murphy, of the *Times*, Bob Barke, of the *Mirror*, Johnny Martin, of the *News*, Frank Roth, of the *Sun*, all talked of him as if he had ruled a supergovernment in New York.

Later, as reporter and editor, I began to get that same feeling about Arnold Rothstein. His body was in a grave, but his influence was a real, live quality in New York City. His name recurred, time after time, in newspaper stories.

He was as newsworthy in 1935 as he had been in 1925.

The election of Fiorello LaGuardia, who ran almost as much against Rothstein as against Tammany Hall, the Seabury Investigation, the Dewey onslaught on organized crime, all concerned themselves with this long-dead man. It came to me that the world in which I lived was partially shaped by him.

I wanted to learn more and more about him so that I could fit him into his proper place in the social history of our times.

I got to know Gene McGee and Maurice Cantor and asked them

to tell me about him. Interviewing Lucky Luciano in Dannemora Prison, I asked him to talk as much of Rothstein as about himself. I searched the files of the New York *Post* and used its wonderful morgue. I owe a great deal to Peter Dinella and his staff for their help.

It was about ten years ago that I decided to write this book. In those years I have interviewed dozens of persons, read scores of books and hundreds of old newspapers. I talked with Murray Stand and James D. C. Murray. I interviewed Grover Whalen. I spent hours talking with Herbert Bayard Swope.

I talked with Ernest Cuneo and with Leo Spitz.

I had a long series of interviews with Carolyn Rothstein Behar, Arnold Rothstein's widow.

I spent many hours with Nicky Arnstein, whom I unashamedly like.

There were many others to whom I spoke, whom I interviewed. Some would talk only if I promised them anonymity. Others would not talk at all, looking over their shoulders as they refused me information. In almost every instance I found great reticence. A quarter of a century and more after Rothstein's death there were many persons unwilling to commit themselves about him.

It seems to me that this proves my basic premise: that the influence of Arnold Rothstein lives on, still survives.

All the conclusions reached in this book are mine. I have used the information given me, but the interpretation of that information is my own responsibility. What I sought were facts. How these facts were fitted into the complete picture was a matter of my judgment alone.

So, to all those who were willing to let me make public acknowledgment of their help, I now say, "Thank you." Those who asked that they remain anonymous, them also I thank.

A special debt is owed to Allen Marple for reasons too many to enumerate.

And to my wife, who helped me prepare this book from thousands of pages of drafts and hundreds of pages of notes, all my gratitude.

Los Angeles, 1958   LEO KATCHER

Chapter 1 Gunshot Wound (Fatal)

At 10:53 P.M., Sunday, November 4, 1928, the desk sergeant at the old West Forty-seventh Street station house in New York, received a call from a police box informing him of a shooting. He immediately wrote a short bulletin, transmitted it to police headquarters on Centre Street. It read:

"Man reported shot in Park Central Hotel, Seventh Avenue and Fifty-sixth Street. Ambulance dispatched."

Shortly before midnight, more details having been given the sergeant, he wrote a second report, which went into the station house blotter:

"Arnold Rothstein, male, 46 years, 912 Fifth Avenue, gunshot wound in abdomen, found in employees' entrance, Park Central Hotel, 200 West Fifty-sixth Street. Attended by Dr. McGovern, City Hospital. Removed to Polyclinic Hospital. Reported by Patrolman William M. Davis, shield #2493, Ninth Precinct."

At 10:53 A.M., Tuesday, November 6, while millions of Americans were casting the votes that elected Herbert Hoover president, some changes were made in this second report.

The word "fatal" was parenthetically inserted after "gunshot wound," and a second paragraph was appended:

"Rothstein apparently had been engaged in a card game with others in room 349, on the third floor of the Park Central Hotel, when an unknown man shot him and threw the revolver out of window into street. Body found by Lawrence Fallon, 31-64 Thirty-fourth Street, Astoria, employed as house detective by the hotel."

1

This report was limited to the little knowledge possessed by the man who wrote it. It contained one major error. Rothstein had not been involved in a card game just prior to his shooting. He had, however, been involved in one a few weeks earlier and his shooting came as the direct result of that game.

The desk sergeant, even had he known this fact, would not have revealed his knowledge. He had good reason for being circumspect. If he knew nothing else, he knew that the shooting of Arnold Rothstein was a matter for the upper echelons of the police department, of New York City politics, and of local and nationwide crime and gambling.

Arnold Rothstein was much more than an ordinary citizen. He was "The Brain," "The Bankroll," "The Man Uptown." His connections came from the top and went to the top, with Rothstein a central switchboard, a one-man nerve center. No ordinary desk sergeant wanted anything to do with Arnold Rothstein. Not with Rothstein alive nor, now, with Rothstein dead.

Of course, during the thirty-six hours between the first report and the last one, the shooting was being investigated. Detectives were not seeking information about Rothstein, because they knew all it was good for them to know. They wanted information about his movements on the windy, sleet-laden Sunday night when he was shot.

Abe Scher, night cashier at the "old" Lindy's restaurant on Seventh Avenue, gave them some facts.

"Mr. Rothstein comes in," Scher said, "it must have been about nine o'clock. Every night he comes here. [Scher, like so many Broadway habitués, spoke most often in the historical present, rather than the past, tense. Damon Runyon faithfully reproduced this patois.] Regular as clockwork, he comes here. Sunday night, Monday night, any night. Everybody knows that.

"Like always, there are some people waiting for him. They are waiting near his table, the same one where he is always sitting. . . . What fellows? . . . Sid Stajer. Fats Walsh. Jimmy Meehan. This Wellman fellow. . . . Who is paying any attention?

"You got to understand. This place, it is like an office for him.

People come in and they are leaving messages for him. All day and night, they are telephoning for him here. It ain't that Mr. Lindy likes the idea, but what can he do? An important man like Mr. Rothstein, you do not offend.

"So, like I am saying, he comes in and he goes to his table. He is saying 'hello' to people and they are saying 'hello' to him. Some fellows, they go to his table and they are talking confidential to him. You know, they are talking into his ear. . . . Did he give any-one money? . . . Who knows? Mr. Rothstein you see, but you do not watch. . . . Does he have his little black book? Is there a time when he is not having his little black book?

"There are phone calls for him. They are wanting 'Mr. Rothstein,' or 'Arnold,' or 'A. R.' I do not ask who is wanting him. One thing I do not do is to be asking questions. In my business you mind your own business, understand?

"Anyhow, this last call comes, it must be maybe a quarter after ten. I tell him he is wanted and he goes to the telephone. He talks maybe a minute. . . . Did I hear anything? . . . The way he talks, you could stand right beside him and not hear anything. Besides, who listens?

"He is finished, he goes back to his table. Then I see he is going outside with Jimmy Meehan. Two, three minutes later, Meehan is coming back in. He goes back to the table and he sits down. Mr. Rothstein, I am not seeing again."

The police located Jimmy Meehan, a florid-faced gambler and grifter. He was an old acquaintance.

"Yeah, that's right," Meehan said. "A. R. gives me the high sign and I follows him outside. He says, 'McManus wants to see me at the Park Central.' He takes a gun out of his pocket and he gives it to me. 'Keep this for me,' he says. 'I will be right back.' Then he walks up Seventh Avenue and I go back inside."

The police teletype carried a "wanted" message for one George McManus, gambler, bookmaker, brother of a policeman and of a priest. "Age, 42. Six feet, 210 pounds. Dark hair and fair complexion. Wanted for questioning. Pick up on sight."

At the Park Central Hotel the telephone operator looked at her records. She found the chit that recorded a telephone call to Circle 3317, the phone number at Lindy's. The call had been made at 10:12 P.M., from room 349. The register showed the room had been taken by a man who had signed in as "George Richards."

Room 349 was empty when the police entered it. A window was open and a wind was whirling the curtains about. There were some empty whisky bottles and some dirty glasses. Ashtrays were filled with cigarette butts, some of them lipstick-smeared. Opening a closet, the police found an expensive, hand-tailored Chesterfield overcoat. Embroidered on the lining was the name, "George Mc-Manus."

A call was made to the Bureau of Identification at headquarters for a picture of George McManus. Minutes later, a motorcycle policeman delivered it. The night clerk thought this was the man who had registered as "George Richards." Later, others were to make a more positive identification.

The house detective, Fallon, told his story.

"I was in the lobby when young Kelly, who works the service elevator, comes running in. He sees me and tells me a man is shot or sick or something in the service stairway. I go with Kelly and I see this man. He is hanging on to the banister with one hand and he is holding his belly with the other. He says, 'Call me a taxi. I've been shot.'

"I send Kelly to look for a cop. I take a good look at this fellow. . . . Sure, I recognize him. Everybody knows Arnold Rothstein. About then, the cop on the beat comes in."

The police questioned Kelly.

"All I know is I am in the elevator when I hear these steps on the stairs. I go to look and this guy is walking down slow. I say, 'Are you sick?' and he says, 'Get me a taxi. I've been shot.' This ain't none of my business, so I go looking for Fallon. Then he sends me for a cop. I come back with the cop."

The cop was Patrolman Davis.

"When Kelly grabs me," Davis said, "I call the station house, like the book says. Then I go to the hotel. I get one look and I know who he is. I ask him who shot him, and he says, 'Get me home. The address is 912 Fifth Avenue.'

"I start writing in my book. I ask him again, 'Who shot you?' He just says, 'Don't ask questions. Get me a cab.' That is when the ambulance arrives. While the doc is looking at him, I am getting the names of all the witnesses. By the time I am finished, they are taking him away."

Among the witnesses listed by Davis were a taxi driver named Abe Bender, and a hotel maid named Mrs. Bridget Farry. Both were volunteer witnesses.

Bender came to Davis holding a revolver. "I am sitting in my hack," he said, "when something comes flying down from the hotel and hits my hack a whack. It bounces into the street. I jump out and go see what it is. When I see it is a gun, I figure I better get it to the cops right away."

When it was pointed out to Bender that he had probably destroyed valuable fingerprints by handling the gun, he answered, "A time like this, who thinks of fingerprints. I am a hackie, not Sherlock Holmes. So, do me something."

Bender's statement was taken down by a police stenographer and he signed it. He was told to remain available for further questioning.

Bridget Farry was the prize witness. She was a loosely fleshed, heavily built woman and a voluble one. Middle-aged, born in Ireland, she had a heavy brogue, a sharp tongue, and an intense eagerness to talk—and talk.

She was the maid on duty on the third floor of the hotel on the night of the shooting.

"I saw," she said, "that the room hadn't been made up during the day and so I went there and knocked at the door. A big feller, Irish as Paddy's pig, comes to the door and says to me, 'And what is it you want?' I tell him I'm the maid and I want to clean up the room.

"'It needs no cleanin',' he says.

"My eyes tell me different. There's these glasses and the dirty ashtrays and also there is a woman in the room. But it's none of my business and if he ain't wantin' the room cleaned up, it's less work for me and the better off I am for it."

Mrs. Farry looked at the picture of George McManus and identified it at once. "Sure, he's the one. I'd know him anywhere."

It developed that Mrs. Farry was acquainted with Rothstein. She had once worked for him in the Hotel Fairfield, which Rothstein owned, and he had been accustomed to giving her a few dollars whenever he encountered her afterward.

"A decenter, kinder man I never knew and I'll be lightin' a candle for him this very night."

Mrs. Farry was also shown another picture, this one of Inez Norton. "I never saw the woman in me life."

Miss Norton, to whom detectives also talked, was blonde, good-looking, misty-eyed, shocked and grieving. A former actress, she was domiciled in the Hotel Fairfield, but had apparently moved in after Mrs. Farry had ceased working there.

Miss Norton, her voice husky, told police she had been with Rothstein early on Sunday evening.

"We had dinner at the Colony," she said, "and then he left me at a movie while he went to tend to some business."

She said there had been nothing unusual about his behavior at that last meeting. "Arnold was his very gay, very normal, very natural self. He was very much in love. He didn't seem to have anything on his mind. [She did not regard this as a non sequitur.] He certainly didn't fear anything. We spoke of many subjects, but mainly of love. He said he hoped soon to be free to marry me. He said everything would be mine—his property and his money. But I cared only for him."

Then she broke into tears.

One other witness was questioned, Rothstein himself.

Early Monday morning, Detective Patrick Flood sat down beside Rothstein's bed in Polyclinic Hospital.

Rothstein, awakening, saw him there. "Hello, Paddy."

"Hello, Arnold. Who shot you?"

"I won't talk about it. I'll take care of it myself."

Flood did not pursue his questioning. He dropped a hand on the white sheet that covered the milk-faced man with the large, brown eyes, and said, "Get well quick, Arnold." Then he left the room. He told the reporters who were waiting there for him, "He didn't tell me anything."

That was the temporary limit of the investigating. In due course, the police would talk with a host of characters. Gamblers. Con men. Gangsters. Dope peddlers. Musclemen. There would be some persons to whom they would not talk. Perhaps because they did not know about them. Perhaps because they knew better.

After all, they couldn't send an alarm out for a Chinese merchant in Hong Kong, a banker in Geneva, an exporter in Antwerp, or a distiller in Scotland. And it would not have been wise to talk with Jimmy Hines, one of the powers of Tammany Hall, nor with Albert Marinelli, whose influence was almost as great.

They did, after a time, talk with the handsome, slender, graying woman who came to the hospital from the apartment at 912 Fifth Avenue, the place Rothstein had called "home." She had been married to Rothstein for twenty years, but she did not know him as well as did many others.

Not as well, for instance, as Nicky Arnstein, con man, charmer, gambler and horse-player, knew him. Nor as well as Sheriff Tom Foley, the Tammany stalwart. Not even as well as pale-faced, jumpy, drug addict Sid Stajer knew him. Or as well as bunko artist, drug-peddling, woman-charming Dapper Dan Collins knew him.

Hoodlums like Jack ("Legs") Diamond knew Arnold Rothstein far better than she did. So did racket king "Ownie" Madden. And "Subway Sam" Rosoff knew sides of him of which she was unaware. The list could be made to include many hundreds.

The people of the United States—nearly all of them—knew of him. And he was many things to many men.

To some millions Arnold Rothstein was the "man who fixed the 1919 World Series." To these he was the defiler of the American institution which ranked just below belief in God and reverence for motherhood.

To the men who wrote the headlines for the tabloids he was "King of the Gamblers."

To Damon Runyon, Broadway's Aesop in a checkered vest, Rothstein was "The Brain," mastermind of New York's larcenous activities.

To novelist F. Scott Fitzgerald, Rothstein was the epitome of socially accepted evil in a corrupting society. Fitzgerald gave Rothstein the name "Wolfsheim" and made him a character in *The Great Gatsby.*

To the editors of the *World Almanac* Rothstein was a "sporting man." They regarded him as so important that for many years they included this notation in the section headed "Memorable Dates":

"1928. . . . Arnold Rothstein, sporting man, was shot in New York City Nov. 4 and died Nov. 6."

Yes, alive and dead, he was many things to many men.

Lloyd Morris, social historian, described Rothstein in his *Postscript to Yesterday,* as "The [J.P.] Morgan of the underworld; its banker and master of strategy."

Herbert Asbury, in his book *The Great Illusion,* called Rothstein "The underworld's big money man and backer of shady enterprises."

Gene Fowler, in his idealized biography of the late attorney, William J. Fallon, *The Great Mouthpiece,* presented a contrary—and minority—opinion. He called Rothstein "an exalted pawnbroker." Then he added, "His pocketbook was his skull; his bankroll, the brains. He was an excellent executive, as we Americans judge these things."

Fowler quoted Fallon on Rothstein:

"Rothstein is a man who dwells in doorways. A mouse standing in a doorway, waiting for his cheese."

All these judgments and descriptions were partially right—which also made them partially wrong. The most apt comparison was probably that made with the first J. P. Morgan. After all, both men dealt in money and in the use of that money to create power. The big difference, of course, was in the separate spheres in which they operated.

Morgan had, or found, legal sanction for the manner in which he got his money and used his power. Rothstein never sought, nor did he have, to sanctify his cynicism. He did not believe that might needed respectability to make it right. He was amoral and therefore subject to neither conscience nor public opinion.

Both men made deep changes in our social fabric. Morgan made big business bigger, stronger, more effective. He perfected the trust and the holding company. He took control of American finance away from the government, moving it to his own office. He imposed his character and beliefs on the American economy.

But Morgan operated within the framework of the law, was subject to it. And so, though his influence is still felt in the world of money, in the world of finance, it is only a tenuous, shadowy influence. The laws affecting trusts affected him. The great depression of the 1929-1933 period brought into power Roosevelt and his New Deal. And the New Deal passed laws which took most of Morgan's power away from his successors.

Rothstein, on the other hand, dealt with the financing of business outside the law. Since that was the case, no laws could change the pattern he created. His heirs live according to the rules he laid down, within the structure he created. Their power and money are greater than his were. But that is because the stakes are greater and the rewards richer.

What was it that Rothstein did?

Basically, he transformed the world of crime from an anarchic into an authoritarian state. He gathered the loose, single strands of crime and wove them into a tapestry. He took the various elements that were needed to change crime from petty larceny into big business and fused them. The end result was a machine that runs smoothly today. Runs as Rothstein made it run.

Its component parts—politicians and lawbreakers—have become one.

He did not do this as part of a grand design. He simply experimented as the need arose. Those experiments which worked became rules of conduct. He was the ultimate pragmatist in a pragmatic world.

The times demanded someone like him. That was his good fortune.

He was gambler, fixer, corrupter, politician, businessman and pawnbroker. His creed was materialism. He dealt in money. He believed, with all his heart, in money.

He was a gambler who played with loaded dice and marked cards. He was a sportsman who denigrated sport. He fixed horse races and prize fights.

He was a politician who bribed and bought other politicians. He started as their errand boy, became their partner. At the end he was their boss.

He was a legitimate businessman and used every illegitimate practice in his business.

His birthplace was New York and he was as much a part of the city as Grant's Tomb, Times Square, Coney Island, and the subway. Anything west of West Street was a strange land. Yet, his influence spread across the continent, reached to Europe, to Asia, to the Caribbean.

He was never convicted of breaking a law, yet he was the Grey Eminence of Crime.

He was the "Big Bankroll" of the underworld.

He was—well, he was Arnold Rothstein, who died of a "gunshot wound (fatal)" on the morning of November 6, 1928, and was buried the next day to the mournful sound of the *Kaddish*, the orthodox Jewish prayer for the dead. It was the second time it was said for him.

In death, he was reclaimed by the faith in which he had been born. He had long before forsaken it. His symbol was not the Star of David but the Dollar Sign. He believed not in the Prayer Book but in the Bankbook.

However, there were no pockets, not even in the shroud of Arnold Rothstein.

Chapter **2** *I Always Gambled*

Y*isgadal, Ve yiskadash . . ."*
The first handful of earth was thrown on the plain pine coffin.

The rabbi asked the Lord's compassion for *"Arkum ben Avrahum ben Dovid."* For "Arnold, son of Abraham, son of David."

Of these three only Abraham survived. A frail, bearded man, prayer shawl about his bent, narrow shoulders, he stood at the grave-side. Beside him was Esther, his wife of half a century. Behind them were their three remaining children, Edgar and Edith and Jack. A little apart was Carolyn Rothstein, Arnold's widow. That had been her relationship with the family for a score of years. A little apart.

This was the family that survived Arnold Rothstein.

He was the seed of Abraham and Esther. What manner of people were the parents who had given him life?

Given life to one whose funeral services were attended by police and gamblers and jailbirds and drug addicts. By reporters and photographers and a motley crowd of curious. Given life to a man who had died a violent death.

Abraham Rothstein was a native New Yorker, born on Henry Street, on the lower East Side. He was the son of David, who had fled the pogroms of his native Bessarabia some years earlier.

Abraham Rothstein had led a model life for his almost threescore and ten years. Orphaned early by his father's death, he had left school to support his mother and his brothers and sisters. He had

11

operated a dry goods store, then entered the cotton-converting business. He had been very successful. He was a rich man.

He was also a man of simple, fixed belief. He believed in The Law. The Law of his faith and the law of his country. He was a disciple of orthodoxy. He was a good man.

A testimonial dinner was given in his honor in 1919. It marked his efforts—and success—in settling a major dispute in the New York City garment industry. He had been chosen by both sides to act as arbitrator because both sides trusted him completely.

Among the guests who honored him at the dinner were Alfred E. Smith, then governor of New York, and Louis D. Brandeis, an associate justice of the Supreme Court of the United States.

After others had talked about him, he talked a little about himself. His talk was brief. "My father," he said, "bequeathed me a way of life. He taught me, above all, to love God and to honor Him. Secondly, he taught me to honor all men and love them as brothers. He told me whatever I received I received from God and that no man can honor God more greatly than by sharing his possessions with others. This I have tried to do."

This was the man whom Governor Smith called "Abe the Just."

This was the man of whom were told innumerable stories of charity, years of public service, rectitude and selflessness.

This was the father of Arnold Rothstein, but no one mentioned the son at this dinner.

Abraham Rothstein lived his private life, like his public one, in strict accordance with The Law. He obeyed the Decalogue. No one commandment above any other, but all with his entire belief.

He lived in accordance with the religion and the customs of his people. Even in relation to his marriage. As was customary, it had been arranged for him. In only one respect was it different. He saw his bride for the first time on his wedding day. But that was a matter of geography.

There were not many Jews in the United States in 1878. Those who did live in the United States retained ties with their home cities and provinces. These ties were centered in the various lodges and societies which had headquarters in every major American city. But the main office was always New York.

The secretary was the guiding hand of these organizations. He kept in touch with the old country as well as the new. He was the keeper of vital statistics, of births and deaths, marriages and confirmations.

A good part of his income derived from a side line. He acted as *shadchen*, or marriage broker. He was Cupid's transmission belt. His records told him when a youth or maiden had reached marriageable age. And he was always ready to locate a proper mate.

There came a time when the secretary visited the home of Abraham's mother. Was it not time for Abraham to take a bride? The mother agreed that it was. Then she listed her son's virtues and asked, "Can you find a maiden who would make him a proper wife?"

The secretary nodded his skullcapped head. "I can. It may take time, but I can."

He went to his office and searched his records. Among them he found the name of Esther Kahn, daughter of Simon and Reba Kahn. The Kahns had come to the United States from the same Bessarabian town as had the Rothsteins.

Now began a series of maneuvers, an elaborate protocol. And these were conducted across the full width of the continent, for the Kahns lived in San Francisco.

The secretary told Mrs. Rothstein, "The Kahns are good, religious people. They are learned. And they are successful. Simon Kahn has prospered and will be able to provide a fitting dowry."

There was nothing exceptional about this; dowry giving was customary.

Mrs. Rothstein agreed that Esther Kahn would make a most suitable wife for her son.

Now the secretary began a correspondence with Simon Kahn. Kahn agreed that it was a fitting time for his daughter to be married. There were some upright young men in San Francisco whom he had under consideration. However, he was open to any suggestion from the East.

It took three months for arrangements to be completed. At the end of that period Esther and Abraham were betrothed. And, for the first time, they communicated directly with each other, exchanging photographs and stilted phrases.

Since Simon Kahn was to bear all the expenses of the wedding, it was natural that the ceremony should take place in San Francisco. The date was fixed and Abraham set out on the long trip.

It had been planned that Abraham would have three days in San Francisco between his arrival and the marriage. Flat wheels, engine failures, and other mishaps ate up the three days. Abraham reached San Francisco just four hours before the time set for the ceremony.

There was barely time for him to meet the girl he would soon be taking to wife. Shyly he exchanged a few words with her in the presence of her parents. He just had time to see that she was a slight girl, of medium height, with lustrous olive skin and oversize brown eyes that filled the top half of her face. Her hair was blue-black.

She saw a thin, gentle-looking young man with a shy smile. His voice was soft and his manner comforting.

They had this brief moment together and then Simon Kahn took his soon-to-be son-in-law in hand. They sat in the curtained, high-ceilinged parlor of the Kahn house and there Abraham had his first, and only, drink of hard liquor.

In a short while the Kahn family, friends and *Landsleit* gathered for the ceremony. The young couple stood beneath the wedding canopy, still strangers, as the rabbi recited the words of the marriage ceremony. At its end, a glass was placed on the floor and the rabbi told Abraham to shatter it. He brought his foot down hard, and the glass splintered.

The rabbi said, "So long as this glass remains splintered, so long shall you two be joined in marriage."

The pair were man and wife.

Years later Esther said, "When we married, we did not love each other. How could you love a stranger? But all the material for love was there. I respected Abraham. I knew he was a good man or my father would not have approved of him. From the first moment he was gentle to me and considerate. Love, of course, came later."

The day after the wedding, the couple left for New York. Ahead was a long journey. For Abraham, it was a journey home; for Esther, it was a journey away from home to a strange world. She was leaving her family, her friends and her youth behind. It saddened her.

Abraham said, "I promise that you will return here many times."

She accepted the promise on faith. She felt that Abraham never made a light promise, for a promise became a debt. And he believed in paying his debts.

Eight days later they were in New York.

Abraham, before leaving, had found a home for them. It was a brownstone on Forty-seventh Street, just west of Lexington Avenue. The neighborhood was quiet, far removed from the business section. And there was a new synagogue only a few blocks away. At that time the district in which they lived was part of Yorkville.

Esther came to this new home in the strange city of New York, a city about which she knew little. When she saw it, it overwhelmed her.

It already had a population of more than a million people living on the island of Manhattan, which then was the city's limit. Boats arrived daily from Europe, carrying new hordes of immigrants. Italians and Germans and Irish and Jews, most of whom settled into the rabbit warren that was New York.

New York was still a boom town, a frontier town. It was ribald, wide open, lawless. The Civil War, like all wars, had bred disillusion and revolt. Morality was honored only in the breach.

Public morals were at their lowest ebb. In New York the remains of the Tweed Machine were being reorganized by one of Tweed's former followers, wryly labeled "Honest John" Kelly. Tweed was dying in 1878, a discredited man because he had been caught. The forces of civic decency had found a victim, but no victory. The politicians were still extorting their tithe from the public funds.

Nationally, of course, the situation was as sordid. The scandals of the Grant administration were slowly coming to light. The railroad barons were milking the public. Drew and Fisk and Vanderbilt and Gould and Belmont were amassing bigger and bigger fortunes from their pillaging.

Private morality was little better. The leaders of the city attended church on Sunday, but profited from the gambling houses and brothels that abounded. Streetwalkers thronged the city, made their headquarters in the Twenties. The Seven Sisters operated seven houses on Twenty-fifth Street, one alongside the other, and would not accept trade except from gentlemen in formal dress and carrying bouquets.

Everywhere so-called dance and concert halls thrived. Harry Hill's was on the "must see" list of every solvent sightseer who visited New York. And a regular stopping-off place for slumming parties. And all these hoped they would be able to see Hill's notorious "Virginia Reel" performed.

This was a tribute which Hill always paid when a distinguished, or very rich, patron came to his establishment. Sometime during the course of the evening Hill would shout above the ordinary tumult, "We will now have a Virginia Reel and, in this number, the girls will take them off."

The girls did. When Harry Hill issued his order, his strippers indulged in no teasing.

There were other places with attraction for moneyed visitors. One was the American Mabille, owned by Theodore ("The") Allen, who proudly informed a Congressional investigating committee in 1868 that he was "the wickedest man in New York." A member of the committee, after seeing the American Mabille and the Prince Bernard, another establishment owned by Allen, said that Allen was modest. "He is," said Congressman Rogers of Pennsylvania, "the wickedest man in the world."

The American Mabille specialized in naked women and raw whisky, but it had an upstairs room where pheasant and champagne were served and in which gambling, rather than sex, was the commodity purveyed.

On a much lower level was Bill McGlory's place. He offered cut-rate vice twenty-four hours each day and it was moot whether his dance hall or its next-door neighbor, the Bucket of Blood, was the scene of greater violence.

The Haymarket was operating, forerunner of the dime-a-dance places of a later generation, but far more dissolute than any of its descendants.

The politicians took their graft from such places. And, often, found their pleasures in them. But it was gambling, and the gambling houses, that provided the regular funds that kept politicians rich and political organizations functioning.

Gambling was big business. It provided sensation and thrill and pyschological outlet for dreams that couldn't be made to come true in any other way. And money. Money for the operators of the gambling places and their partners, the politicians.

Morrissey's was still running in 1878, though its founder, John Morrissey, ex-prize fighter, ex-congressman, builder of Saratoga, was dying in his home near the United States Hotel in Saratoga. Morrissey's place was headquarters for Tammany politicians, just as the gambling house and saloon of Colonel Isaiah Rynders, United States marshal for New York, had been a score of years earlier.

The Republican politicos made their headquarters in Allen's Prince Bernard Hotel and, later, his "Square Deal Club." It was at the Prince Bernard that Republican boss Thurlow Weed accepted a campaign contribution of $25,000 for Lincoln's re-election campaign in 1864 from Allen.

Most elegant of all the gambling houses was that of Joe Hall, who welcomed politicians of both parties and asked only that they bring well-filled wallets with them.

The world of Joe Hall, of The Allen, of Billy McGlory, and of the stuss houses and three-card monte games was alien to Esther and Abraham for a long time. It was to become known to them through their second son, a son who would follow in direct succession to John Morrissey and Richard Canfield as the foremost gambler in the world.

Their first child, a son, was born on East Forty-seventh Street in 1880. He was named Harry. Arnold was born in the same house in

1882. By that time, the house had grown too small and the neighborhood was already undergoing a change. It was no longer part of the country, but a part of the Tenderloin District of the city. The Rothsteins moved to a new home on East Seventy-ninth Street.

Three more children were born to the Rothsteins. They were Edgar, Edith and Jack, in that order.

At the synagogue, in the business world of which he was a part, at meetings of the Bessarabian Society, it was always remarked that Abraham was among the most fortunate of men. He had a good wife, a fine family, a thriving business. None envied him, for he was a devout, hard-working man of integrity who shared what he had with the less fortunate. His good fortune stemmed from his good life, his piety, his belief in The Law.

Wearing his phylacteries and his prayer shawl he daily intoned blessings unto God and thanks. And when he spoke of his family it was always as though nothing marred his happiness, as though nothing could mar it.

Still, from the beginning there was something disturbing about Arnold, the second son. He wasn't gay, outgoing, a child of laughter, like his older brother, Harry. He was a baby that did not laugh, an infant who looked out at the world through great brown eyes that were so like his mother's, but so different in that they never sparkled with kindness.

When Arnold was barely three his father was awakened one night by a strange sound. He ran to the room that the two boys shared. There he found Arnold standing over his brother, a knife in his hand. Abraham took the knife from him and pleaded, "Why, my son? Why?"

"I hate Harry." That was all the answer he gave and, having given it, he withdrew into silence and himself.

There was only one time that Arnold showed deep emotion as a child. It happened in 1888 when Abraham redeemed his wedding promise to Esther and she took the long trip to San Francisco to see her family. She took Harry, the eldest, and Edith, then the baby, leaving behind Arnold and Edgar (Jack was not yet born).

The first night she was gone Abraham was startled by the sound of heartbroken weeping. He found Arnold hidden away in a deep closet. Abraham sought to take Arnold in his arms, but the boy repulsed him.

"You hate me," he said. "She hates me and you hate me, but you all love Harry. Nobody loves me."

Abraham tried to tell Arnold of his love for him, of Esther's love for him. "You are our son. We love all of you alike."

"It's a lie. If she loved me, she wouldn't leave me. She'd take me and leave Harry here."

Some six months before he was murdered, Arnold Rothstein told this memory to John B. Watson, the noted psychologist. He added, "I think I remember this better than anything else that ever happened to me." And then he said, "It was the only time I ever really cried."

From the beginning he found ways to live within himself. He rebuffed companionship. He sought dark places—cellars, closets—in which to play. He liked the dark.

And he lived in Harry's shadow. Harry was a brilliant student. He was cheerful, gregarious, a leader. And he left a difficult inheritance for his brother. He took away much of his identity, for Arnold was never just himself. He was Harry's brother.

Arnold turned to close-mouthed resentment. He was uninterested in his schoolwork. He wasn't stupid; he just didn't care. By the time he reached the fifth grade he had fallen two full years behind and his brother Edgar had caught up with him. From then on Arnold stayed with his class. Edgar explained this. "I'd do all the homework and Arnold would copy it and remember it. Except in arithmetic. Arnold did all the arithmetic. He loved to play with numbers."

The Rothstein children all were sent to *Chedar*, Hebrew school. Arnold was an even worse student here. He was truculent, a truant. And he refused to learn anything.

Harry was even more brilliant in his religious studies than in his secular ones. The Hebrew language came easy to him. He had a deep interest in the history, religion and culture of his people. So deep that when he was thirteen he told his parents that he wanted to study for the rabbinate.

This brought an added happiness to Abraham. His people had always placed a high value on learning, especially religious learning. To have a son who was a *melamed,* a scholar of The Law, who wanted to be a rabbi, was a great honor.

But a son like Arnold brought shame.

Abraham tried to reason with Arnold. He told him of the centuries during which the religion had been created, of the teachings that had resulted. "You should be proud of being a Jew."

"Who cares about that stuff? This is America, not Jerusalem. I'm an American. Let Harry be a Jew."

Reluctantly Arnold continued sporadic attendance at Hebrew school until his confirmation. But he put aside the phylacteries and the prayer shawl that were given him as presents. "I've had enough," he said. He never wore these gifts.

Hebrew school was replaced by another school, the streets and alleys of the city. He began to gamble. He matched pennies with other boys as soon as he had pennies of his own. A policeman caught him shooting dice behind coalboxes in an alley and brought him home to Abraham.

"Gambling is a sin," Abraham said. Arnold paid no attention. What did his father know anyway?

Arnold Rothstein gave one of his infrequent newspaper interviews in 1921. He was asked about how he became a gambler. "I always gambled," he said. "I can't remember when I didn't. Maybe I gambled just to show my father he couldn't tell me what to do, but I don't think so. I think I gambled because I loved the excitement. When I gambled, nothing else mattered. I could play for hours and not know how much time had passed."

Then he added, "I wasn't different from the other kids. Everyone gambled."

This was almost true. Wherever one turned there were gambling places. They ran openly and took pennies, nickels, dimes and dollars. It was enough to call down the wrath of the righteous, and one of these, the Rev. Charles H. Parkhurst, grew very wrathful indeed. In a sermon, delivered at the time when Rothstein was growing up, Dr. Parkhurst declared:

"The political harpies that, under the guise of governing the city, are feeding day and night on its quivering entrails . . . are a lying, perjured, rum-soaked and libidinous lot. . . . Gambling houses flourish on the streets almost as thick as the Roses of Sharon. . . . These are eating into the character of what we think are our best and most promising young men."

Rothstein could hardly be described, even then, as "one of the best and most promising young men," but gambling was eating into his vitals. He watched the three-card monte operators on the streets. He lurked in shadows and watched the lower East Side stuss games in operation. "Stuss" was a New York version of the old Western gambling game of faro, but the odds against the players were considerably higher.

Rothstein played dice and poker with other young strays. When he was fourteen he began to keep a record of his winnings and losses. These were usually in sums less than a dollar, but he kept a careful account. And he won more than he lost.

He guarded his money carefully—and carried it with him always. He was stingy and yet was given to occasional splurges of generosity. He would stand treat just for the sake of the approbation and thanks of those whom he treated. Edgar recalled, "It was always the biggest, toughest boys whom he treated. I guess he wanted to get them on his side."

Arnold wanted to be liked and this was a way of buying affection. Or a semblance of it.

He found odd jobs in poolrooms. A "poolroom" originally was a place in which lottery tickets were sold. Lottery, because of the manner in which winnings were paid off, was called "pool." Since lottery tickets were sold all day and the drawings were not held until late in the evening, proprietors of poolrooms installed billiard tables to occupy their customers during the long waiting periods.

The game of billiards was either too slow or too difficult for the hangers-on. They devised a game of their own, first called "pocket billiards" and later "pool."

When Arnold had nothing else to do he practiced on the billiard tables. He became adept at the game and as the players began to gamble on it he gambled with them. He began to make his pocket money from this source. He became so expert that one poolroom operator, "Florrie" Sullivan, paid him a regular fee to represent the house. That meant Rothstein was available to play all comers and he shared in any winnings that Sullivan might make by betting on him. He also had the privilege of betting on himself.

He managed to finish two years of study at Boys' High School, but left school for all time in 1898. He was sixteen and he told his father there was nothing left for him to learn in school. He would finish his education on the streets.

But what did he need of schools when there were such places as gambling houses, poolrooms and the prop room of Hammerstein's Victoria Theatre on the corner of Forty-second Street and Seventh Avenue?

There was a dice game in the prop room every Monday. That was the slowest day of the week and the game originally was begun by employees of the theater as a way of killing time. Soon friends of the employees joined the game. Word spread and young toughs and young "sports" became regular participants.

Willie Hammerstein made a few attempts to halt the game, but these were abortive. He was alone against a motley group that included "Monk" Eastman, "Whitey" Lewis, Herman Rosenthal, "Dago" Frank, and members of the Hudson Duster and Gopher Gangs who were terrorizing New York.

The prop room provided the scene of Rothstein's higher education. There, in minuscule, he conducted the type of operations that were to continue for thirty years.

To start with, he did his first moneylending at these games. He always carried his bankroll with him, money accumulated from shooting pool, from running errands, from poker and dice games. And money he had earned by working sporadically for his father. He always knew how much money he had, but that didn't stop him from counting and recounting it. He liked the feel of silver, of bills, in his fingers.

He would make his loans on Monday, payable the next Monday.

The interest rate was high; for every four dollars borrowed, five had to be repaid.

It was both a profitable and a precarious business. The I.O.U.'s given Rothstein didn't have much value on the open market place. But Rothstein had a "collector" who went after overdue accounts. This collector was Monk Eastman.

Probably no tougher strong-arm man ever existed than Eastman. He was bullet-headed, with a broken nose, cauliflower ears, heavy jowls. He was impervious to fear and cold-bloodedly cruel. He was a gun fighter, a knife fighter and a fist fighter. Intellectually he was hardly more than a moron, but he didn't need brains for his living. Brute force and cunning were enough and he had sufficient of both these.

Monk Eastman was the leader of one of the toughest gangs in New York. He was also the pet of "Big Tim" Sullivan, Tammany boss of the East Side. Eastman was a big help on Election Day and whenever else Sullivan might need him. He had a tremendous loyalty to Sullivan and some of that loyalty carried over to Arnold Rothstein.

Even then, when he was barely sixteen, Rothstein hung around Sullivan's headquarters. He ran errands, made himself useful, translated for Sullivan when one of his Jewish voters appeared at the club with a request or a complaint. Sullivan considered Rothstein a bright young man with a great future. (He felt the same way about another young loafer named Herman Rosenthal.)

Rothstein had met Eastman at the Sullivan club. The gangster had taken a liking to the younger man. And so, when Rothstein went into the moneylending business, he told Eastman about some of his recalcitrant clients. Eastman usually had one of his henchmen serve as the immediate collection agent. It took little time for word to get about that welching on Rothstein was unhealthy.

In those beginning days Rothstein also learned some lessons about finance. One lesson was that money bred money. The more there was available to lend the more interest would be forthcoming and, like an endless belt, the more money there would be to lend. So Rothstein looked about for ways to build his bankroll.

Abraham Rothstein owned a big, solid-gold watch. He rarely carried it, preferring to keep it in a drawer of his desk. Arnold would often slip the watch from its hiding place when he needed spare cash. He could always pawn the watch for thirty or forty dollars and the interest he paid the pawnbroker was considerably less than he would receive from the proceeds.

It was an elementary lesson in getting other people's money to work for him, and Rothstein never forgot it.

Rothstein heard laments at Hammerstein's about there being few places for a dice game, such as this one, available. He searched about and found a vacant old barn near Water Street. The watchman who had the place in charge was quite willing to rent it to Rothstein for three dollars a night.

In return for providing a place to gamble, Rothstein collected "vigorish."

The exact derivation of "vigorish" is indeterminate, but it probably stems from the word "vicarage" which was defined as "the small or privy tithes that accrue to a parish vicar." Rothstein extracted a "small or privy tithe" from each bet made in the game he promoted. In the long run the word really changed very little in meaning when removed from its ecclesiastical background to that of the underworld.

By the end of his sixteenth year Arnold Rothstein had accumulated more than five hundred dollars, a large sum for that day. No wonder that Big Tim Sullivan looked at him as a "comer," a promising young man with a great future. And Sullivan was a man who could turn that promise into reality.

Timothy D. Sullivan was known both as "Big Tim" and "The Big Feller." He was the political boss of that area given the general name of "The Bowery," on New York's East Side. He was a professional politician. That meant he was kind to "widders and orphans." He bought coal in the winter and ice in the summer for the poor. He got jobs, fixed violations of city ordinances, arranged for immigrants to become citizens, attended confirmations, circumcisions, ordinations and *bar mitzvahs*.

He wore his iron hat in a synagogue and removed it in a Christian place of worship.

He was always ready with monetary help. He provided doctors, lawyers and even undertakers whenever the need for these arose. All he asked in return was that the people of the Bowery vote the straight Democratic ticket on Election Day. It seemed a cheap price for them to pay. Sullivan knew it was he who was paying the cheap price, but he never thought of the public as composed of people.

He would, and did, say proudly, "I never turned anyone away from my door." By the standards of his day and his vocation he was not an evil man.

He was big, broad-shouldered, with a perennial smile on his face. He was sentimental, with large eyes that could brim with tears at mention of children suffering, Ireland, or cruelty to anybody's mother.

The best picture of his character and beliefs was given by Big Tim himself at a monster political rally that closed the 1909 campaign in New York. He had been attacked in an article in *McClure's* magazine, and he chose this occasion to answer. The place was Miner's Theatre on the Bowery, owned by Sullivan and his partner, John Considine.

First, Sullivan took up the charge that he was wealthy. "I am worth something," he said, "and there is no reason why I should not be. I'm an average downtown boy with a good clear head and it's always clear, for I don't drink or smoke. But I haven't changed my residence since I got my money and I ain't going to. I was born among you and I'm going to die among you."

Then he turned on his attackers. "The trouble with the reformers is that they don't know our traditions down here. That's why they think because I've got a little money, there must be something wrong, that I must be getting money in some crooked way or I wouldn't stay here. I'll tell you why I stay here.

"I was born in poverty, one of six children, four boys and two girls. The boys used to sleep in a three-quarter bed, not big enough for two, and the girls in a shakedown on the floor. Some nights there was enough to eat and some nights there wasn't. And our old mother used to sing to us at night and maybe it would be the next day that we would think she'd been singing but that she had gone to bed without anything to eat.

"That's the kind of people we come from and that's the kind of mothers that bore us down here. If we can help some boy or some father to another chance, we're going to give it to him. The thieves we have down here ain't thieves from choice. They are thieves from necessity and necessity don't know any law. They steal because they need a doctor for some dying one or they steal because there ain't any bread in the house for the children. . . .

"I've never professed to be more than the average man. I don't want you to think I'm very good, for I've done a lot of wrong things. I'm just an average man, but I've told you of that old mother of mine and what she did for me, and I want to say here, before you all, that there is no man on earth who believes in the virtue of women more than I do. . . .

"Fourteen years ago I began giving Christmas dinners and shoes away to the poor. Someone has said Sullivan gives the people a little turkey and a pair of shoes on Christmas and robs them the rest of the year. As I'm the Sullivan that does this, they mean me. Now I'm going to tell you how I got that idea of giving away shoes.

"It was way back in '72 and a boy named Sullivan was going to the Elm Street school and there was a Miss Murphy who was a teacher. This boy had an old pair of shoes and she asked the boy to stay after school. He thought some other boy had done something and put it up to him and he wasn't going to stand for it. So he said, 'Miss Murphy, if I've done anything let me know, because I want to get away and sell my papers.' She told the boy he hadn't done anything and she gave him an order. The order was to Timothy Brennan, brother of a big Tammany leader, and he gave me a pair of shoes.

"I needed them shoes then and I thought, if I ever got any money, I would give shoes to people who needed them and I'm going to buy shoes for people as long as I live. And all the people on earth can't stop me from doing what I think is right no matter what names they call me."

This was a public performance before his own people. In it he took advantage of their emotions, which were basically the same as his own. He meant every word he spoke, believed it to be true. Evil, like beauty, was to him something that was in the eye of the beholder, and when he looked at himself he saw no evil.

Sullivan was an intelligent man. He knew his business, which was politics, and the place he occupied in the business. He gave a cold, hard appraisal of his function to a reporter for the New York *World*.

"Every community," he said, "has to have some man who can take the trouble to look out for the people's interest while the people are earning a living. It don't make any difference whether he's tall, short, fat, lean, or humpbacked with only half his teeth. If he's willing to work harder than anyone else, he's the fellow will hold the job. They're not always grateful by any means and when they catch a man with a four-flush, no matter how good his excuse, it's 'skidoo' back to the old home for him.

"And so, after all, there isn't much to it to be a leader. It's just plenty of work, keep your temper or throw it away, be on the level and don't put on any airs, because God and the people hate a chesty man."

Whether there was much or little to it, Sullivan was a leader. He had come up the ladder, from shoulder bumper to boss, under the aegis of Richard Croker and Tom Foley, who was to be sheriff of New York and the political godfather of Alfred E. Smith and James J. Walker. Sullivan believed in Tammany and, without ever having heard or read what Aristotle had written, accepted the fact that man was "a political creature."

And political organizations are a necessary part of democracy.

Sullivan had a number of protégés. Among them were Charles F. Murphy, who would be the last of the absolute bosses of Tammany, and James J. Hines, who would succeed Sullivan as the power be-

hind the boss in Tammany. And sell that power for a pittance to a
gangster.

Sullivan also encouraged other bright young men, among them
Arnold Rothstein and Herman Rosenthal. He saw successful futures
for them, not in politics but in gambling. "You're smart Jew boys,"
he told them, "and you'll make out as gamblers. That business takes
brains."

Hand in hand with politics and gambling went the saloon. Every
corner saloon was a local headquarters for politicians. Frequently
the saloonkeepers were the district leaders. Orders for food and
clothing usually came from the saloonkeeper.

Most saloons had gambling rooms. All of them were clubhouses
for the young men of the district, especially the tough, rowdy element who made up neighborhood gangs. These young hoodlums
were the shock troops of the political army, always available to
rough up opponents, wreck competition, repeat at the polls.

Tim Sullivan made his start as a Bowery saloonkeeper. He was
still interested in saloons when he died. His office was in the ornate
saloon that carried his name. His brother Paddy ran the Hesper
Club, which was the Tammany district headquarters and was more
gambling house than saloon. His stepbrother, Lawrence Mulligan,
had a saloon that also housed the Larry Mulligan Association. In
addition, Sullivan was part owner of the Metropole Hotel.

Sullivan could truly offer, as Jimmy Walker did so many years
later, to match his "private life against anyone's." But that did not
prevent him from doing business, or associating, with thieves, gangsters and crooked gamblers. He abhorred the scarlet women and
their cadets, yet he saw nothing contradictory in taking his cut of
the protection which they paid.

Sullivan ranted against "crooks," but he gave such as Monk Eastman a literal license to steal.

Rothstein admired Sullivan greatly. It might have been that he
found a father image in him. Certainly Sullivan had qualities that
would appeal to Rothstein, qualities which Abraham Rothstein did
not possess. At any rate, from the first time he came to Sullivan's
attention Rothstein continued to ingratiate himself with Big Tim.

He knew he could profit from this relationship. And learn from it.

One of the first things he learned was that men universally respected, and yielded to, power. Money gave Sullivan much of his power. Rothstein decided he would make the money first and the power would inevitably follow.

Chapter **3** *Look Out for Number One*

Arnold Rothstein passed into adolescence an introverted, silent young man. He lost his early chubbiness, leaned down. His home life was a continual battle with his father, a battle that was fought with recriminations, pleas and promises by the older man and met with silence and twisted lips by the younger.

His relations with his brothers were peculiar. Harry might as well have been a stranger. But he spoiled the two younger boys, bought them presents, gave them pennies. Jack, the youngest, was quite bright and Arnold, who had fought studying all his school career, encouraged the youngster continually. "You're smarter than Harry," he said. "Go ahead and show them."

Arnold was seventeen when he told his parents, "I'm leaving home."

Surprisingly, he had taken a job as a traveling salesman for a line of hats and caps. His father was pleased that he had taken a job, expressed the hope that being on his own might change him. Arnold heard him out, shrugged, and left the house.

His territory took him into upstate New York, Pennsylvania, and West Virginia. He traveled this route for almost two years, being moderately successful. As his own boss, he could play pinochle, shoot pool, play poker with other salesmen and with the local "sports" in the towns on which he called.

He was in Erie, Pennsylvania, during his second year on the

road, when he received a telegram telling him that Harry, the beau ideal of the family, had died suddenly of pneumonia.

When Arnold returned home, the orthodox services had already been held, and the family was sitting *shiva* for the dead youth.

The mirrors were covered. The family sat on boxes. Abraham's clothes had been rent. But not more than his soul and his spirit. He had aged a decade in a night. Esther sobbed quietly. The younger children, awed and frightened by their first contact with death, were red-eyed from weeping.

Arnold was enveloped by the grief. He, too, sat *shiva*. He was one of the *minyon*, or quorum, of ten males who prayed each night and each morning for the eight days of *shiva*.

After all, he was still hardly more than a boy. This was a moment of crisis in his life. He was, for the time being, a part of the family. Harry's death was a bond between him and his father and there had been no real bonds before, except that of birth, between them.

And there was also the element of guilt. Years afterward Rothstein told his wife, "Somehow, I had the feeling that I was responsible for Harry being dead. I remembered all the times that I'd wished he was dead, all the times I had dreamed of killing him. I got to thinking that maybe my wishing had finally killed him."

The feeling of guilt obtruded into Rothstein's dreams. For years he had a recurrent dream in which Harry would appear and say to him, "I'm not dead. Go into my room and you'll find me there." Sometimes Rothstein would awake from the dream and start for Harry's room.

Arnold made an attempt to replace Harry in the life and affections of his parents. For three months he stayed with them. He gave up his job and went to work in his father's factory. He went to the synagogue a number of times. He spent his off hours at home, not even visiting poolrooms.

His parents seemed unaware of the effort he was making. Abraham was lost in grief and prayer, his thoughts fixed on his dead son, his affections still centered on him. And Esther merely grew more remote.

A quarrel, as always, climaxed this period. Arnold felt rejected. His old belief that he was unloved and unwanted had been strengthened. One day he packed up his clothes and walked away from the home of his parents. He never went back to spend a night under their roof.

Rothstein moved into the Broadway Central Hotel. He was a slim, rather handsome, youth. His cheeks were chalky, never taking on color. His eyes were the most striking feature of his face. They were oversize, softly brown in moments of ease. But whenever he was under tension of any kind the eyes appeared to harden and then grow hooded.

He was filled with energy, unable to relax even for a moment. He was a man who had no inner resources; his own company bored him. His only reading matter was the newspaper and he read only the sports pages.

He had to be part of a crowd, yet he didn't like people. When he joined others he was nearly always an onlooker, not a participant. He stayed on the fringe, smiling, affable and eager to please. He was a good listener. He wanted to know all about everyone else. He fought to keep anyone from knowing anything about him.

He found a job as a cigar salesman. This kept him involved with owners of hotels, saloons and gambling places. With some of these he formed a series of surface friendships. His habit of listening made him a good salesman, because it caused people to think he was really interested in them and their problems. So, though there was no actual intimacy, there was a temporary community of interest.

He made a good living selling cigars. He later said, "I averaged a hundred a week. That was a lot of money for a man, let alone a kid." And he added to this by playing pool. He started by playing for small stakes. As his bankroll, and his skill, increased he began to bet larger sums. Soon he was spending part of every night at the poolroom owned by John J. McGraw, manager of the New York Giants baseball team.

John McGraw was one of the stellar lights of the sporting world. He was the highest-paid manager of the best and most successful baseball team in the world. It was Jim Mutrie, captain of the team who, being asked, "Who are the Giants?" replied, "The Giants? We are the people."

Rothstein liked being around McGraw. He liked being around Tod Sloan, the highest-paid jockey in the world, and Stanley Ketchel, the best fighter, pound for pound, in the world. And these two bosom buddies of McGraw's were at the poolroom night after night.

Broadway always paid special tribute to the best and biggest in any field. Just being the best marked an individual off from the common herd. It resulted in the individual's being held in esteem. The best jockey. The best distance runner. The biggest gambler.

Arnold Rothstein, at that time, set his eyes on being the best in a limited field. He wanted to be the best pool player on Broadway. It would give him a place in the hierarchy of Broadway, a place to start from. And he knew that where he went from there depended upon his ability and his bankroll.

That was one other gauge of a man's place in the Broadway spotlight. The size of his bankroll. The public size, that is. The man with a million in the bank didn't rate with the sport who flashed a thick roll of hundred-dollar bills. The roll was real because the money could be touched, seen, spent. The bankbook was just a piece of paper with a number written on it.

The bankroll had another special virtue. It was always available. Its owner could take advantage of a sudden opportunity, didn't have to wait to fill out a withdrawal slip. Or cash a check.

"Money talks," he once told an interviewer. "I learned that fast. The more money the louder it talks."

The cigar salesman made a good living. He lived frugally, did not dissipate. Each week the roll in his pocket grew a little thicker. He knew he could never attain his ultimate aim by simple economies, but these could start him on his way. He didn't like long-range projects. He was essentially a short-term, quick-turnover man. Even when he bet on a horse race, he preferred a sprint to a distance race.

Rothstein pursued a fixed course. He worked at selling cigars until he had accumulated $2,000. He decided that this was sufficient to base an entry into gambling as a profession. He quit his salesman's job. He would never again work for anyone else. All the rest of his life, no matter what else he might be, he would always be a professional gambler.

His first job was runner and collector for a bookmaker. It was not difficult to make this connection, because most persons thought this a most unpropitious moment to enter, or remain in, the field. For the second time in three years a committee of the state legislature was conducting an investigation into gambling, crime and politics in New York City. A daily parade of witnesses was giving damning testimony.

A cry for reform was coming from many sources, the loudest emanating from the pulpit of the Rev. Dr. Parkhurst. Almost as shrill were the demands of the New York *Evening Sun* and the New York *Post*.

But Rothstein was not taking his cue from either the pulpit or the editorial pages. Tim Sullivan had patted him on the back and told him to go ahead. Sullivan was not worried by the investigation, nor was Richard Croker, boss of Tammany Hall. There had been investigations before and there would be later investigations. But nothing would really be changed.

The situation in New York—the connection between crime and politics—could not be eradicated unless politics was abolished. And politics, for good or evil, was part of the democratic process. And part of the price of freedom.

For that matter, the investigations were part of politics also. They were weapons in the hands of the opposition, which controlled the state legislature.

The state of New York could be divided into two parts—New York City and all the rest.

The city was dominated by immigrants, and the children of immigrants, who had come from Middle Europe, Italy and Ireland, bringing with them the ideas, the customs, the morality of their

native lands. This population was growing ever more Catholic, with
the values of that religion.

Upstate, which meant the rest of the state, was still predominantly
Protestant, predominantly Anglo-Saxon. It was a stronghold of the
Puritanism that had dominated the colonies, carried over for almost
a hundred years after the Revolution.

The city was a Democratic stronghold; upstate was Republican.
The State Constitution, long ago drawn, was weighted heavily in
favor of upstate elements. (Al Smith remarked wryly in 1921 that
"it was unconstitutional for the Democrats to control the state legislature.") Republicans, therefore, always had a ready weapon to
use against Tammany. An investigation ordered in Albany.

U.S. Senator Thomas Platt, called the "Easy Boss," controlled
the Republican party. He carried on a war against Croker. But it
was a surface war, fought with mock bullets. A well-read man, a
student of history, he was aware that the battle between city and
country was centuries old. In ancient Rome it had been *urbs* versus
rus. In Cromwell's England, between Cavaliers and Roundheads.
(Was not Cain a landholder and Abel a shepherd?)

So, what he fought for was momentary advantage and not the
annihilation of Tammany.

Three years earlier Platt had ordered a New York City investigation. It stemmed, as did this present one, from charges made by
Dr. Parkhurst and backed by newspapers. The Lexow Committee,
as it was called, had revealed just enough to show there was substance to the charges and then been liquidated.

The reason advanced had been that Dr. Parkhurst had not been
able to provide "actual proof."

But this was not the true reason. That reason was an agreement
entered into between Platt and Croker. It provided that Platt would
end the hearings and, in return, Croker would give a share of New
York City patronage to Platt. Among other things, six Republicans
would be appointed to judicial posts.

Croker later maintained that, in addition to calling off the hearings, Platt promised repeal of certain state laws restricting home

rule in New York City. And that this repealer legislation was supposed to precede the judgeships.

Platt charged he had shown good faith in calling off the Lexow Committee and expected Croker to deliver on his end before he ordered the new legislation.

During this stalemate New York City elected a reform mayor. Croker accepted this philosophically. He told Lincoln Steffens, then a reporter for the *Evening Post*, "[The] people could not stand the rotten police corruption. We'll be back after the next election; they [the people] can't stand reform either."

He was proved right when Mayor Strong, the reformer, was beaten by Tammany.

Platt repeated his demand for the judgeships and Croker refused the demand. Platt ordered another investigation, this one called the Mazet Investigation, after the chairman of the committee which conducted it. The Lexow investigation had been ended because Parkhurst had not offered "proof." Mazet's was predicated on Platt's assertion that now Parkhurst did have proof. And that proof was bolstered by evidence gathered by Steffens and by Jacob A. Riis, the *Evening Sun*'s great reporter.

Mazet began holding his hearings. Like investigators before him and investigators who would follow him in New York City up to, and including, Thomas E. Dewey, he was fully aware of the "ground rules" which governed such inquiries.

Politicians of all parties have certain mutual interests. These must always be safeguarded. Therefore the ground rules.

In the Mazet hearings, as in those of the Lexow Committee, the targets were the police. Steffens, in his *Autobiography*, told the reason for the ground rules and showed how they were applied in this instance.

"[The accused police officers] had behind them the most powerful politicians in both parties whom they could threaten to involve in their testimony; and the politicians could, with threats, call upon statesmen and businessmen high up. Once started, no one could foretell where the exposure would stop; it was indeed like a fire. . . . The investigation was a worry . . . for the underworld and indeed for the upper world. . . . The pressure upon the Commission was irresistible . . . and my guess was [the commission] had to agree to keep the revelations within the bounds of the police and their dealings with vice and small business."

There were moments when it appeared that Frank Moss, special counsel to the commission and counsel for Dr. Parkhurst's Society for the Suppression of Crime, might ignore the ground rules. One such moment came when Moss called Croker as a witness.

Moss wanted to know about certain financial melons that Croker had shared as the result of franchises granted by the Board of Aldermen and special laws passed by the same body.

Croker, a squat man, thick-chested and thick-armed, with a scrubby beard emphasizing his strong jaw, fought back against this line of questioning. He called it a modern inquisition. He tried to trade blows with Moss, but he came out a loser. He admitted he was not a politician for the glory involved.

Moss asked, "Then you are working for your pocket, are you not?"

"All the time, the same as you," Croker answered.

Others, it was revealed, worked for their pockets also. These included members of the police, the judiciary and the District Attorney's office.

As the inquiry went on, some gambling houses were closed. The streetwalkers were chased off the streets. Others were arrested and found their regular bailbondsmen were not available. There were a number of police transfers, resignations and retirements.

The public was informed of corruption within the police department, learned that gamblers, prostitutes and even burglars bought protection. The going rates for appointment to the police department, and promotion within it, were made public knowledge.

It was at this time, and under these circumstances, that Rothstein became a gambler. Like Croker, he did not believe the people could stand reform.

His pay as runner and collector was $25 a week plus commissions on any bets he might get. He was not interested in this small take; he at once began to look for ways to increase his take-home pay.

An old-time bookmaker called "Kid Rags," whose real name was

Max Kalish, was an apprentice with Rothstein. When Rothstein was killed, Kalish told a reporter, "He couldn't stay on the level. Right away he began 'past-posting.' [This meant placing a bet after post time, when the result of the race was already apparent.] When I called him on it, he told me it wasn't wrong, just smart. He said now I was wise to it, I ought to do some of it myself. It was easy money and no one had a right to pass up easy money."

Kalish went on to tell of Rothstein's philosophy as a youth. "He used to say, 'Look out for Number One. If you don't, no one else will. If a man is dumb, someone is going to get the best of him, so why not you? If you don't, you're as dumb as he is.' Rothstein was always looking for a little bit the best of it. He used to say that just a half-point [one-half of one per cent] could mean thousands over a length of time.

"He knew percentages and knew how to take advantage of them. I learned a lot from him."

Rothstein did not work for the bookmaker long. Somehow he was prospering too fast, and his employer didn't like that. By 1902 Rothstein was working for himself. His office was his hat. He booked bets on horse races, ball games, elections and prize fights. And he gambled on his own, mostly shooting craps, but often in poker games.

He was a small operator, but that was the way he wanted it. He explained, "Never get into a game that you can't bull." That meant a man was a fool to play against a bigger bankroll. The secret of winning was to have enough money to lose one more bet than anyone else could afford to lose.

That was why he stayed away from the big games that such men as Richard Canfield, Davy Johnson and Bill Busteed operated. He knew about these men and their games, envied them their money and their standing in his world. He longed for the day when he would be in their class, but he was realist enough to know that day was still to come. In the meanwhile he would not overmatch himself.

As a young gambler he went to the places where the sports congregated. He became well known at Jack's and Shanley's, at Rector's and Considine's, at the old Waldorf, with its Peacock Bar, and at the Knickerbocker, where Maxfield Parrish's painting of Old King Cole dominated the room.

He made regular calls at the Hesper Club and Big Tim Sullivan's saloon. He was available for any errand or favor that Sullivan might want of him. He even voted in the election of 1901, though he was still two years below the legal age.

Rothstein made a lot of acquaintances, but few friends. One of these was Nicky Arnstein. Arnstein was handsome, debonair, part confidence man, part gambler. Tall and slender, with a baritone voice that he used like a musical instrument, Arnstein outranked Rothstein in those days.

"He was just a kid," Arnstein recalled. "He didn't look like a gambler. His face was not impassive, but a kaleidoscope of emotion. When he played, he smiled and grunted and scowled and laughed hoarsely. He looked pleased and he looked worried. But those expressions told his opponents nothing because they told too much. Of course, if anyone had been able to read Arnold's eyes, it might have been different. But no one could read his eyes. They were always hooded."

Bit by bit Rothstein increased his bankroll. At the end of 1903 it had reached $5,000. He was doing well at a time when other gamblers were doing badly.

Reform was back again. William Travers Jerome was district attorney and he was conducting repeated raids on what had been sacrosanct establishments.

The Allen, now past seventy, closed the last of a string of gambling houses he had been running for more than a half century. This was the "Square Deal Club," on West Third Street, just east of Sixth Avenue. Allen's place wasn't raided. He closed it voluntarily after it was revealed that he had contributed more than $6,000 to Jerome's campaign.

Canfield, also, closed up in 1903. A member of the Vanderbilt family lost $100,000 at a single sitting at Canfield's and gave the gambler an I.O.U. The Vanderbilt honor was at stake, so the I.O.U. was paid, but the Vanderbilt family brought pressure on Jerome to close up Canfield's.

One midnight, Jerome led a raid on the famed gambling establishment on East Forty-fourth Street, next door to Delmonico's. The raiders broke in and wrecked the place. Canfield, gambler by profession, art collector and bibliophile by avocation, did not reopen. He felt that he had been betrayed, that there were no longer "gentlemen" players and "gentlemen" politicians. He hung Whistler's portrait of him, called "His Eminence," in his library and gave himself over to enjoying the masterpieces he had accumulated through the years.

"Honest John" Kelly closed his downtown "store" and retired from gambling temporarily. It would not be until 1907 that he would reopen at 156 West Forty-fourth Street.

Men like Allen, Canfield and Kelly were public figures. Jerome, politically ambitious and publicity wise, directed his attacks on them. There was no value in going after unimportant gamblers like Rothstein.

This was a time when Rothstein maneuvered carefully. He never pushed himself beyond safe limits.

His activities were diverse. Primarily he gambled. On anything. But he was still lending money, still charging high interest for that money. And he was already advancing funds to "operators" like Nicky Arnstein, who might be temporarily down on their luck and in need of working capital.

He was not averse to going into legitimate enterprises either. Not if they offered a chance of a big return. He was a silent partner in an automobile agency and in a number of drugstores.

The bankroll grew larger. By the end of 1906 it mounted to $12,000.

He always carried the cash with him. It was a thick, green billboard, advertising his ability and his success. And it had another value. It gave Rothstein a feeling of assurance that he was progressing. Whenever he had self-doubts he could count his money. Whenever he had a sense of inferiority he could flash his roll.

This might irritate others, but he did not care about others. It didn't matter to him that he wasn't liked. What did matter was that his bankroll got respect.

He obscured his personality. He was well-mannered. He dressed quietly. He was abstemious. His personal life was above reproach. It is a peculiarity of gamblers that they are almost monkish outside their trade. Nearly all of them are monogamous. Such eminent psychiatrists as Dr. Ralph Greenson and Dr. Edmund Bergler hold to the theory this is because gamblers exhaust themselves emotionally in their gambling.

Dostoevski, in his letters and diary, tells how gambling gave him orgiastic pleasure.

But Rothstein was not the same type of gambler as Dostoevski. In him there was none of the feckless daring, the thoughtlessness, the intoxication. He was a cold-blooded businessman and gambling was his business. Yet he lived the same type of controlled life that other gamblers did.

What was the reason?

His youth and upbringing, of course. The background from which he had evolved, on which he had turned his back, but which was a daemon he could not cast out. He grew up at a time when sex was a taboo subject. He came from a family where it was never mentioned. He connected sex and everything concomitant to it with the religion of his fathers.

Outwardly he had discarded that religion. He was no Jew. But inwardly there was a vestigial fear, a vestigial superstition. No matter how much he tried to tell himself that Judaism was nothing to him, actually it was a great deal to him. He wanted no part of its virtues; he could not discard its faults.

His people separated women into two groups, "good" women and "bad" women. He accepted that separation. Until 1907 he had no interest in good women and a fear of bad women. But in 1907 he fell in love.

The girl was Carolyn Greene, barely nineteen, an actress. She was slight of build, of medium height. Her hair was reddish-brown and her eyes were gray-blue. She had a small part in the play, *The Chorus Lady,* which starred Rose Stahl.

They met one evening at Churchill's. Rothstein was immediately attracted to her. And she to him. "He was quiet, well-spoken, with a nice smile. I had no idea he was a gambler," she said, "for he looked and acted like a successful young businessman or lawyer."

Rothstein asked her to have dinner with him and she accepted. They had a number of other dinner dates. Then, without a word, he ceased seeing her.

This surprised her, but what surprised her even more was to be told that Rothstein was questioning anyone who might have some idea of her private life. Did she have any boy friends? What was her reputation? Did anyone know anything bad about her? (He was not interested in anything good.)

Carolyn seethed. She sought Rothstein out and upbraided him. "How dare you ask people about me? What business am I of yours?"

Rothstein smiled and said, "A man has a right to know all about the girl he's thinking of marrying."

The answer was so unexpected that she was at a loss for words. Before she could recover Rothstein had tipped his hat and walked away.

A short time later Carolyn was invited to a supper party by George Bauchle, the attorney who was a poker-playing crony of Rothstein's. When Carolyn reached Delmonico's and asked for Bauchle's party, she was led to a table for two where Rothstein was sitting. He rose and said, "I'm the party, a party of one. I hope you're not angry."

She was angry. But she was also amused and flattered. And hungry. Besides, she had dressed for a party, looked forward to one, and she was determined to have one. So she remained.

This was the official beginning of Rothstein's courtship. His inquiry was completed and he was satisfied with its results. Carolyn belonged among the "good" women.

Rothstein did not lay rapid-fire siege to a woman's heart. He had so many interests that time for romance had to be rationed. But he saw Carolyn at regular intervals. Like all young men going acourting, he preened his tail feathers.

"I'm going to be a big man someday."

"A big gambler, you mean," was her answer. She was by now aware of his profession.

"What's wrong with that? It's a business. But I'm not going to be a gambler all my life. When I have enough money I'm going to go into a big business."

"How much is enough?"

He laughed. "I don't know. But I've got a start." He took his bankroll from his pocket and spread it on the table.

"Put that money away. It doesn't impress me and you're a fool to show it off that way."

He shook his head. "You don't understand, Carolyn." He spoke very seriously. "This—" his hands touched the money with caressing fingers—"this is going to make me big and important. I know how much money means. I'm going to have more and more of it. Nothing is going to stop me."

She believed him. "I had to," she said. "It was as if he were taking an oath or praying to the only God he could conceive of."

During this period Rothstein indoctrinated Carolyn into the peculiar world in which he lived. She met politicians like Big Tim, Charley Murphy and Tom Foley; newspapermen like Herbert Bayard Swope, Ben De Casseres and Bruno Lessing; gamblers like Vernie Barton and Tom Shaughnessy; wits like Wilson Mizner and Grant Clark, the songwriter.

She met all these, but it was a long time before she met Rothstein's family. That came more than a year after Rothstein's courtship began. "I want you to meet my family," he said.

"I'd like to."

He looked away from her, spoke with less assurance. "I've got to take you there," he said. "Believe me, it doesn't matter what they say or think. I'm a stranger to them. I live my own life."

"But you say you have to take me to them."

He nodded. "That's right. It doesn't make any sense, but that's the way it is. It's something I have to do."

She said, "Maybe you're not such a stranger to them after all."

But this he would not admit.

They went to the brownstone on West Eighty-fourth Street where the Rothsteins now lived. It rose four stories, a twin to its neighbor on each side. It was high-ceilinged, commodious, luxurious. It was a home that befitted a wealthy merchant. It was filled with massive pieces of furniture and the Rothstein family.

Esther had lines on her almond-shaped face. Her brown eyes gleamed under shadowed lids.

Abraham was a patriarch in a skullcap. He was dressed in his formal black, his spare figure a little bent.

There were the two boys, Edgar and Jack, caught between two worlds. They were heirs to the past, but unsure as to whether they would accept the legacy or, like their older brother, reject it.

And Edith, the sister. She was shy, wide-eyed.

There was constraint in the parlor. Everyone sat on the edge of the overstuffed furniture, thoughts as stiffly balanced as their bodies.

Finally, Abraham asked the inevitable question. "Are you Jewish, Miss Greene?"

"My father is Jewish and my mother is Catholic. I have been brought up as a Catholic."

"But you will change your religion if you and Arnold should marry, will you not?"

She did not drop her eyes from his. "No, Mr. Rothstein."

He nodded slowly, his lips twisted into a wry smile. "My son," he said, "is a grown man. I cannot live his life for him. If you should marry him, you have all my wishes for your happiness, but you cannot have my approval. How could I approve losing my son?"

"But you would not be losing him."

Abraham still smiled, a smile close to weeping. "If he marries outside his faith, he will be lost to me. That is The Law."

When Rothstein took Carolyn home, she said, "Someday you'll hate me for coming between you and your family. I don't want that to happen. Maybe we ought to stop seeing each other."

He laughed bitterly. "It was just the way I knew it would be. Maybe I just wanted to hurt myself. But I won't let it change anything about us. I love you. I want to marry you. My father said I lived my own life. Well, it wouldn't be much of a life without you."

"You're always talking about percentage. This time it's against you. Have you thought of that?"

"Sometimes I buck the percentage. There are ways to even things up. I love you. Will you marry me?"

"Yes," she said.

The ceremony took place in Saratoga, New York, on August 12, 1909. This was in the heart of the racing season. Herbert Bayard Swope was best man and Margaret Powell, who later married Swope, was maid of honor.

And in the house on Eighty-fourth Street, when Abraham Rothstein was informed of the marriage, he tore his clothes and ordered that the mirrors be covered again. He put on his prayer shawl and for the first time recited the *Kaddish* for the second of his sons.

Chapter 4 A Well-known Sportsman

Marriage added a new dimension to Rothstein's life. Or, more accurately, it made it a schizophrenic life.

There was always a part of him which wished to conform, to belong, to accept the protective coloration of normalcy. That was the part of him that turned back to his beginnings, to his parents, to their world. To a world that lived by established social rules, that had a strict code of social morality and social behavior.

In that world a man married a "good" woman. She made a home for him, provided him with stability.

Rothstein had uprooted himself from such a life, but he still wanted a fixed place in the world. And he used the one criterion he had: the world of his fathers.

That was why he kept on telling Carolyn that someday he would cease gambling. It wasn't that he thought of it as reforming, but as conforming. Without Carolyn, that idea was impossible. With her, it was always a potentiality.

She had been part of show business, but not deeply involved in it. Her background was conventional. A middle-class family with middle-class ideas. When she became an actress, it wasn't revolt. It was just that she liked to sing and dance. After all, she went home every night after the show.

Carolyn was aware that she was married to a gambler, but there was little social stigma to his business. Gambling was not regarded as sin per se. Not even as a major vice.

The gambler was, a half century ago, still a romantic figure. He was a man who took long chances in a world that believed in the long chance. He mixed with gentility, with society. A Canfield could be friend and intimate of the great artist Whistler. Only a few years earlier, John Morrissey had sat in Congress, been the companion of Commodore Vanderbilt and August Belmont. A "The" Allen could sit down beside Thurlow Weed, campaign manager for Abraham Lincoln.

E. Berry Wall, the Beau Brummel of American society in the days of Newport's greatness, wrote in his autobiography, *Neither Pest nor Puritan* of how Leonard Jerome was able to meet financial needs after his daughter had married Lord Randolph Churchill. This happened about the time that Jerome's grandson, Sir Winston Churchill, was born.

Jerome had promised his daughter a dot of $10,000 yearly, and this money had come from renting his town house to the Union League. After a time the Union League built its own clubhouse and Jerome found himself in bad straits.

"When his friends found Leonard in such a position," Wall wrote, "they got together—men like Colonel Lawrence Kip, Pierre Lorillard, James R. Keene, the Van Burens, and other members of the Knickerbocker and the Union Club. They decided to take over Leonard's house, opening a club where one could play baccarat and poker. . . .

"These men offered Leonard Jerome twenty-five thousand dollars a year rent, which he accepted, and the place was turned into a [gambling] club. . . .

Gambling—even the ownership of a gambling house—was something a gentleman could do, though he could not go to work.

This was a period of chaos. The economic world had seized upon Darwinism as a rationalization for its conduct. It was still the fag end of the era of "Robber Barons." And certainly these men—Drew, Fisk, Gould, Vanderbilt—had all been gamblers.

It was a consciousness of this that could lead Carolyn Greene—sharp-minded and realistic—to believe that her husband could use gambling as a means to an end. That he could step from that world into any other that he wished and for which his talents were best suited.

In 1909 Rothstein was barely inside the periphery of the complex world of politics, gambling and crime. How could Carolyn know that he was to move, as though propelled by a centripetal force, to its very heart? The force would not touch her directly. That was why, for a score of years, she could believe that sometime he would quit gambling.

She would not accept the signs that were apparent from the day of her marriage.

During the rest of that 1909 Saratoga season Rothstein made book, played cards and dice. Carolyn went to the track with him each day. Then, after the four of them had dinner, she and Margaret Powell found ways to amuse themselves while Rothstein and Swope went gambling.

Saratoga was a delightful place for a honeymoon. Even for a honeymoon for one. The Grand Union and United States Hotels were beautiful structures with extraordinary service. There were the baths, the tennis courts and a theater. The town was a gathering place, as it had been sinoe before the Civil War, for the rich and the famous.

In addition to these charms, to the cool nights, and to the fresh breezes, there were the race track and the casino.

John Morrissey had built the original race track during the Civil War. At the same time he had opened a Saratoga branch of his Manhattan gambling house. It was these attractions which had brought the three great Union heroes of the Civil War—U. S. Grant, William T. Sherman, and Philip Sheridan—to Saratoga. They had also brought the Vanderbilts, Jim Fisk, James G. Blaine, Samuel J. Tilden, August Belmont and other titans.

Arnold Rothstein began a yearly pilgrimage to Saratoga in 1904. With the other bookmakers who operated at the track he came to Saratoga aboard the "Cavanagh Special," the day before the racing season opened.

The Special was a de luxe train, composed of Pullman cars, diners and, for those temporarily down on their luck, day coaches.

It was named in honor of James G. Cavanagh, arbiter of the betting ring since 1897.

Cavanagh occupied a position among bookmakers like the one Judge Kenesaw M. Landis was to hold in baseball and Will H. Hays in the motion-picture industry. He was the head of the Metropolitan Turf Association, a closed shop of bookmakers who handled bets at all the New York State race tracks. Bookmakers could not afford to air their disputes openly, nor could they permit public differences with their patrons. Someone had to be the court of last, and absolute, resort. That was Cavanagh's position.

He ruled on who could—and who could not—join the Association. The final accolade was when a bookmaker became a regular on the Special.

In 1909 Rothstein made his sixth trip as a regular. Like the horde of others aboard, he felt and hoped this would be a big season. Also like many of them, he feared this might be the last season.

Charles Evans Hughes, a stern moralist, was governor of New York. He had prodded the legislature into passing a law which banned bookmaking. This law had been rigidly enforced during the metropolitan season, when the horses ran in Democratic-dominated New York City and its environs. The result had been a dismal season for bookmakers.

Racing had long been proclaimed "the sport of kings." Its promoters maintained its purpose was "to improve the breed." But it had developed, when the common men found they could not bet, that they were not very interested in a royal sport. And there were mutterings that Henry Ford and some others in Detroit were making improvement of the breed a matter of small importance.

The bookmakers, realists all, knew the one purpose of racing was gambling. Without it there would be no racing. Their hope rested in Saratoga.

Saratoga, of course, was in New York. However, it was in upstate, Republican, New York, and its citizens always voted the straight Republican ticket.

The assemblyman from Saratoga had voted for the Hughes Bill, but Saratogans did not hold it against him. They took it for granted he had voted against bookmaking in New York City, where it was gambling, not against bookmaking in Saratoga, where it was a "business."

Saratoga's principal industry was gambling. Its economic life was dependent upon the money that flowed in during the month of August. Natives expected that the law would not mean the same thing in pure, churchgoing, Republican Saratoga that it meant in sin-ridden, corrupt, Tammany-bossed New York City. Besides, didn't good Republicans own the race tracks, the hotels, the boarding-houses, the stores and shops?

If Saratogans reached this feeling on the basis of reason, the book-makers reached the same conclusion on the basis of cynicism. They knew that the convention which had nominated Hughes, which had written the antibookmaking plank into the Republican platform, had been held in Saratoga the previous August. Held there so that the delegates, fresh from doing their moral duty, could go out to the track and relax.

They found their cynicism justified when they arrived in Sara-toga. They were told that word had been received that there would be no interference with their trade at the Saratoga meeting.

There was jubilation among the betting horde. They drank a toast to Cavanagh. Rothstein drank his in milk.

He was not then an important member of the bookmaking world. He did not rank with "Tiffany" Wolfgang, with Davy Johnson, with "Hummingbird" Tyler or Tom Shaw. His customers would not in-clude such plungers as "Pittsburgh Phil" Smith, Riley Grannan, John Sanford, the carpet manufacturer, or Joshua Cosden, the oil millionaire. He was just another bookmaker with a limited, albeit quite thick, bankroll, who had to guard against being cleaned out by one big bet.

In the era of bookmaking it was possible for bettors to leave the race track with more money than they had brought with them. They were engaged in a guessing contest with a bookmaker and, some-times, they could outguess him. Agreed that the bookmaker had the percentage going for him, he could still lose.

Today, of course, with pari-mutuel betting, this is no longer possible. The bettors merely gamble against each other. The various states, the race tracks, the local communities, all scoop their percentage off the top of each bet. The state practices a new, and highly profitable, type of "vigorish." The machines merely act as conveyor belts for cash, charging fifteen per cent for their use.

Rothstein, then, had to be chary of his bankroll. He didn't want one big bet, but a lot of small ones. And he always sought means by which to protect himself. The best means was to have a bigger and bigger bankroll.

This was no more than he had known back in the days of the Victoria. And, as in those days, he utilized the hockshops. This time, however, it was not his father's big gold watch that went into pawn, but Carolyn's jewelry. He had given her many gifts during their courtship. Now he borrowed these back.

He explained his reasons to Carolyn. "I don't need the money, but I might. It gives me room to maneuver. Besides, it's one way of using someone else's money. I can lend it out at a lot more interest than I'm paying."

In those days, and afterward, he would discuss the philosophy of his business with her, but never the actual business nor any specific plans. He armored himself against any intrusion into his thoughts. He said, "If one man knows something, it's a secret. If two know it, eleven know it. When three know it, a hundred and eleven know it." This form of geometrical progression was in no textbook, but it was axiomatic to him.

He had a successful season at Saratoga, winning about $12,000. "Your husband is going places," he told Carolyn, spreading the money on the counterpane of the bed in their hotel room. "I've got plans."

He revealed these plans when they returned to New York.

He was going to open his own gambling house. To that end he rented two brownstones on West Forty-sixth Street. They would live in one and the other would be his place of business.

To operate safely, Rothstein needed protection. He had a location and a bankroll, but these were not enough. He went to Tim Sullivan to get protection.

Sullivan, always sentimental, was delighted that Arnold had married. Sullivan believed in marriage, big families and the straight Tammany ticket. His wedding present to Rothstein was protection—with one condition attached. Rothstein was to take one Willie Shea as his partner.

Shea was a ward leader who, for a number of years, had held a job as a building inspector. The pay was small, but the graft was big. Every construction job needed Shea's approval. The result was that Shea had amassed a large bank account.

Recently, however, he had incurred the anger of his superiors. A matter of poaching on someone else's preserves. A complaint had been made to Sullivan, with the suggestion that it was time someone else took over from Shea, some poor and deserving youth whose mouth was watering for the chance. Since Shea had broken one of the rules of the game, Sullivan had to accede to the request.

Shea was now out of work. He wanted to get back at the trough. It was Sullivan's idea that he and Rothstein become partners. Sullivan told Rothstein, "Willie can put up part of the bankroll."

Rothstein did not argue. He would have preferred being on his own, but that hadn't worked out. By accepting Sullivan's "suggestion" Rothstein was placing Sullivan under an obligation. And, besides, he would have the use of someone else's money.

Sullivan arranged a meeting of Shea and Rothstein. Shea was a little man, cocky, short-tempered, miserly and suspicious. In addition, he was violently anti-Semitic. After the meeting Shea went to see Sullivan.

"How can you tell what a Jew's thinkin'?" he demanded. "They're different from us."

"Rothstein's a good boy," Sullivan said. "And smart. You stick with him and you'll make a lot of money."

That was one argument that could win over Shea. His cupidity was greater than his intolerance. He entered an agreement whereby he posted half the bankroll, and then proceeded to look out for his interests. He was determined that Rothstein wouldn't outsmart him.

Since Shea was always inside the gambling rooms, Rothstein acted as "outside man," the partner who made the contacts, lined up players, joined in social activities with the players. It also permitted him to diversify his activities. He not only kept his various eggs separated, he frequently divided yolk from white and kept these apart.

He continued to lend money. Through Sullivan he met George Considine, brother of Sullivan's partner, and the two ran a poker game in the Metropole Hotel. He also made book, though the heat was still on bookmakers.

A "friendly" poker game, begun in the Broadway Central Hotel some years earlier, still went on. Now, it was the "Partridge Club," and it held its meetings at the Metropole or at Jack's or Shanley's.

When Rothstein had been just another face—a name—in the background no one had bothered to react to him. Now, however, others did. In this world in which he lived men sought out each other's weaknesses so they could profit from them.

Because Rothstein was not a good mixer, because he had a supercilious twist to his lower lip, he irritated many people. They didn't like a man who appeared to be self-sufficient, whose attitude they felt was superior. Certainly Rothstein was given to being dogmatic. And he had a habit of referring to other people as "chumps."

There was a group who made their headquarters at Jack's who especially disliked Rothstein.

This group included Wilson Mizner, already known for his sharp tongue, Jack Francis, a successful gambler, Tad Dorgan and Hype Igoe, both of whom were sports writers and cartoonists. There was a touch of insularity in all these, overladen with anti-Semitism. As Mizner said, they didn't like the smart-aleck sheenie. They plotted to put Rothstein in his place and make a profit for themselves in the process. None of them was averse to a little lawful larceny.

They agreed among themselves that they had discovered Rothstein's weakness. It was vanity. They decided to make that vanity costly to him and profitable for them.

Rothstein still played pool regularly. At times he found an unwary individual who would gamble with him on the result of a game. The Broadway regulars obeyed a strict set of rules. When one of them found a "pigeon," no one interfered with the plucking.

And the regulars had seen Rothstein pull out even the tail feathers from suckers.

Mizner and his group decided that they would hit at Rothstein through his supposed strength. To that end they brought Jack Conway from Philadelphia to New York. Conway was a "gentleman sportsman." He was an expert amateur jockey, both on the flat and over the jumps. And he was an expert pool player, so good he had defeated a number of professionals in matches at the Philadelphia Racquet Club, of which he was undisputed champion.

Mizner was certain Rothstein did not know Conway. However, there must be no direct challenge. Anything so straightforward would only raise suspicions in Rothstein's mind. The whole thing had to be carefully plotted.

The group waited their chance. It came one night at Jack's. They were seated at their regular table when Rothstein came in. He said "hello" and accepted an invitation to have a cup of coffee.

For a time the talk was strictly "shop." Prize fights, baseball and horse racing and bits of gossip of Broadway. Then, casually, Francis started talking about pool and billiards. They discussed great players like Alfred De Oro and Jake Schaefer, and Willie Hoppe. In an offhand way, Francis said that their guest, Conway, was probably the best amateur pool player in the country.

Rothstein, caught off guard, said in his soft, irritating voice, "You're wrong. You're a hundred and ten per cent wrong."

Mizner snapped the jaws of the trap. "Name someone who can beat him and for how much."

Rothstein immediately grasped that he had been maneuvered into an untenable position. He could try to laugh it off, but that way he would lose face. The word would quickly spread that he had backed down. On the other hand, he had tremendous confidence in himself. He, too, had beaten professionals. He took out his bankroll, peeled off some bills. "I'll bet $500 I can beat Mr. Conway."

Even if he lost, all he would lose would be money. It was a cheap price to pay for keeping up his front.

It was agreed that they would play to 100 points and, since Rothstein had been challenged, he chose the site of the game, John Mc-

Graw's Billiard Parlor, alongside the old Herald Building. By insisting on this site, Rothstein was coppering part of his bet. He owned a piece of the business and the money the spectators would spend would yield him a profit.

It was eight o'clock on a Thursday night when they began their match.

It was quickly obvious that both men were experts. Conway won the first match by a few points. Smiling, Rothstein paid off and asked for a return match. Conway's backers were willing. Rothstein won this time and there was an immediate demand for a rubber game to settle which was the better player.

Rothstein won this rubber match, collected his bets. He started to walk away from the table but was halted by Francis. "How about another set of three games?"

Rothstein laughed, said, "I can play all night." He thought he was kidding.

They played the second set and, again, Rothstein won two out of the three games. He was now more than $2,000 ahead. By this time, the room was so crowded that McGraw had barred the door against any more spectators.

Again Conway asked for another match. Again Rothstein agreed. And, again, Rothstein was the winner. It was now past closing time and McGraw announced that play was finished for the night. The crowd and Conway's backers would have none of it. They wanted further action.

Mizner offered to pay and tip the attendants if they would stay on. Someone in the crowd started passing a hat and it was filled with change and greenbacks; this money was given the boys who were racking balls, keeping score and waiting on the spectators. McGraw shrugged his shoulders and agreed to let the game go on.

By sunrise, Rothstein had won another $3,000. His supporters in the crowd had also won large sums. Conway won occasional games, even a number of matches, but he was never able to pull even. Each time he appeared to be coming close, Rothstein would beat him.

After each match it was Conway who said, "Just one more."

Friday morning passed and then Friday afternoon. The players were served sandwiches and black coffee between their turns at the table.

By Friday evening both men were playing raggedly. Their reflexes had slowed and their eyes kept misting. But the man who was behind would not quit and the man who was ahead was amenable to playing until collapse. He was on velvet and ready to go on.

It was McGraw who finally called a halt to the game. At four o'clock on Saturday morning, after more than thirty-four hours of continuous play, McGraw refused to allow the balls to be racked again. His remark, as reported by Donald Henderson Clarke in *In the Reign of Rothstein*, was, "If I let you go on, I'll have you dead on my hands."

Rothstein did not reveal how much he had won. Mizner and his group said they had lost more than $10,000.

After the players washed and had some black coffee, they went to a Turkish bath. Arrangements were made there for a rematch, this time in Philadelphia, for a side bet of $5,000. However, this never came off. Some of Conway's friends talked him out of it, saying it was degrading for a gentleman to match himself against a professional gambler.

However, the newspapers which reported the match did not call Rothstein a gambler. Instead, the *Mail* referred to him as "a well-known sportsman," and the *World* called him the "son of a wealthy businessman."

In all that was written about him in the ensuing years he was to be identified as a gambler. And never again would he be primarily identified as the son of the father. No, he would have an identity of his own.

That was something he wanted very much.

Chapter **5** *Better Luck Next Time*

Like all gamblers, Rothstein was always hunting the big win, the killing. His day-to-day activities paid for overhead—"the nut"—and yielded a small and steady profit. This was not enough, however, to fatten his bankroll to the point where he could compete with a Davy Johnson or a John Kelly. For it to grow that large he would have to strike a bonanza.

The odds on this eventuating were long; but there was always the chance. He was operating in an era when great fortunes were being made by men who took all kinds of gambles and loved to play high.

As "outside man" for his gambling house Rothstein was always searching for a "mark." This was gambling argot for a rich man who thought he could beat the house. "Making your mark" meant proving the sucker wrong.

There was fierce competition among gamblers for marks. And a code of ethics. One gambler had the right to try to cut in on another's mark, but it was a gross violation to tip off the sucker. Rothstein came close to breaking the rule in the case of Ohio Columbus Barbour, head of the Ohio Match Company, and Barbour's close friend, J. R. Graves, builder of the Polk Street railroad station in Chicago.

Barbour and Graves, their fortunes made, came to New York in 1910 in search of culture and excitement. Barbour especially had an interest in art. His appearance in New York was reported in the newspapers and excited interest among both art dealers and gamblers.

Barbour became a regular visitor at the art galleries and quickly fell in with another art connoisseur, a suave, gentlemanly, world traveler who could speak with authority on the Renaissance school, the Flemish school, and the paintings of El Greco. Barbour had great enthusiasm, but little knowledge. He asked his new-found friend if he would go to Europe with him and Graves to assist the pair in buying art treasures.

The world traveler reluctantly agreed. His name was Nicky Arnstein.

There have been few like Nicky Arnstein. Whatever his antecedents—and Nicky has told so many stories that there is no way of knowing the truth—Arnstein has always shone with a patina of culture. His comments on art made sense, even to professionals. And his manner and bearing were such that it never entered Barbour's mind that Nicky was anything but what he said he was.

For some weeks Nicky and Barbour visited salons and museums in New York and then they prepared to leave for Europe, accompanied by Graves. The smart boys of Broadway had watched Arnstein bait his line, hook his fish. And they were waiting to see how big that fish would be when Arnstein landed him. Among those who had watched was Arnold Rothstein.

He wanted a "piece" of Barbour. Knowing Arnstein, he had gone to him and tried to arrange for Arnstein to steer Barbour to his poker game. Arnstein had refused. That wasn't what he had in mind. Nor did he want to surrender his fish for a steerer's fee of ten per cent.

Rothstein didn't give up easily. He booked passage on the same liner as that on which Arnstein, Barbour, Graves—and a fourth individual, Harry Holland—were to sail. Holland was an expert "mechanic," or card manipulator. He looked like Henry Hicks, from Hicksville, a man who had operated a general store, made his pile, and was now enjoying it.

The first night out, Arnstein saw Rothstein in the dining salon. Rothstein gave him a high sign and they met on the deck. Rothstein made a forthright proposition. He would give Arnstein a flat $10,000 for the privilege of sitting in on any poker games played during the voyage. Arnstein's answer was a polite, but firm "No."

Rothstein, frozen out, spent the entire voyage watching a four-handed poker game in which Barbour and Graves lost $100,000, mostly to Holland. Rothstein did not get off the boat when it docked, retaining his room for the return trip.

Rothstein, however, found his own mark a short time later. This was Charles Gates, son of John W. ("Bet-a-Million") Gates. The father idolized the son and gave him everything he wanted. This applied especially to money. Young Gates, a pale copy of his father, tried to emulate the older man as a gambler. He did not succeed. However, John W. Gates did not mind. Money meant little to him. He had made his fortune through the invention of barbed wire, added to it as one of the prime movers in creating the combine which became the United States Steel Corporation.

Young Gates was amiable, pleasant, a soft touch. He was a little shopworn by the time Rothstein got around to him, but his money was newly minted.

Rothstein first encountered Gates at the Café de l'Opéra, a restaurant on Forty-second Street and Broadway. Rothstein made no secret of his business but insisted that he liked young Gates as a friend and didn't want him as a customer. For more than a month he fenced off any suggestions by Gates that he would like to try his luck at the Rothstein gambling house. Instead, Rothstein would suggest they go to the track or spend some time at establishments other than his own.

Gates, however, wanted action against Rothstein. He even said he would enjoy becoming a player in the Partridge Club poker game. Rothstein had no desire to build up his mark only to share him with such accomplished, and rugged, gamblers as Swope and Harry Sinclair, the oil millionaire. Finally he reluctantly agreed to permit Gates to play in his gambling house.

The help were primed for Gates's visit, especially Willie Shea.

Shea's relationship with Rothstein was not a trusting one. Even though he handled the money, was the "inside" man, and had made a good profit from his partnership, he still distrusted Rothstein. He frequently complained to Big Tim that he was being cheated. Somehow, he was sure, Rothstein was getting the best of him. For a long time he wasn't quite certain how this was being done, but finally he decided he knew.

He told Sullivan that Rothstein was using George Young Bauchle, whose relationship with Rothstein now included that of lawyer and client. Bauchle was having a phenomenal run of luck, playing faro.

There is a special term in faro for the last three cards—it is "last turn out of the box." Anyone playing against the house who called these cards in the order in which they would appear got 4 to 1 for his money. Bauchle just could not seem to miss on calling the last turn.

Shea changed dealers on Bauchle, even took over the box himself. It made no difference; Bauchle continued to win. Shea then demanded that Rothstein bar Bauchle from playing in the gambling house. Rothstein refused.

Barring Bauchle would imply one of two things. Either Bauchle was dishonest or the house would welcome only players who lost. Impugning Bauchle's honesty without proof could not be countenanced. And the other alternative would mean the end of the gambling house. So Bauchle continued to win and Shea continued to grumble.

This was the situation on the November night when Gates, accompanied by Vernie Barton, gambler and part-time steerer for Rothstein, came to the house to play.

Rothstein greeted his young friend and suggested that he go easy.

Barton, too, suggested that the play be moderate.

Gates agreed. He bought two $100 stacks of chips and played the colors on the roulette wheel. His luck was bad, however, and the chips were soon gone. Gates bought three more stacks. He lost this money also. Rothstein commented that this wasn't Gates's night and said perhaps Gates should call it quits.

Gates, however, thought differently. Roulette was not his game. Faro—bucking the tiger—was. He bought another $500 in chips and said he would only play until he was even and then he would cash in and he, Rothstein and Barton would go out on the town.

It turned out that faro was not his game either. At dawn he wrote out a check for $40,000 to cover his night's losses. It had been an expensive night.

Shea was given the check to cash. Then the entire group—among them Gates, Rothstein, Shea and Barton—went out for breakfast. While they were eating, Shea remarked that it might facilitate matters if Gates would accompany him to the bank, where Shea would cash the check.

Always obliging, Gates agreed. After breakfast he and Shea took a cab and rode off to the bank. Rothstein headed for home. Barton, who was entitled to ten per cent of the take for "steering" Gates to the game, said he would be at the gambling house that night to collect.

Rothstein woke Carolyn to tell her of the big winning. "With this money added to the bankroll, we can go after more of these highfliers. It makes us solid." He went happily to bed.

That evening when Rothstein went to the gambling house he was told that Shea was not there though it was hours after his regular arrival time. Never before had he allowed play to begin without him. Nor had Shea appeared by midnight. By that time, however, reports of his activities had reached Rothstein.

One of the first to bring these to Rothstein was Vernie Barton. "Shea's on the town, drinking champagne, and telling everybody that he put one over on you."

"Go find him and tell him I want to see him."

Barton took this message to Shea.

"Go back," Shea said, "and tell the Jew I've got the money and I'm going to keep it. If he wants his share, tell him to collect it from what Bauchle stole."

Barton reported this to Rothstein. "What are you going to do about it?"

"I'm going to think about it."

Rothstein finished thinking the next afternoon and went to see Big Tim Sullivan. Sullivan had already heard the news. "What do you want me to do?" he asked.

"Nothing. Let him keep the money."

"The whole forty thousand?" Sullivan was incredulous.

Rothstein nodded. "It's cheap. Look at it this way. One-third of it was his anyway. He has eight thousand coming to him out of the bankroll. We've been averaging about a thousand a week in profit. What it comes down to is that he's taken $15,000 for his share of the business. It's worth a lot more."

Sullivan chuckled. "That dumb Irishman should've known better than to try to outsmart you."

Rothstein took a piece of paper from his pocket. "I had Bauchle draw this up. It's a quitclaim. When I find him, I'm going to get him to sign it."

Sullivan slapped Rothstein's back. "Whatever you do is all right with me."

Rothstein found Shea at the Knickerbocker bar. The absconding partner was both drunk and truculent. When he saw Rothstein he announced he had no intention of giving him "one damn dollar out of the Gates money."

Rothstein said, "Okay, Coakley." This was a favorite expression, one he would use all his life. He put the quitclaim on the bar and said, "Sign this and you can keep the money."

Shea had been anticipating trouble, as had the onlookers. Now, when there was none, he blustered even more. "Thought you could put something over on me, didn't you? Well, I was a lot too smart for you."

Rothstein didn't answer, just gave a fountain pen to Shea. The latter quickly affixed his signature.

"We're quits now," Rothstein said. "The money's yours and the place is mine."

Much of Broadway was pleased with what it regarded as a come-down for Rothstein. The man who called so many other people chumps had been made into a chump. He had been taken. But then Broadway had some second thoughts and realized that Rothstein wasn't a chump after all. Maybe the price was high, but he had rid himself of Shea. And business was good at the gambling house.

Shea, too, sobered up and took stock. He went to Rothstein and pleaded drunkenness. He offered to pay over the $40,000 and re-enter the partnership. Rothstein said, "Get out of here before I throw you out. You're a crook and a welcher."

Shea left, muttering that he would go to Sullivan. He did go, but he was refused help. "Nothing doing," Sullivan told him. "You thought you were putting one over on Arnold. Well, now you know you got to get up mighty early in the morning to do that."

Even though he had not profited from his first big mark, Rothstein felt he was ready to take on some others. There was no paucity of potential customers. They included Edward O. Wolcott, U.S. senator from Colorado; Julius Fleischmann, the yeast king; Francis Kinney, manufacturer of Sweet Caporal cigarettes; Louis Ehret, the brewer; Joseph Seagram, the Canadian distiller; and drug manufacturer John Staley of Pittsburgh.

These men were all successes in their fields. They were highly successful in business. Yet, when it came to gambling, they were as much suckers as Charlie Gates or Willie Vanderbilt, who were living high off money that had been made for them. They tried to beat the percentage in New York and Saratoga and, when they failed, were ready to come back the next night.

There was nothing petty about their gambling. They played for high stakes, often in six figures.

With Shea gone, Rothstein did not have time to scout continually for such players. Instead, he put greater dependence upon steerers. And his best steerers turned out to be women.

A great many of the big gamblers liked feminine company. They particularly liked women of the theater. Rothstein cultivated a number of musical comedy beauties, especially Lillian Lorraine and Peggy Hopkins. He gave them presents of lovely, expensive bags, of equally expensive perfume.

He played a game of cat-and-mouse with Peggy Hopkins. He took her to the track with him and told her he was betting for her. At the end of her first visit he told her she was a thousand dollars ahead. When she asked for the money, he said it was chicken feed, that he would really make a killing for her.

Miss Hopkins was slightly avaricious and the idea that she might make a thousand dollars an afternoon—with no strings attached—appealed greatly to her. So, she was back at the race track the next day and, again, was a winner. And, again, she did not get her hands on the money. This went on for four days, at which time she was a "winner" of almost $5,000. She wanted the money very badly, but Rothstein told her that he had a sure winner going the next day and he was going to put the whole $5,000 on the horse.

Peggy tried to talk him out of it. She said she was happy with her winnings and would be glad to settle for the lesser sum. But Rothstein would have nothing to do with such an idea. When you gambled you gambled for high stakes, you shot for the moon. And, after all, what did she have to lose? Not a penny of cash.

The next day Peggy was waiting for Rothstein. What was the name of the horse? In what race was it running? What were the odds? Rothstein put her off.

Three races were run, and each time in answer to her look of inquiry Rothstein shook his head. But as the horses went to the post in the fourth race, Rothstein said, "This is it!"

"Which horse?" Peggy asked.

"You'll find out soon enough."

The starter got the horses off.

"Which horse?" Peggy demanded.

Rothstein watched as the horses reached the first turn. "The one in the lead," he said.

Peggy let out a sigh of relief. The front-running horse was leading by open daylight. What Peggy didn't know was that the horse was a notorious quitter. She found out, however, when the horses reached the backstretch. The horse on the head end faded and fell back. It was next to last when the race was over.

Peggy was so disappointed that she started to cry. Anger and frustration were mixed with her disappointment.

Rothstein tried to placate her, but it took a great deal of placation to make up for "her" $5,000. Finally Rothstein said there was an easy way for her to make another $5,000. All she had to do was bring one of her wealthy friends to Rothstein's gambling house.

Peggy listened to Rothstein's proposition. Then she asked, "Suppose he wins?"

"Then it will be up to you to see that he pays you off."

It was not long after this that Peggy began to make Rothstein's gambling house a stopping-off place when she was out with a "gentleman." One evening she was able to bring a group that included Stanley Joyce, whom she later married (and whose name she kept long after they were divorced), Percival H. Hill, of the American Tobacco Company, and a pleasant-looking girl who had once appeared in a show with her, Bobbie Winthrop.

Joyce was known to enjoy gambling and it was he whom Peggy had steered to the house as a player.

Hill was a big bettor at the race tracks and, in August, an occasional visitor to the Saratoga gambling houses. However, he was not regarded as a plunger. Everything being relative, a small bet for him might equal a lifetime's earnings to others.

Rothstein greeted the group as they entered. He knew Joyce and Hill casually, as he knew almost everyone who was part of Broadway or the gambling scene. His primary interest was in Joyce. He accompanied Joyce and Peggy to the dice table, told the stickman to take good care of his friend, Mr. Joyce. Then he left them and took his place at the back of the room where he could observe everything happening.

Hill went to the faro table, stayed there a short time, then began to play roulette.

Rothstein saw that Bobbie Winthrop appeared at a loss. Fearful she might suggest that the others leave, he joined her, asked if there was anything he could do for her.

"I don't understand any of these games," she said.

He offered to explain them to her.

"It doesn't matter," she said. "I don't have any money."

Rothstein signaled to Tom Farley, then asked Bobbie if she would like anything to eat or drink.

"A chicken sandwich," she said. "I've never tasted champagne. Could I have champagne?"

"You can have anything you want. Champagne for the lady, Tom."

Rothstein was explaining roulette to Bobbie when John Shaughnessy, his pit man, walked to him and signaled he wanted to talk with him. Rothstein excused himself, moved a few steps away. "What is it?"

"He's in the hole for $60,000 and wants more credit. He wants the limit raised too."

Rothstein looked at Joyce, who was holding hands with Peggy and seemed in the best of humors. "He doesn't look like a big loser."

"I don't mean Joyce. It's Hill."

Rothstein let out a soft whistle. "How much cash has he lost?"

"About $4,000. The rest is on paper."

"I'll talk to him." He called to Bobbie, "Be right back." Then he walked toward Hill.

As of that moment, the $60,000 Hill had lost was the largest amount anyone had ever dropped in Rothstein's gambling house. Rothstein knew he could cut off Hill's credit where it was, but that would downgrade both him and his establishment. On the other hand, if he gave Hill further credit, Hill might well recoup his losses.

There was another consideration. Would Hill honor his losses?

Rothstein had only seconds in which to make a decision.

He reached Hill. "I hear you've been running in hard luck, Mr. Hill."

Hill said, "Slightly. I've made some errors of judgment. I would like the limit raised." He took it for granted that there was no question of his getting further credit.

"How much credit would you like, Mr. Hill, and what limit?"

Hill turned to the croupier. "What do I owe you?"

The croupier totaled the chips in his rack. "Sixty thousand, sir."

Hill said, "I'd like another $40,000 and a $500 limit on the numbers, with no limit on anything else."

Rothstein said, "Of course." He turned to the croupier. "Give Mr. Hill his chips and he can name his own limit."

Rothstein had taken the gamble that an I.O.U. for $100,000 was no more of a risk than one for $60,000; Hill would honor the greater sum as readily as the lesser. He felt the odds were with him. He was raising the limit for a loser, something he was always pleased to do. Hill, an amateur gambler, would press his bad luck, hoping it would turn. That was in Rothstein's favor. As a professional, he knew that bad gamblers raised the stakes when they lost and tried to play safe when they were winning.

As Rothstein walked away from the table, he said, "Mr. Hill, your credit is any limit you want to set. That's the only limit in effect tonight. Good luck." This was also part of his gamble. He was flattering Hill, buttering up his ego.

Rothstein rejoined Bobbie Winthrop, went with her to the faro table and tried to teach her how that game was played. She listened, watched, shook her head and said, "I'm not very good at games."

They returned to the sideboard and Tom Farley provided her with more champagne.

Rothstein pointedly avoided the roulette layout. He watched the dice game awhile. He even took over the faro bank. He could hear the roulette wheel spin, hear the click of the ivory ball, the sudden silence when it came to a halt. He depended upon the sounds that came from the crowd that was watching to tell him what was happening.

The crowd—the players—were always against the house. The house was the common enemy.

All other play slackened. Rothstein went back to the sideboard. Bobbie was still there. They were talking about the shows on Broadway when Lou Betts, one of the housemen, came over and whispered, "He's in for a hundred and fifty." A little while later Shaughnessy sidled past. "Two hundred."

A little before four in the morning, Shaughnessy came by again. "Two-fifty."

Rothstein asked Tom Farley to give him a glass of milk.

"Champagne," Bobbie said, "tastes better." She was giggling.

Rothstein had not finished the drink of milk when he saw that Hill was through playing. He excused himself.

"My judgment did not improve," Hill said. "If you will give me an I.O.U., I will sign it."

Tom Farley handed the chits to Rothstein. He added them as though he did not know the total. He looked up surprised. "These come to $250,000." He offered them to Hill to check. Hill said, "That's what I thought."

Rothstein took a blank chit, inscribed, "I.O.U. $250,000," and handed it to Hill.

Hill took the paper and a pen from Rothstein. He wrote, "Please pay to bearer the above sum," across the bottom, and signed it. "If you will present this to Mr. Sylvester in my office tomorrow, he will honor it. Good night."

"Better luck next time," Rothstein said.

The group of four now prepared to leave. Peggy found an opportunity to whisper to Rothstein, "When do I get my money?"

"After I get mine." He threw a quick glance at the paper in his hand. It represented—no, could represent—more money than he had ever had. Or it could prove just a piece of paper with some mocking words scrawled on it. He would know soon enough. Now, all he could do was wait.

He went to the door with the group, said good night to them. To Bobbie he said, "Come again." He lowered his voice so the others could not hear. "I think you're lucky for me."

The play for the night was over. Farley and his helpers began to clean up. Liquor and cigars went back into the sideboard. Housemen covered gambling layouts.

After a time only Rothstein, Shaughnessy, Betts and Farley remained. They sat at a covered poker table. The I.O.U. rested on the black table cover.

It had been a big night. Joyce had lost $17,000. Other gamblers had dropped some thousands too. Even without Hill's big loss, this would have been one of the more profitable nights since the gambling house had opened. Hill's loss, however, made it something very different.

Rothstein, like the others, stared at the I.O.U. After a time he reached over, picked it up, folded it and put it in his watch pocket. "I'm going home, Thomas. Lock up."

Whatever he felt, he kept it from the others. Only when he had reached his home, a few doors away, did he let go his grip on himself. He went into Carolyn's bedroom and awakened her. "There's something I want to show you." He walked to the library.

When she joined him there, he was seated in a big leather chair. His shirt was open at the throat. He had removed his collar and tie. His face was flushed and perspiration beaded his forehead, his upper lip, his neck. Her first thought was that he was ill. "What is it, Arnold? Don't you feel well?"

He handed her the I.O.U. It was wet with his perspiration.

She read it in the dim dawn, then read it again. "The poor man. Can he afford it?"

Rothstein brought up a short, husky laugh. "He could afford ten times that much and never miss it. What I want to know is, is it good?" He rose and started pacing the room. "A quarter of a million," he said. His voice was low, husky. "If it's good, I'll buy you the biggest diamond in New York. I'll buy you the best fur coat. Whatever you want, I'll buy it for you."

"What I want won't cost anything. All I want is a promise."

"What kind of promise?" He was quickly wary.

"I want your promise that you'll stop gambling if this I.O.U. is good."

"Let's wait and see if it's good. Besides, it's not all mine. I have to give their cut to Lou and John. Then there's the ten per cent to the steerer who brought Hill to the place. And I have all the other expenses."

"But that will still leave you a lot of money."

"We'll see," he said. Then he made her a concession. "Why don't you smoke a cigarette while I have some milk and cookies?" He hated her to smoke. Somehow, it wasn't ladylike.

"I'll make a deal with you," she said. "You quit gambling and I'll stop smoking."

He didn't answer her. Instead, he went to get his milk and cookies. They were waiting for him, as they always were, in his bedroom. He came back to the library. "I've got butterflies in my stomach," he said.

He got a few hours' sleep, was bathed and shaved and dressed by eleven. He had a cup of coffee with Carolyn. "No point in waiting and wondering." He spread the I.O.U. before him. "I'll know in an hour if this means anything."

He took a taxi to the office of the American Tobacco Company and went to the suite occupied by Sylvester, who was treasurer of the company. A secretary greeted him and asked him his business.

"It's personal. I've been sent to Mr. Sylvester by Mr. Percival Hill."

The secretary went to an inner office, returned, and said, "Mr. Sylvester will see you."

Sylvester looked up as Rothstein entered. "What can I do for you, Mr. Rothstein?"

Rothstein walked to the desk, laid the I.O.U. on it. "Mr. Hill told me to give you this."

Sylvester read the note, glanced up at Rothstein. "This is a gambling debt, I presume."

"In a sense. I gave the money to Mr. Hill. He lost it."

Sylvester drummed on the table with his fingertips. "I doubt that this is collectible at law."

Rothstein's face showed nothing. "Some have been, Mr. Sylvester. It's not my intention to go to law, however."

Sylvester again drummed on the desk. "I am going to pay this—this—draft. You accepted it in good faith, at least with as much good faith as a gambler accepts any I.O.U. However, I am informing you now that I will not honor another such I.O.U., not even for five cents. Do we understand each other?"

"We do," Rothstein said.

Sylvester called his secretary back into the room. "Make out a check for $250,000 to the order of . . .?" He looked inquiringly at Rothstein.

"Arnold Rothstein."

"To the order of Arnold Rothstein," Sylvester said. "I will sign it and then you will accompany Rothstein to the bank and he can have it certified." He looked at Rothstein again. "Is that satisfactory?"

"Most satisfactory."

"Now, if you'll excuse me, Rothstein, I have work to do." It was a complete dismissal.

Rothstein said to Carolyn, "He treated me like dirt. Well, I've got a quarter of a million dollars and that makes me as good as he is."

She took advantage of the opening. "You can be better. You could be richer than he is. You could go into any business and be a bigger man than Sylvester."

"We'll see," Rothstein said. "Right now, it's too soon to make plans." He started from the room. "I better go tell the boys that everything is all right."

She stared at the door long after he had gone. She knew that there had been two big losers in the past few hours. Percival Hill and Carolyn Rothstein.

Chapter **6** *Outward Order and Decency*

Arnold Rothstein had evolved into a man of importance in his world. The poolroom hustler, dealing in small change, had become the big gambler, the well-known personality.

It had taken ten years of effort. And ten years of luck. His marathon pool match with Conway had raised him from anonymity. When he turned the tables on Willie Shea, people began to talk of his cleverness. His intelligent operation of his gambling house, his use of Broadway beauties as steerers, caused these same people not only to talk about his cleverness but to believe in it.

More important than these factors, however, was Rothstein's continuing relationship with Big Tim Sullivan. Sullivan's power and influence were at their zenith. He was the man behind the man who was the absolute ruler of Tammany Hall, Charles F. Murphy. And he was also the man behind Arnold Rothstein.

Sullivan was a very rich man and his wealth had come to him by, and through, politics. He controlled gambling in New York—an illegal activity—and boxing, a legal activity. He operated a string of theaters, owned saloons, hotels and slum realty.

The source of his wealth and power was his control of small-time crime and small-time criminals. The graft that came his way came from a century-old source. From vice and gambling in its various forms.

It was no secret that New York City was corrupt. The wiser politicians sought to keep this corruption under control. And under cover. This was the duty of the police department. William J. Gaynor, who was a Tammany mayor and a good mayor, not necessarily a contradiction, expressed best what was expected of the police department.

He said it was the duty of the police to "preserve outward order and decency."

Gaynor expected no more of the police in the battle against corruption. He knew the police were an integral part of that corruption.

Gaynor knew he owed his office to a political machine. His private morality was greater than he expected public morality to be. But, since he was in politics, he knew he was part of what Lincoln Steffens, a short time earlier, had called a "system." Later Herbert Bayard Swope would call it "The System." That system called for—depended upon—the alliance between political machine and crime.

Democracy's greatest strength remained its inherent weakness. So long as the majority ruled it was necessary to get the votes of that majority. All was fair in politics. The spoils justified the means.

Sullivan could say after an election, "One district went 388 votes for us and 4 for the other fellows. They got one more vote than I expected, but I'll find the fellow." He was confident he would. And just as confident that he would change that vote.

Sullivan did not like to talk about how he got his 388 votes. One of his lieutenants, however, did give an anonymous interview to *Harper's*, which appeared in the October, 1913, issue.

In the period before the Australian ballot, on which candidates of all parties were listed on the same ballot, voters asked for either a Democratic or a Republican ballot and then deposited it in the box. There was no way to split a ticket. One year Sullivan was suspicious of some of his followers. He ordered that every Democratic ballot be impregnated with a strong, and lasting, scent.

As each voter emerged from the polling place, an official "smeller" was waiting to sniff his hands.

This was a sharp practice, but a legal one. Far more prevalent and more important were the illegal practices, of which "repeating" was the keystone. Repeating, of course, meant the casting of more than one vote by the same man.

The anonymous politician gave an insight into one of Sullivan's favorite methods. It required men with "lilacs," that is, men who were bearded. He was asked if a smooth-faced man could not as easily vote as a bearded one.

"He can vote just as well onc't, but one vote lets him out if the inspectors are inclined to make trouble. Big Tim said when you use repeaters in the district, always get guys with whiskers. . . .

"When you've voted them onc't with their whiskers on, you take 'em to a barber and scrape off the chin fringe. Then you vote them again with side lilacs and a moustache. Then to a barber again and off comes the sides and you vote 'em a third time with the moustache. If that ain't enough, and the box can stand a few ballots more, clean off the moustache and vote 'em plain face. That makes every one of them good for four votes."

The repeaters were made up of floaters, Bowery bums, panhandlers, panderers and gangsters. These latter coerced, intimidated and used physical force to get votes for the politicians who paid them. When need arose, they stuffed ballot boxes or stole them and threw them into the river.

The price for prostituting the democratic process was cheap. Repeaters were paid a dollar for each vote. The gangsters were better cared for. A few were given sinecure jobs. Most, however, received extralegal privileges, like the right to shake down bordello operators, operators of shady hotels, and small gambling places. If arrested, they could depend upon the district leader to get a word to a magistrate, who would then mete out mercy with a soup ladle.

For all their value, the gangsters received relatively little. Ten dollars was big money. But, instead of money, a Monk Eastman was given a sense of power, of importance.

The gangsters were errand boys for the politicians. They were at the bottom of the underworld scale in the period before the First World War.

The gamblers stood somewhat higher. Still they operated on sufferance and could not tell what price they would have to pay. They could always be sacrificed as a display of civic righteousness.

The man at the top was always a politician. And working directly with him there was always a high police officer. All graft was strained through him. He was the "bagman."

These two—politician and police officer—held the power. No gambler—not Canfield or Kelly or Busteed or Johnson or Rothstein —could operate without approval from the top. No hoodlum—not Eastman or Paul Kelly or "One Lung" Curran—had immunity or received favors except from the top.

The reason was money. The politician controlled the pocketbook.

There was a steady, day-to-day, take for the politician. What was paid him in driblets became a raging torrent by the time it reached him.

The *New York Times*, in one of its many efforts to show how corruption operated and how much money it yielded, printed an estimate of the yearly graft paid to the protectors of gambling. It listed the different operations, and their yield, as follows:

Pool rooms, 400, at $300 monthly	$1,440,000
Crap games, 500, at $150 monthly	900,000
Gambling houses, 200, at $150 monthly	360,000
Gambling houses (large), 20, $1,000 a month	240,000
Swindlers, 50, at $50 a month	30,000
Policy	125,000
TOTAL	$3,095,000

The *Times* said that this gambling graft went to a "secret gambling commission" that was composed of the "head of one of the city departments, two State Senators, and the dictator of the poolroom syndicate of this city, who was before the Mazet Committee and is allied with Tammany Hall."

New Yorkers who were involved had little difficulty identifying the men whom the *Times*, for reasons dictated by the libel laws, had not specifically identified. They were Tim Sullivan, then a state senator, Senator McCarren of Brooklyn, Frank Farrell, an important gambler who owned the New York Highlanders baseball team (later to become the New York Yankees), and William J. ("Big Bill") Devery, chief of police.

--- --- top, of course, was Sullivan. And at that time Devery was his bag man. Later there would be a split and the two would fight each other bitterly.

This type of organization went back to the 1840's, when Isaiah Rynders, Tammany leader, United States marshal and gambler, set it up. He was succeeded by A. Oakey Hall, who became mayor of New York, and the order of succession went through the Tweed and Croker regimes to Sullivan.

The policemen who had acted as collectors—and enforcers—included Inspector Alexander Williams, who gave the "Tenderloin" its name, Devery, and, after him, a handsome, ambitious, driving police lieutenant of German ancestry, Charles Becker.

Under Sullivan and Becker the control was strongest, the returns greatest. It was Becker who used the strong-arm methods, who believed in force over persuasion. This could be because, when they formed their partnership, Sullivan was already rich, already powerful, and already a sick man. The pair dominated the world of graft and crime.

Becker had a lust for wealth and power. He was intelligent, single-minded and stubborn. It was his ultimate aim to succeed to the power and perquisites of Sullivan. Like Devery, he had political ambitions. Unlike him, he hoped to work through Tammany and not against the machine.

Circumstances appeared to favor Becker's ambitions. In 1911 Big Tim Sullivan became seriously ill, the victim of paresis. His mind was affected and he had to be kept under constant watch. Some attempts were made to keep his condition a secret, but these failed. Finally there was a public acknowledgment when a triumvirate, made up of Sullivan's brother, Florrie, his nephew, Jim, and Frank Farrell took over as leaders of Sullivan's old district.

This was a mark of Charley Murphy's loyalty to the man who had made him head of Tammany Hall. But the triumvirate, together, were not the equal of Big Tim alone. Divided power and responsibility—in Russia it is called "collective leadership"—means diminution of both. The group was able to hold local political leadership since Murphy gave them control of patronage.

But a vacuum was created in relation to the control of gambling and graft.

Two men sought to fill this vacancy. One was Becker. The other was Tom Foley, long-time friend of Murphy, astute politician and in the tradition of Tammany. Foley's lieutenant was a rising young district leader, a former blacksmith, James J. Hines.

Murphy was publicly neutral, but privately favored Foley.

Becker wasted no time in maneuvers or strategy. He turned to the gangsters and chose one of them to enforce his rule on the underworld. The man he chose was Jacob ("Big Jack") Zelig.

Zelig, like Becker, was using another man's misfortune as a steppingstone. Monk Eastman had been sentenced to ten years in prison soon after Sullivan became ill. No other politician had moved to help Eastman. A large number seemed happy to see him put away.

Becker gave Zelig carte blanche. He could use any methods he wished, so long as these resulted in Becker's getting the graft and the power that emanated from control of gambling and vice. For a year it appeared that Becker would win out. He seemed on the way to becoming the power that he wanted to be.

The money was coming in regularly. And it was big money. The gangster army was taking its orders from Becker. They were available to him for any service, especially that required Election Day.

However, as seems inevitably the case, the seeds of his destruction rested within his character. His stubbornness, his vanity, his faith in force—which had brought him so far—destroyed him. The instrument of that destruction was a small-time gambler, a poor failure of a Broadway "sport," named Herman Rosenthal.

Rosenthal and Arnold Rothstein had started together. They had served their apprenticeships under Sullivan. He had called the pair "smart Jew boys." He had been only half right. Rosenthal, whatever else he was, was not smart. And his ambition far overextended his ability.

Rosenthal had opened a number of gambling places, and all these had failed. He was a bookmaker who could not win, despite all the odds in his favor.

Each time that Rosenthal was in trouble he went back to his old patron, Tim Sullivan, and Sullivan helped him. In 1912 Rosenthal's principal source of income was the gambling concession at the Hesper Club. This had always been remunerative. Even Rosenthal should have been able to make it pay. But he did not.

Because of Rosenthal's connections, and because the game he ran was so small-time, there was little reason why Becker and Zelig should have molested him. After all, there was an unwritten rule that the game at the Hesper Club was sacrosanct. But it was just that rule which probably motivated Becker.

His vanity fed on success, became megalomania. He had to show that he did not fear, or respect, either Tim Sullivan or those who still depended upon his protection. Pushing Rosenthal around, making him pay tribute, would be proof of that.

Becker gave Zelig orders to collect from Rosenthal as he did from other gamblers. Rosenthal refused to pay. He told Zelig that this was Tim Sullivan's game, above threats and coercion. "You better pay," Zelig told him. "Sullivan's out and Becker's the boss now."

Rosenthal told this to Florrie Sullivan, who suggested that Rosenthal meet force with force. To that end, Rosenthal made an alliance with a group of hoodlums led by Bridgie Webber and Sam Paul. Webber, a former lieutenant of Eastman, wanted to force Zelig out as Eastman's successor and take over himself.

There were no secrets in the underworld. Becker heard about this new alliance as soon as it was formed. He met it characteristically. A gang of toughs, led by Zelig, was sent to take care of Webber. They broke into Webber's clubhouse, wrecked it, and beat Webber almost to death. The revolt was crushed even before it had begun.

Again Rosenthal went to Florrie Sullivan. This time he was told there was no point to fighting Becker. He was advised to make a deal. Reluctantly Rosenthal did so. Becker became his partner in the game at the Hesper Club.

The shotgun alliance was a most unhappy one. Rosenthal was bitter. He called the partnership a form of robbery. He told everyone—Rosenthal was a man who insisted upon taking the world into his confidence—that as soon as Sullivan had recovered his health, Big Tim would straighten Becker out. His simple mind could not conceive that the time was past when Sullivan could help anyone.

Becker ordered Rosenthal to keep his mouth shut. That was as effectual as King Canute's famous order to the sea.

Becker then ordered two raids on the Hesper Club! Rosenthal was arrested and fined.

The final blow came a short time later. Becker's press agent had been charged with killing a man in a crap game. Rosenthal, like all gamblers, was told to contribute to a defense fund. His assessment was $500. Rosenthal refused to pay.

A few days later, on his way home from the Hesper Club, Rosenthal was assaulted by a gang of hoodlums. He was left half-conscious and the last thing his assaulters told him was that the beating would be repeated unless he anted up the $500.

But Rosenthal had a stubbornness equal to Becker's. He tried to find means of fighting back. He asked Tom Foley for help, but was refused. He went to Rothstein, who told him he was fighting a losing battle.

Rosenthal turned to whisky for solace. This made his tongue even looser than usual. And with each drink he felt more and more injured and insisted upon telling the story of his injuries. One who heard that story—most of which he already knew—was Herbert Bayard Swope.

Swope was the *World*'s expert on politics and the underworld. No one could have better fitted the job. The tall, elegant, red-haired Swope was a man about town, a man who loved to gamble, a man who had friends, acquaintances and connections on every level. Nowhere were his connections better than in the world of politics. He was the friend of Murphy, of Foley, of Sullivan. And also of Charles S. Whitman, Republican district attorney of Manhattan.

Whitman was able and ambitious. He had his sights set on the governor's chair in Albany and, after that, possibly the White House. He looked on his present job as a jumping-off place toward his higher ambitions. What he wanted was some big case—some big scandal—that would give him front-page publicity and a reputation.

It came to him through Swope.

Swope was many things, but he was primarily a newspaperman. The story was the thing. His first allegiance was to his newspaper. So, although he knew that he would strike at many persons with whom he was friendly, many with whom he was intimate, he set out to get Rosenthal's story.

It was not that Rosenthal could tell Swope things he did not know or suspect. Ever since Lincoln Steffens had written *The Shame of the Cities* it had been public knowledge that there was a strong bond between crime and politics. But Rosenthal was the first person who could give names, dates and facts. Rosenthal was the first person "on the inside" who might give details that could be proved. He could document the charges.

Steffens had written that "a system exists." Swope wanted to give the details of that system. And so, in his stories, he was the first to capitalize the initial "s" in the word. He began to write of "The System."

His initial step was to talk separately with Rosenthal and Whitman. He arranged a meeting between the gambler and one of Whitman's assistants. At this meeting Rosenthal gave a general picture of what he was prepared to talk about.

Now Rosenthal made the first of a long series of errors. He was not quite bright and was unable to realize how precarious his position was. His one protection was complete secrecy, but he felt that it was publicity. He believed he could scare Becker off by letting word seep out that he had talked with the District Attorney's office.

Within hours, Rosenthal told a dozen people "in confidence" of his visit to Centre Street. He said that he was putting the skids under Becker.

Rosenthal's "secret" quickly was common knowledge. One of the first to hear it was Tom Foley. Foley called Arnold Rothstein and told him to get hold of Rosenthal and shut him up. "Get that stupid son of a bitch out of town," Foley told Rothstein.

Rothstein sent John Shaughnessy to find Rosenthal and bring him to the Rothstein home. An hour later Rosenthal was there.

Rothstein let Rosenthal know what he thought of him. The mildest name he called Rosenthal was "fool."

Rosenthal defended himself. "If the Big Feller [Sullivan] was here, Becker would be pounding a pavement."

"The Big Feller isn't here. And if he was, he'd tell you to keep your trap shut. All you can do is make trouble for a lot of people."

"I don't want to make trouble for anyone, only Becker. They ask me about anybody else, I won't tell them. Only about Becker."

"They're smarter than you are. They're not interested in doing you any favors. Whitman is only interested in Whitman and the Republicans. He'll crucify the Big Feller."

But Rosenthal continued to be stubborn. "They can't make me say what I don't want to say."

Rothstein took out his bankroll and counted off $500. "Beansy," he said, "you've got to get out of town. You stay away until this thing blows over. Here's enough money to get you out. If you need more, let me know."

"I'm not leaving town," Rosenthal said. "That's what Becker wants me to do. I'm staying right here."

No arguments could sway him. He was convinced that he could use Whitman to destroy Becker. He could not see anything beyond that, could not understand that he was a key not to the destruction of Becker but to The System.

Finally Rothstein gave up. He informed Foley he had been unable to muffle Rosenthal.

For some unaccountable reason Whitman delayed talking with Rosenthal or arranging to have him go before a Grand Jury. This delay permitted Becker to act.

Jack Zelig was then in the Tombs, charged with assault. There he was visited by a gambler named "Bald Jack" Rose, who later testified that he had gone as Becker's emissary. According to Rose, he transmitted a blunt order to Zelig. Zelig was to hire some professional thugs and have Rosenthal killed before he talked.

Zelig, again according to Rose, agreed. Zelig was freed from the Tombs. On the outside, he was given a bankroll of $2,000 and told to use it any way he saw fit.

Shortly thereafter Zelig hired his execution squad. It was made up of a quartet known as "Gyp the Blood," "Lefty Louie," "Dago Frank," and "Whitey Lewis." Their original names were Harry Horowitz, Louis Rosenberg, Francesco Cirofici and Jacob Seidensheiner.

All four had records that attested to their capabilities. Gyp the Blood had been "sheriff," or bouncer, at some of the lowest dives and saloons on the East Side. He was regarded as the equal of Monk Eastman or "Eat 'em Up Alive" Jack MacManus in that capacity. Once, dared to prove his strength, he had cracked an opponent's spine over his knee.

Whitey Lewis was a former prize fighter who had renown as a blackjack wielder and slugger. He was Zelig's personal bodyguard.

Lefty Louie was a pickpocket, a roller of drunks, a gunman. He was also quite a ladies' man and had a string of prostitutes working for him. One of his specialties was the "badger game," that old swindle in which an irate "husband" discovered his wife and a stranger in the process of cuckolding him.

Dago Frank was simply a killer. A dope addict, he was without fear when hopped up. His was probably the first gun for hire in New York City on a free-lance basis.

If this first step was quickly undertaken, none of the events that followed was marked by speed. Actually, few crimes have been marked by such ineptitude on the part of all concerned, criminals, police and law-enforcement agencies.

Had there been any efficiency shown, the history of New York— and of Arnold Rothstein—would have been markedly different.

Finally, the group set a date for Rosenthal's murder—July 7, 1912 —and a place—the Garden Café on Seventh Avenue.

The four men marched into the restaurant on that night and surrounded the table at which Rosenthal sat, having dinner with his wife. Dago Frank and Lefty Louie had their guns in their hands. But they took no action. Instead, the four just stared hard at Rosenthal for a long minute and then turned and walked from the room.

They explained that the reason they had not killed Rosenthal was because his wife was present. It would be a breach of gangland etiquette to murder a man while his wife was on the scene.

However, though they did not kill him, they frightened him. He finally realized that he was in danger. He told everyone that he had changed his mind. He was no longer interested in talking to Whitman.

Among those he informed was Swope. But he also told Swope he was still determined to destroy Becker. Swope offered him a means. Why not tell the full story of Becker to the *World?* It did not occur to either of them that Rosenthal was inviting his own death.

Rosenthal did not weigh the consequences. He saw this as an opportunity to get even, to avenge his long list of injuries. Swope was his friend, would wield the dagger that would strike down Becker. Eagerly, Rosenthal started to talk. And he talked for hours. When he had finished he accompanied Swope to a notary, where he signed an affidavit that all he had told Swope was the truth.

With the biggest story of his career—one of the biggest of all time —Swope rushed to his office and handed his sensational scoop to the desk.

It appeared, together with a copy of the affidavit, on the morning of July 13.

Rosenthal had given a complete picture of his relations with Becker. He told of their "partnership" in the Hesper Club, listed the graft that he had paid to Becker. He also had provided a list of other gamblers, their location, and the price all of these were paying for the right to operate.

The story, of course, was a sensation. What would happen next? Nothing, for twenty-four hours.

On July 15 Whitman sent a detective to bring Rosenthal in for questioning.

At the District Attorney's office, Rosenthal for the first time in his life had nothing to say. He told Whitman he had no statement for him and refused to go before the Grand Jury. No amount of hammering could change his mind. Finally Whitman told him he could go.

As Rosenthal left Whitman's office he became aware that he was being followed. He managed to elude his trailer and, seeking some haven, rushed to the Rothstein home on West Forty-sixth Street. He found Rothstein there. "I've changed my mind," he said. "Give me the money and I'll get out of town."

"You waited too long," Rothstein said.

"Let me have the five hundred," Rosenthal pleaded. "I'll go 'way someplace and hide."

"You're not worth five hundred to anyone any more, Beansy," Rothstein said.

"Then you can go to hell." Rosenthal stormed from the house.

The next day Rosenthal experienced another change of mind. He went on his own initiative to see Whitman. He was ready to talk.

He repeated what he had told Swope and added more. He poured out all his bitterness. He waited for his statement to be typed out and then he read it, corrected it, added to it. He told Whitman he was ready to go before the Grand Jury. He left Whitman's office shortly after midnight.

It was known to the authorities that Rosenthal was a marked man, yet neither Whitman nor the police offered to give Rosenthal any protection. The District Attorney said later that none had been asked. The police never offered any explanation.

Still being trailed, Rosenthal went from the District Attorney's office to the Metropole Hotel on West Forty-third Street. He went to the bar, had a drink, then went into the dining room and ordered a big meal that included a porterhouse steak.

The Metropole, owned by the Considines and Sullivan, was a gathering place for the sporting crowd. This night, as on all nights, it was filled with gamblers, politicians, theatrical people and newspapermen. Rosenthal was known to virtually all of them, yet not one person spoke to him. No one answered his greeting. Heads were averted from him.

In a spirit of almost hysterical courage, Rosenthal ate his meal and continued to sit at the table. He drank a half dozen cups of coffee. At intervals his eyes would sweep the crowded room and then go to the door. It was as if he were waiting for death to come to him. His wait ended shortly after two in the morning.

A waiter told him some friends were outside the restaurant and wanted to talk to him. Such was Rosenthal's stupidity, or innocence, that he asked no questions but rose from the table and walked into the street. An automobile was parked at the curb, directly in front of the restaurant. A voice called, "Here, Beansy," and Rosenthal started toward the car. When he was a yard from it, a fusillade of bullets erupted from inside the car. At least four entered his heart. He was dead before his big body hit the sidewalk.

The car roared off.

It took two weeks to find the killers, though their identities were known to the police, the District Attorney and the underworld. Ironically, the police officer who conducted the search was Lieutenant Charles Becker.

After the four were rounded up, they immediately implicated Zelig. When Zelig was arrested, he in turn implicated Rose and Becker. He said the pair had paid him to hire Rosenthal's killers.

Becker was arrested on July 29, the day after Zelig agreed to turn state's evidence.

Trial of the four gunmen was set for October 6, 1912. Becker's trial was severed from that of the others, and set for early the next year.

On October 5, 1912, the day before Zelig was scheduled to testify against the gunmen, he started to board a streetcar at the corner of Second Avenue and Thirteenth Street. A man standing beside him pulled a gun and shot him to death. He was Phil Davidson, a petty hoodlum, who was arrested, tried and sent to prison for second-degree murder.

Even without Zelig, Whitman had enough evidence to convince a jury that the four gunmen were guilty of first-degree murder. They were sentenced to die and were executed on the night of April 13, 1914.

When they died, Becker was still in jail. He was still fighting for his freedom. And powerful forces were at work to secure that freedom for him.

Other forces, even more powerful, and other men, however, were no longer interested in Becker. His usefulness to them was over. They knew that changing times had caught up with The System, that it was now necessary to divorce the police department from direct control of vice and graft.

It was not that The System was obsolete, but that this one part of it was. It was an essential part, so a substitute had to be found for it. A new kind of bag man, a new "man between," was necessary.

While Becker was in prison the search for this man was conducted by Charley Murphy. He looked for a man who would be able to adjust to a changing world, in which crime, like everything else, was changing. He wanted a man who could treat crime as business—big business—and who would help organize it on business principles.

So, even while others thought that only saving Becker could save The System, Murphy had already decided that saving Becker was a matter for Becker to worry about. He was no longer necessary to The System.

Chapter **7** *Sir Charles*

The immediate happenings after the Rosenthal murder gave no sign of the coming change. Instead, they fell into the pattern of the past, beginning with a new investigation of New York City, this one headed by State Senator Curran.

The underworld and its immediate protectors were resigned to this. The investigation would supply headlines. Some individuals would have to be sacrificed. But the investigation, they believed, would have no lasting effects upon The System. Any more than the actual murder of Rosenthal would have lasting effects—except upon Rosenthal.

On this thesis, the underworld and most of its protectors—not all, not Murphy—acted to protect their immediate interests. It had a long list of historical precedents for its cynicism. But the underworld, always literal, lacked the imagination to sense that a change was necessary. It substituted a part for the whole and decided that, because Becker was in danger, The System was in danger; because Becker was to be tried, The System was to be tried.

The underworld acted in the only way it knew to save itself.

The first step was to raise a defense fund for Becker. Gamblers, bordello operators, thieves, saloonkeepers—even the police themselves—found they were expected to contribute. Some did and some —at first—did not.

The Curran Committee hearings were held before Becker went on trial. They were given the details of how this fund was being raised by Mrs. Mary Goode, a brothelkeeper. Mrs. Goode was a most co-operative witness, not because she wished to put herself out of business but because she wanted to remain in it.

Her testimony revealed that she was not opposed to paying for protection, that she regarded this as a necessary expense. What she resented was that the price was rising so much faster than her income and, because of competition, she could not pass it on to her customers. She brought her problem into sharp focus under questioning by Emory R. Buckner, chief counsel for the committee. Here is part of the transcript of her testimony.

Q. (by Buckner) What is the matter with the police?
A. The Becker pocketbook, you know.
Q. The Becker pocketbook?
A. They want your life now. . . . Why should it take $100 to bail a woman out of jail? I will tell you. . . . It is the Becker pocketbook. The $100 is split between the lieutenant and the bondsman. That is the Becker pocketbook. . . . Whoever heard of $100 to bail a woman out until Rosenthal was killed?
Q. You say the prices are being raised?
A. They are making a fortune. . . . I said it before. It is the Becker pocketbook.

Mrs. Goode was especially bitter because, as she explained, she ran a "respectable disorderly house." Asked to define this, she said, "Well, a respectable house can be run, for instance, by a woman who only lets gentlemen in. She never lets gunmen in or convicts."

After Mrs. Goode left the stand, others told of their experience with the "Becker pocketbook." This gave the investigators and the general public information which the underworld had long had.

Pressure was exerted not only on small fry like Mary Goode but on individuals with "connections" like Honest John Kelly.

Kelly was told that he was expected to put up $2,500 for Becker's defense. He informed the policeman who came to collect that he would not put up one "plugged nickel to defend Becker." He added that he had never liked Becker, did not like him now.

Kelly went even further. He told a reporter for the *Tribune*, "If Becker is convicted and sent to the chair, it will be no loss to the community."

At this time Kelly was operating a lavish gambling house at 156 West Forty-fourth Street. It numbered prominent politicians, millionaires and society scions among its clientele.

On the night of December 14, 1912, while play was at its height, a squad of police raided the place. Carrying picks, axes, crowbars and battering rams, the raiders used them on furniture, paintings, mirrors and gambling equipment.

Kelly and his employees were badly mauled.

Other gamblers, with one notable exception, heeded the warning. They paid their assessments.

The exception was Arnold Rothstein.

His protection came from a higher, more potent, source than Becker. It derived from "14th Street," from Tammany Hall itself. It came straight from The Boss, straight from Murphy. It came from Tom Foley, now Murphy's closest adviser.

It even came from the regency which had been appointed to protect Big Tim's empire but could do little except liquidate it.

It was not personal affection or loyalty based on long association that was behind this protection. It was need. While Becker waited, first in the Tombs and afterward in Death Row at Sing Sing, for a reversal of his conviction, a new trial, some miracle, someone had to take over many of his functions.

Long before Becker died in the electric chair, Murphy had picked his successor. He had chosen a man who, he felt, fitted into the changing world.

For a half century following the Civil War a jungle morality was prevalent in the United States. Might made right, and if there was need for any scientific credo to justify it, Darwin's Theory of Natural Selection was present, rationalized into "survival of the strongest."

This was the era of the "Robber Barons" in business and finance. Vanderbilt, Astor, Fisk, Drew, Gould, Morgan and Rockefeller made their own morality.

So, too, did the absolute political bosses, like Tweed and Croker among the Democrats, Thurlow Weed and Tom Platt among the Republicans.

Since they got away with their depredations, these became their own excuse for being. There was no call for conscience to be attached to pragmatism, like a caboose on a freight train.

However, a revolt against this rabid individualism began soon after the turn of the century. It was led by Theodore Roosevelt, whom Tom Platt had called "that crazy cowboy in the White House." Roosevelt insisted that teeth be put into the Clayton and Sherman antitrust, antimonopoly acts, and that these be rigidly enforced. He gave backing to a Pure Food and Drug Act. He thought in terms of the general welfare, rather than in terms of big business.

The Robber Barons fought him. However, there were a few exceptions among them who sensed that compromise was better than warfare. One such was Judge Elbert H. Gary, whom Morgan had placed at the head of Morgan's greatest trust, the United States Steel Corporation.

In his biography of Morgan, *Morgan the Magnificent*, John K. Winkler told how Gary came to side with the angels. After taking his new position, Winkler wrote, Gary found that "he was in a nest of thieves. . . . When Gary came to New York [to head United States Steel] he believed the charges of immoralities and irregularities against Big Business were merely the mouthings of demagogues. Sadly, through actual experience, he came to realize that many of the men who controlled Big Business possessed the morality of alley cats."

To men like Gary it became obvious that the dictum of Commodore Vanderbilt, so long accepted as Scripture, must be scrapped. The public refused any longer to be damned.

Instead, the public rose against those who had so long preyed upon it. It turned its anger, its frustration, against business, finance and politics. It demanded a return to Puritanism, a moral reform.

It got not reform but the appearance of reform. Even as the antitrust laws were being enacted, business was retaining the best lawyers to find loopholes in them. The same was true in the case of all other regulatory legislation.

Politics and politicians were even more vulnerable than business. Politics was directly responsible to the people in the sense that it required votes. Every citizen was a stockholder in politics.

Charley Murphy was among the first to grasp this. He had the intelligence, the astuteness and the historical awareness that his task called for.

Murphy was different from all his predecessors who had led Tammany Hall, from Aaron Burr through Dick Croker, in one major respect. Where these others had developed flamboyant personalities, Murphy subdued his. He sought to melt into a gray background. It was the possession of power that mattered to him, not the flaunting of it.

Murphy was born in New York, had grown up in the old Gas House District. He was physically powerful and a fine athlete, so good that he was offered an opportunity to play professional baseball. He rejected this, preferring to enter politics.

This he did through the classic route, ownership of a saloon. A shrewd businessman, he prospered and by 1890 owned four saloons, the biggest and most important being located at Twentieth Street and Second Avenue. This saloon was the headquarters of the Anawanda Club, the district Tammany club.

In 1892 Murphy became Tammany leader of the Gas House District. He worked hard. M. R. Werner, in his *Tammany Hall,* reported that "Murphy stood against a lamp-post on a Second Avenue corner every night about nine o'clock, and anybody in the district who wished to see him called to discuss business or pleasure."

He performed the basic duty of a district leader. He delivered the vote. Like Sullivan and other politicians, he also distributed largess. However, Murphy went beyond them in his philanthropies. He gave some $4,000 for the relief of victims of the blizzard of 1888. He contributed $1,500 to the mission maintained by Dr. William S. Rainsford, rector of St. George's Protestant Episcopal Church. This was J. P. Morgan's church.

Robert A. Van Wyck, elected mayor of New York in 1898 by the Democrats, appointed Murphy to the dock commission. A fellow commissioner was J. Sergeant Cram, a Harvard graduate, member of a wealthy, social family. The two, Harvard aesthete and Gas House strongboy, became close friends. Cram taught Murphy how to wear a dress suit. He also interested him in reading books, especially history.

The revelations of the Mazet Committee resulted in a victory for reform in the next election and Murphy became a private citizen. He organized the New York Trucking and Contracting Company. Shortly afterward Dick Croker went into semiretirement preferring to live in England, raise bulldogs and race horses.

A triumvirate took over control of Tammany. Its members were Murphy, Daniel F. McMahon and Louis F. Haffen. Quickly Murphy emerged as the strong man of the trio. Late in 1902 he became sole leader of Tammany Hall.

Murphy did not attain absolute power in Tammany without a struggle. No opponent was more troublesome than Bill Devery, the former chief of police. Devery, in his years in the department, had built up a strong following and made a fortune. Out of the department, Devery saw, with Croker's retirement, a chance to grasp Croker's power for himself.

Devery won his first contest easily, becoming Democratic leader of a West Side district without much of a fight. Murphy, however, refused to admit Devery into the inner circle at the Hall. Devery then announced that he was a candidate for mayor and would run against the Reform Mayor, Seth Low, and the Tammany candidate, George B. McClellan, son of the Civil War general, a Tammany favorite who had made a good record as a congressman.

One of the ironies of the campaign that followed was a charge by Tammany that the gambling element was behind Devery. Devery replied to this charge: "There ain't no one behind me but Devery's shadow."

When Murphy and his followers continued this line of attack, Devery responded, "And touchin' on and appertainin' to collectin' graft from dives and poolrooms, if I'm the man that's doin' the boss collector act, tell Murphy that he'd better hurry up and send me around his hush money from that house not far from Twenty-seventh Street and Lexington Avenue. . . . The trouble with that fellow is that he's got a red light hangin' around his neck and consequently he sees red in whatever direction he looks."

Devery's hardest blows were thrown at Murphy's efforts to attain respectability. He called Murphy "Sir Charles," and said, "Since Charley Murphy has got to runnin' with J. Sergeant Cram, he's turned up his trousers at the bottom and he's wearin' glasses. Soon he'll be dividin' his name in the middle."

Murphy, however, had the last laugh. It resulted from Devery, rather than he, getting the backing of a true symbol of respectability.

The Devery versus Murphy fight received national publicity. When it was at its height, Carry Nation came to New York, with her hatchet. One of her first stops was at Devery's headquarters, where she had a long, private talk with Devery. Emerging from the building, she was asked for a statement by reporters.

"I want to say," she announced, "that I approve of Mr. Devery's campaign. He isn't a Democrat or a Republican. He is a Prohibitionist."

It took Devery some time to convince his followers that he was not going to cut off the supply of free beer at his headquarters.

Tammany beat both Devery and Seth Low, thus proving again Croker's axiom that New York City could not abide reform for more than one term.

With Tammany returned to power, Murphy's contracting and trucking company leased docks from the city and then re-leased them at a profit that ran as high as 5000 per cent. The company also received contracts from such business stalwarts as the Pennsylvania Railroad, for whom it excavated the site of the Pennsylvania Station.

Murphy became a millionaire. He owned an estate on Long Island, complete with a nine-hole golf course. Here, he and Cram and a number of selected guests could enjoy the sport far from the gaze of his Gas House friends and associates.

Murphy had two business offices. One was Tammany Hall, where people who wanted to see him sat and waited. The other was the second floor of Delmonico's restaurant, where he received those persons whom he wanted to see. Opposition newspapers called this "The Scarlet Room of Mystery."

Murphy worked assiduously at whitening the Tammany sepulcher. In the course of this campaign he first fought publisher William

Randolph Hearst, then joined him, and ultimately fought him again.

In 1905 Hearst ran for mayor of New York as the candidate of the Municipal Ownership League. His biggest issue was that Murphy and the private traction companies were in league to profit at the expense of the city and its millions of users of public utilities.

McClellan won a second term, defeating Hearst. Even though Tammany used all its force of floaters, of gangsters and ballot manipulators, the victory was by a narrow margin. Hearst demanded a recount. It was granted him.

As Hearst later accurately charged, Tammany took no chances that the result might be upset. Thousands of ballots cast for Hearst on the East Side, where he had a large following, disappeared. They were stolen and thrown into the East River by gangsters and hoodlums. In addition, other thousands of ballots were printed, marked for McClellan, and placed in ballot boxes that were supposed to be secure from such tampering.

The man responsible for safeguarding the ballots was Tom Foley, sheriff of New York.

Hearst's bitterness was directed more at Foley than at Murphy.

A year later the Democrats held a state convention to choose a candidate for governor. There had been rumors—which few believed —that Murphy had made a deal with Hearst to give Hearst the nomination. These rumors proved fact. Murphy pushed through the nomination against the personal wishes of the delegates. He used threats, promises and money.

State Senator Thomas F. Grady, one of the delegates, publicly apologized for his vote and called it "the dirtiest day's work of my life."

The Republican candidate was Charles Evans Hughes, who had come into prominence as chief investigator of the insurance scandals in the state.

Hearst lost. He blamed his defeat on a lack of vigor on the part of certain Democratic leaders, among them McClellan, Foley, Tim Sullivan, and Senator Patrick McCarren, the Brooklyn Democratic leader who was one of the biggest gamblers in the country. He could hardly have had any reason for expecting their support.

Just before the convention at which he was chosen, Hearst sent a telegram to the Indianapolis *Star*. In it he described McClellan as an "election thief" and Sullivan as "a keeper of dives and lord protector of crooks and criminals." He used similar appellatives for Foley and McCarren.

Murphy survived a revolt after the election. Some of his friends pointed out that, while Murphy had given the nomination to Hearst, he had done little to get the vote out for the publisher. They explained Murphy's action as Machiavellian. He had succeeded in destroying Hearst as an important political factor.

(How wrong they were! Some twenty-six years later Hearst, still recalling the events of 1906, would throw his support to Franklin Delano Roosevelt against Tammany's own Alfred E. Smith, and thus help gain a presidential nomination for Roosevelt.)

Actually Murphy had used Hearst, as he used Cram and August Belmont and Thomas Fortune Ryan, as window dressing for Tammany. It was part of his long-range plan for making Tammany appear to be not a tiger but a pussycat.

Perhaps it derived from the books Cram had caused him to read, perhaps from intuition, but, whatever the cause, Murphy knew important changes were needed in The System.

Long before Rosenthal was murdered, Murphy knew the old manner of regulating, and profiting from, lawlessness was near its end. Business had washed its face and demanded that politics do likewise. New York City had emerged from its frontier stage.

Murphy had taken no drastic steps before Rosenthal was killed; the need was not yet apparent to others. Afterward, however, he moved quickly. He gave orders that open prostitution be ended, that the red lights be extinguished. He told the police to close the storefront gambling joints.

Some of the perquisites of the gangsters were canceled. Their total immunity from the law was no more. This had actually preceded the murder and one of the victims of that order had been Monk Eastman.

These acts pleased Murphy's respectable friends. They were good for business.

Murphy had another motive for his actions. He wanted to cut down the power of the police. The meat on which various uniformed Caesars had fed had been the graft from vice and gambling. Battening on such food, Williams, Devery and Becker had gained both wealth and power. They had built personal political followings.

Devery had challenged Murphy. Becker was on his way to make a similar challenge when Rosenthal was killed. Murphy was determined that no one would rise within the department to fill Becker's outsize shoes.

Murphy knew that reducing police graft would also reduce political graft. But, already, he had found other sources, less malodorous, of revenue. These were given the contradictory term "honest graft."

Such graft included payoffs from those who did business with the city, who built its buildings, its schools, its hospitals, its streets and its sewers. From those who sold supplies and services to the city. From those who insured its buildings.

This type of graft appealed to business as well as to politicians. It resulted in a friendly relationship, and business replaced the gangster, the panderer, the gambler, as the source of money with which to prime the political machine.

Business provided Tammany with the major share of its campaign funds for local elections. The Republicans, by custom, hit the business jackpot in national and state elections.

But Murphy needed more than money to operate a winning political machine. He needed at least one more vote than the opposition. Gangsters and the underworld were sources of votes, legitimate and illegitimate. Yet these were the very people whom he was alienating by his drive for a "clean city." He could not discard them; he still depended upon them the first Tuesday after the first Monday each November.

It was obvious that, if he took away one source of revenue from this element, he must provide another. Therefore, some gambling, some vice must continue. And new opportunities must be provided to replace the old ones. Business, in addition to paying direct tribute, would have to yield an indirect tribute to the gangsters.

This revenue would come from exploitation of both business and its employees. Murphy knew that not the substance but the form of graft and its sources, of gangster revenue and its sources, would be changed.

He knew further that there would have to be a substitute for Becker. A man whose relationship to the new graft would be even more important than Becker's was to the old. A man of business. But a man without any desire for political power.

A man who understood the value of money and how to make it. A man who had money and knew how to use it. A man, neither policeman nor gangster, who could act as a transmission belt between the two. A man of substance, who could employ, bribe, underwrite and finance.

On the night of July 30, 1915, Charles Becker died in the electric chair in Sing Sing.

A group that included Arnold Rothstein, Vernie Barton, Tad Dorgan and Nicky Arnstein kept a vigil in Jack's restaurant. A gold pocket watch, its case open, ticked away on the bright, bare, white tablecloth.

At exactly eleven, a stillness descended on the room. It was as if here, some twenty-five miles from the scene, all of them were waiting the click of a switch, the hum of electric current. For the words "I pronounce this man dead."

They did not know—not even those vitally concerned—that something more than a mortal man was dying in Sing Sing. An era of crime and politics also was being pronounced dead.

Not by a doctor of medicine but by a professor of politics, Charles F. Murphy. He had already chosen the man who would succeed Becker in the coming age. The substitute part which would keep The System functioning.

The man he had chosen picked up the gold watch from the table, snapped the case together, and replaced it in his pocket. He took out a bankroll, a big bankroll, and said, "Well, let's go look for some action."

The man—and the bankroll—were symbolic of the new era. The man was Arnold Rothstein.

Chapter **8** *A Tailor-made Man*

Murphy did not simply reach out his political scepter, tap Rothstein on the shoulder, and say, "I dub thee 'the man between.'" The choice was made over a period of time. Circumstances made the choice for Murphy as much as he made it for himself.

The most important factor was that Rothstein was at hand. He and Murphy had known each other for more than ten years. In that period Rothstein had grown in stature, in wealth. He had become a person of prominence in his own world, though little known out of it.

He had that basic quality for which Murphy was looking—a business sense. Whatever he did he did as a businessman. He ran his gambling house in that manner. And had made it the most successful, the best operated, in New York. He had had the vision to expand his bookmaking enterprises from a retail to a wholesale level. His customers now included other bookmakers.

Back in 1910 happenstance had made him a bail bondsman. A confidence man, "Plunk" Drucker, had been arrested, arraigned and bail set. Drucker appealed to Tom Foley to get him released. Foley called Rothstein, asked him to post cash bail for Drucker overnight, to be replaced by some other collateral the next day.

Rothstein posted the bail, learned the high premiums charged for this service, and went into the business himself. It soon became automatic for Foley and other politicians, when they needed such a service, to call on Rothstein to perform it. He always did—and at a profit.

And Rothstein in the meantime had made connections with reputable bonding and surety companies. He paid them less interest for the money they advanced to him than he charged. His risk was greater, on paper, but not in actuality. Those who were freed by his efforts knew he meant it when he said, "God help you if you don't," when they gave their word to appear at their trials.

Important as Rothstein's business ability was to Murphy, just as important were other qualities he possessed.

Rothstein was one of Tim Sullivan's boys. That was a solid bond between him and Murphy.

Rothstein was a man who could keep his mouth shut.

Rothstein was a man who did not drink, who did not pop off.

And Rothstein, perceptive, shrewd, knew the score.

Over a period of time Murphy, Foley and young Jimmy Hines began to call on Rothstein for repeated services. These could include anything from posting a bond to ballot stuffing. And Rothstein always delivered.

He had, step by step, become the man between.

The relationship was far from one-sided.

There is the story, undoubtedly apocryphal, of the young man who sought a loan from J. P. Morgan. Morgan refused him, then invited the man to walk the length of Wall Street with him. The man accepted and they paraded the street, Morgan's arm on the young man's shoulder. As Morgan left, he said, "Walk into any door on this street. You'll find you now have credit for any amount."

Substitute Broadway for Wall Street, Murphy for Morgan, and Rothstein was in the same position as the young man. Murphy figuratively walked at Rothstein's side. His arm was on Rothstein's shoulder. Rothstein knew how high a credit rating this gave him.

The "Becker pocketbook" did not molest him. The police did not interfere with his gambling operations. Lawyers, fixers, people in trouble, sought him out. He was a pipeline to "Fourteenth Street." If you wanted a favor from the Hall, Arnold Rothstein could expedite it, assure it, for you. And so you paid him.

Billy Gibson, for instance, wanted a license as a boxing promoter. He approached Rothstein, who went to Foley. And Gibson got his license.

Gibson was grateful. To show his gratitude, he made Rothstein a present of a part interest in a rising young fighter, named Benny Leonard, whom he managed. All during Leonard's great—and profitable—career, Rothstein received ten per cent of his earnings.

Someone else had trouble with a building inspector. Rothstein could take care of that. A bookmaker was having trouble with the cop on the beat. Rothstein took care of the cop. A boy was in trouble and a worried father wondered if there was any way Rothstein could help. There was.

In return, Rothstein took cash. Cash was real. It was something that could be fingered, looked at. Added to the bankroll.

That had grown too large to be carried in its entirety. Some of it was even in a bank. But he always carried sufficient to meet any emergency, any sudden demand. Yes, he had a great deal of money, but he still knew exactly how much. In 1913 it amounted to almost $300,000.

That was big money at a time when a million dollars was still a legendary sum. No gambler had ever had that much, though Canfield had come close. His estate was almost $800,000. Honest John Kelly, when he retired to live off principal the rest of his life in Florida, announced he had plenty of money, more than $200,000.

The gang leaders of the day had little money and their followers even less.

This would alter. A new world would dawn for the gangsters. Their field of operations would change. Business, demanding respectability, would call on the gangsters for fresh activities, call on them and pay them off. It would do it quietly and surreptitiously, like the married man visiting the one brothel in his small town.

Rothstein would help effect that transition. He would have a part in the change, a part in the profits.

That was the reward for being the man between.

The Rosenthal murder, the new-broom technique of the reform administration which followed it, affected Rothstein's operations. It was not safe to operate a regular gambling house. To meet this, Rothstein created the "floating" game. His was truly the "oldest, reliable floating" game that was pictured in *Guys and Dolls*. A game which, though operated by the same man, was never held twice in a row in the same place.

It had one drawback. Players had to be informed where the "action" would take place. Rothstein took it on himself to pass this information along. It was then that he began to stand in doorways, the habit which William J. Fallon derided when he described Rothstein as "a mouse waiting for a piece of cheese."

He expanded his bonding business. He became an agent for a number of insurance companies. He invested, though lightly, in an oil-drilling company. He became a part owner of the Simplex Motor Car Company and its agent and distributor in New York.

He could come home one early morning and say to Carolyn, "We're rich."

They moved to an apartment on the corner of Broadway and Fifty-second Street. The main quarters comprised eight rooms and two baths, with separate quarters for a maid and a butler. The rent was high for the time—$2,400 a year.

It was a lovely apartment that Carolyn worked hard to furnish and decorate. But it was still a place where he hung his hat, slept and changed clothes. He spent more time at Jack's than he did there. Later he would spend less time in his different homes than he spent, first, in Reuben's restaurant on upper Broadway and, later, at Lindy's.

People who wanted to see him looked for him outside his home. They knew that some time each night he would appear at Jack's or at the Metropole or at the Knickerbocker Hotel. The best waiting place, though, was Jack's.

For everyone but Carolyn. She waited at home. Their relationship was on a plateau. Asked, he would swear, his voice tight in his throat, that he loved her. He lavished gifts on her. He bragged of her appearance. He bragged even more of her fidelity. He claimed he was the only man on Broadway who could locate his wife at any moment of the day or night.

Sometimes the telephone by her bed would ring at two, three o'clock in the morning. She would answer in a sleepy voice and Rothstein would say, "Sweetheart, I want you to tell Tom [or Dick or Harry] 'hello.'" She would say "hello," and try to go back to sleep. Someplace on Broadway, Rothstein would add some newly won money to his roll.

He trusted her as he trusted no one else. He would confide his doubts and his worries. He could put aside front—pretense—with her.

Yet even this was not enough to allow him to let down his guard completely. If two people knew a secret, it was no longer a secret.

She was a fifty per cent confidante, an adviser, a friend.

But he could not move outside himself. That was why, no matter what else she was to him, she was never completely a wife. Never completely a woman of flesh and blood. She was an idealization, a statue.

The conflict took its toll of him. Nearly always it made him psychically impotent. When he cried, she comforted him.

Once, years later, he talked of it to a psychologist. He told him of his feelings of shame and guilt. He told him how he felt about "good" women and "bad" women.

He talked about his mother a great deal in that one, long interview.

The psychologist tried to tie the two women together—mother and wife. Rothstein did not listen. This was dirty talk.

But, surprisingly, Rothstein did not say anything about Bobbie Winthrop.

With Bobbie, Rothstein had no feeling of guilt, no sense of shame. She was no mother image, no "good" woman as Rothstein separated the good from the bad.

She came to the gambling house quite often. She was still Rothstein's luck charm. The gambling did not interest her; Rothstein did.

She was a good-looking woman, blonde, with large, staring, blue eyes. She had a good figure, had appeared in a number of shows as a dancer. But her talent was limited and her ambition even more limited. She liked existing.

She was understanding and undemanding. She was like a pet cat, grateful when she was stroked, expecting that she would be fed and housed and given a warm place for her own. Better looking, for instance, than Peggy Hopkins, she never thought of her looks as tools of a trade, something of value.

Rothstein set Bobbie up in an apartment. He gave her money for her needs, which were slight. The apartment was security, a place that was hers, where she belonged. And she had a kind master.

The relationship extended over a dozen years. It began in 1913, when Carolyn made her first trip to Europe. In the beginning it had no complications for Rothstein. Carolyn was away. But that changed when she returned.

As Carolyn Rothstein told it in her book, *Now I'll Tell*, she learned of the relationship almost by intuition. She casually opened a copy of *Town Topics*, a forerunner of the gossip columns, and saw an item that read: "A tailor-made man prominent in the guessing fraternity is being seen nightly in the Broadway restaurants with beautiful Bobbie Winthrop."

It was the "tailor-made" that jabbed her intuition.

She asked Rothstein the direct question that same night and he confessed. Confessed as though he had been waiting for the chance, feeling that, by his admission, he must gain absolution.

"Then there's only one thing for me to do," she said. "I'm going to get a divorce."

"But you can't. I love you." His self-control left him. His voice broke. "You can't leave me. I don't know what I'd do if you left me. I'll give her up. She doesn't mean anything to me. You can't leave me, Carolyn."

She stayed. She had to agree with Rothstein that Bobbie had taken nothing from her, nothing at all. And there were other reasons.

"I loved Arnold," she said. "He was cheating on me, but whose fault was it? I didn't know. Whatever part of Arnold was mine, I still had. I think I had it all his life."

Rothstein used the affair with Bobbie to flagellate himself. It preyed on his mind. A dozen times he would assure Carolyn that it was over. Once he showed Carolyn a check for $10,000. "I'm giving it to her and sending her home to her family. Some place in Pennsylvania. This will end it for good. Aren't you glad?"

"If you do it, I'll be glad."

He did not do it.

There were periods when he did not see Bobbie. Once for three months. Then, one night, he visited her and it was as if he had seen her only the night before. No recriminations. No tears.

This was what provided her hold on Rothstein. She did not ask for anything. She just waited.

Once Rothstein gave her a sealed envelope containing $100,000 in bonds. "It's for you," he said. "Do what you want with it."

Two months later he came to her and said, "I have to have those bonds back."

She went to a bureau, opened a drawer. She removed the sealed envelope, returned it to him. She had never opened the envelope.

One morning in 1925 Carolyn was awakened by Rothstein. He sat on the edge of her bed. "Bobbie's dead," he said. "She died yesterday. I'd like to go to her funeral if you'll let me."

"If you want to go, I won't stop you."

He hung his head. "I want to go."

The funeral was in the morning and was over in plenty of time for Rothstein to get to the race track. He never mentioned Bobbie to Carolyn again. It was possible that he never thought of her again.

During the course of the years Rothstein was seen with a number of women. Broadway talked about him and Lillian Lorraine, him and Peggy Joyce. The talk did not bother him. Neither of these women meant anything to him. They were primarily employees, steering suckers to his gambling rooms.

His life was the making of money. Cards and dice and handbooks and bankbooks were closer to him than anything else. A man had to be single-minded, single-purposed. That is, if the man was Arnold Rothstein.

Still, there were times when he felt the need of something more. He would go to the home of his family. Whether alone or with Carolyn, there was always a pane of glass between him and his father, him and his mother. He knew that Abraham still lit a mourning candle each year on the anniversary of his marriage. A candle that burned all night. A candle for the second son, *yahrzeit* for the second son.

He tried to strike back at his father through his two brothers. He competed with Abraham for the affection of Jack and Edgar. He used money as his weapon, for there he could compete on equal grounds with Abraham. He gave money to the boys. He bought them presents. He bought them tickets to ball games and prize fights and the theater.

You could do anything with money. He was sure of that. You could even buy love.

This was Rothstein in 1913. Rothstein at the moment when he started to scale the heights he had chosen as his own particular Everest.

Chapter 9 — Pigeons and Partridge

By 1913 Canfield was long gone. The Allen was dead. John Kelly was temporarily out of business. William Busteed, Sam Emery, Dinky Davis and John Daley had closed their doors and disappeared.

Only Rothstein remained. Milk-faced, drowsy-lidded, he sat at a green-covered table and played cards. Or stood at the back of a room and watched his employees and his customers as the roulette wheel spun or the dice hit the backboard. His runners picked up horse-racing bets all over town. And in an office on Forty-sixth Street other employees kept a record of the day's play.

To those who had preceded Rothstein as kingpin of gamblers gambling had been a way of life. To him it was a living. These others had taken chances, accepted the sportsman's adage that "where you can't lose, you can't win." They backed their judgment. Rothstein sought out, schemed for, games where he could not lose. He wanted to make chance a negligible, not a determining, force.

It is an anomaly that Rothstein, who was so many other things, should be remembered as a gambler. That is probably the result of the glamour that the word "gambler" evokes. It recalls memories of Mississippi River sportsmen like Edna Ferber's Ravenal. It conjures up the picture of Bret Harte's Oakhurst.

Rothstein was a gambler, of course. He was a crooked gambler. Wherever he could he rigged the chances in his favor. He took it for granted that the people he played against did the same thing. But he worked on the theory that he was smarter than his opponents, that he knew the law of averages better.

Rothstein had a hand in more gambling coups than any other man who ever bet on horses or took a hand in a card game. Or made a wager on a prize fight or a baseball game. Rothstein probably made more money out of running gambling houses than any other operator of gambling houses. Yet, basically, gambling was not his major interest after he became the biggest, most important gambler in New York.

It was merely the most spectacular.

A number of happenings pushed gambling into the background of Rothstein's activities. The first was the passage of the 16th Amendment to the Constitution. That stated in stark terms:

"The Congress shall have the power to lay and collect taxes on incomes, from whatever source derived, without apportionment among the several states, and without regard to any census or enumeration."

This was the first of two constitutional amendments which would have a potent effect upon Rothstein and his career.

For gambling to be big business it required big gamblers. It needed men like young Gates, like Hill, like Sanford and Kinney. Men like these gave the opportunity for big winnings. And, until 1913, men like these kept all the money they had made or inherited. They did not have the Department of Internal Revenue as partners.

The income tax, though its levy was comparatively light, hit many of the free spenders.

It also coincided with the rise of the New Puritanism. Beginning with the turn of the century, that tide of reform which was to culminate in prohibition rose higher and higher. The wealthy became aware that they had better not flaunt their wealth or their playful vices. And gambling, which had long been regarded as a peccadillo, was now looked on as a vice.

The war that followed the Income Tax Amendment was also to play a part in cutting down potential gamblers. It gave a feeling of personal and social responsibility to many of the children and grandchildren of the Gilded Age.

The first to feel the effects of these changes were the small gamblers, the operators of stuss games and poolrooms. The last would be Rothstein.

He would continue to operate gambling houses for a decade. But there would be no continuity to his operations. He saw what was happening, prepared for it, adjusted to it.

The Partridge Club was the first of his gambling games to go. He always pretended it was a friendly game, but this was taken seriously by no one, least of all Rothstein.

The players in this game changed from year to year. Toward its end it numbered such men as Harry Sinclair, Charles Stoneham, who had bought the Giant baseball team from Andrew Freedman, Swope and the writer Bruno Lessing, among the regulars. Also a regular was George H. Lowden, broker and amateur sportsman.

Lowden was one of those gamblers who never seemed able to win. His losses ran high, well into six figures. It seemed, however, that there were always fresh resources for Lowden to tap. Seemed that way until Lowden was arrested, charged with forgery in the abstraction of securities amounting to $300,000 from the vaults of his firm.

At Lowden's trial it was testified that he had used these securities as collateral for a $100,000 loan from Rothstein. He had been unable to redeem the securities. Lowden was convicted of forgery and sent to Sing Sing. A civil suit was then instituted against Rothstein to secure the return of the bonds.

Rothstein was defended in this trial by George Young Bauchle. The defense offered was that Rothstein had merely acted as an agent for Lowden. He swore that he had not been the lender, that a brokerage firm, now unfortunately bankrupt and out of business, had been the actual lender.

A check of the bankruptcy courts revealed that there had been such a firm as Knott, Temple and Company. It had failed, with no assets. Somehow, all its books and records had disappeared.

It also developed that one of the partners in the bankrupt firm had been Charles Stoneham.

Stoneham, called as a witness, testified that, to the best of his knowledge and recollection, Rothstein had told the truth. He was sorry but he could not recollect what had happened to the bonds. After all, it was just one transaction in hundreds—even thousands—completed by the brokerage firms in which Stoneham held varying interests.

Rothstein won; the case against him was dismissed.

There were two consequences. The Partridge Club ceased to function and it became public knowledge that Rothstein and Stoneham had close business relations. How close was to be revealed years later in the course of a number of trials and hearings.

At about this same time Rothstein reluctantly closed his gambling rooms on West Forty-sixth Street. They had become too well known.

Rothstein did not want to go out of the gambling-house business. He looked about for a location where he could operate without too much fear of the law. The place he found was in Hewlett, Long Island.

Wealth and society had begun to throng Long Island. Rothstein liked to be where the money was. In addition, the law-enforcement agencies were not too active in enforcing antigambling statutes. The price for protection was not so high that it made a "nut," or overhead, that gave the profit to the protectors and only the labor to the gambler.

As an added protection—how Rothstein liked to have his bets coppered!—he chose as the site of his new casino a building and piece of real estate owned by State Senator Reynolds, a potent political figure on Long Island. Rothstein was not alone in the purchase. His partners were the Considine brothers, with both Nat Evans and Vernie Barton cut in on the profits.

Whereas the Forty-sixth Street house had been a gambling house pure and simple, with a cold buffet, liquors and cigars available, but not exceptional, the Long Island place was operated like a country estate. The first place had been opened on as small a scale as possible; this new one was operated lavishly.

The house was located on spacious grounds. These were beautifully landscaped and included garden paths and a rippling brook.

Rothstein staffed the house with expert help. Thomas Farley, still with him, acted as butler and overseer. The stickmen and dealers were required to wear evening dress. The dining room was one of the best in the country. Rothstein hired the entire staff of Sherry's for the opening and kept two of the chefs for the period that the house operated.

The menus offered the finest dishes. They differed from most menus in that they did not carry prices. Rothstein, to paraphrase J. P. Morgan, believed that a man who had to know how much it cost to eat couldn't afford to eat.

Entry to the gambling house was by invitation only. However, anyone who was known able to afford to lose a few thousands was able to get an invitation.

Rothstein was aware of the value of snob appeal. He told Damon Runyon, "People like to think they're better than other people. As long as they're willing to pay to prove it, I'm willing to let them."

Rothstein operated here for three years and won a great deal of money. His own estimate was that the profit ran to a half million dollars. But each year the place showed less profit and each year the local authorities grew more rapacious in their demands. By 1919 it was apparent to him that further operation would enrich no one but crooked cops and politicians. He sold the estate.

However, Saratoga was still running wide open. Bookmaking was not legal, but operated in a shadowland where it was not illegal, provided certain precautions were taken. This was the era of "oral betting," when no actual records were supposed to be kept.

The authorities were the victims of twin pressures. First, there was the paid-for pressure of the bookmakers. Second, there was the influence of many of the "best people" who wanted racing to continue and knew that it could exist only if betting was allowed. The gamblers put their pressure on Democratic politicians and office-holders. The better people, who provided so much of the campaign funds for Republicans, exerted their power on that party.

So Saratoga remained the "Spa," the Monte Carlo of America.

The Rothsteins still went to Saratoga each year on the Cavanagh Special, celebrated their wedding anniversary there.

In 1917 Rothstein was approached by a gambler named Henry Tobin, who had a gambling house in Saratoga but no bankroll to enable him to function. Tobin was an old-time gambler with a good reputation. Rothstein gave him $35,000 as a bankroll. But he exacted a high premium.

The loan was to bear interest of a flat ten per cent, due immedi-

ately after the Saratoga season closed. And Rothstein was to share
equally in any profits made by Tobin.

Tobin accepted the terms because they offered him the only
chance he had to operate. Tobin, moreover, was receiving something in addition to money from Rothstein. He knew Rothstein
would be eager to make his profit as large as possible. Tobin thus
was getting Rothstein as a steerer for his game.

The deal worked out satisfactorily for both Tobin and Rothstein.
In 1917 they split a profit of more than $100,000 and in 1918 the
profit was even higher.

It was not until 1919 that Rothstein opened his own gambling
place in Saratoga. This was soon after he had sold out on Long
Island.

He followed the pattern he had set in Hewlett. Through an in-
termediary he bought the magnificent summer home of Mrs. George
A. Saportas, just north of Saratoga. This he immediately remodeled,
spending $100,000 in the process.

He told Carolyn, "I'm going to make it the finest place Saratoga
ever saw. I'll make them forget all about Morrissey and Canfield."

He didn't quite cause the memories of his predecessors to be cast
into limbo, but he did build the most luxurious gambling place in
the United States. He called it the "Brook," and it was a combination gambling house, cabaret, night club and restaurant. There was
not a specialty served at any of the fine restaurants in New York
City that was not available at the Brook. And, of course, there were
no prices on the menu.

Rothstein wanted only the best people as customers. To him,
"best" and "wealthiest" were synonymous. He had no other gauge
than money by which to judge and, because that was his criterion,
he held that there was no other. Originally it was intended that evening dress be mandatory, but Rothstein had to relax this rule because of Sam Rosoff.

Rosoff, a hulking man with a loud voice and no manners, was
the builder of most of New York's subways. He was a power in
Tammany. And a gambler in the tradition of "Bet-a-Million" Gates.

However, he was not a man who was known for his style of dress. He was as likely to wear overalls as a white tie.

When Rosoff appeared at the Brook, demanding action, no one questioned what he wore. Like the characters in the Hearst paper cartoons, he looked as if clothed in dollar bills.

The Brook was the scene of the highest play in the history of Saratoga gambling. Among its players was a quota of "war millionaires," but also such standbys as Joshua Cosden, the oil magnate. Cosden dropped $300,000 one night, $200,000 the succeeding night. On the third night he won $20,000 and insisted on telling everyone about how lucky a gambler he was.

Another oil millionaire, Harry Sinclair, was a high bettor. This was before Teapot Dome, of course. Sam Hildreth, who trained the horses in Sinclair's enormously successful Rancocas Stable, was also a big bettor. Hildreth was a gambling man from way back, an old friend and client of Rothstein's. He and Rothstein had been partners in some of the biggest betting coups ever made in the history of racing.

Charles Stoneham, with his double chin and flabby stomach, second only to Rosoff's, played at the Brook night after night. Stoneham had many interests now. In addition to his brokerage houses and the ownership of the Giants, he owned a string of racing horses and operated the gambling casinos in Havana, Cuba.

Stoneham was involved in one of the oddest gambling sessions that ever took place in the Brook. He sprained a foot and was immobilized for a few days. Bored by his enforced chair-borne state, he telephoned Rothstein at the Brook. "What color came up last on the wheel?"

"The black."

"Bet a thousand for me on the red next turn."

"You're on. The wheel is spinning." An instant later, Rothstein said, "You win."

For more than three hours Stoneham gambled by telephone. When he was done, he had lost some $70,000.

However, Sam Rosoff was probably the biggest plunger who played the tables at the Brook. Burly, red-cheeked, outrageously overweight, Rosoff would waddle to the wheel and start betting thousands on each turn. However, his favorite game was dice. He was the only gambler who made Rothstein uneasy. That was because Rosoff had no respect for money. He never figured odds or percentages, but made his bets whimsically.

And he made his own rules too. The limit was what Rosoff made it, not what the house wanted. Not if the house wanted Rosoff's trade. And Rothstein did. A gambler like Rosoff could break the bank and, a number of times, Rosoff came close.

One night in August, 1920, Rosoff had a streak of luck. By eleven o'clock he was more than $400,000 ahead. Rothstein needed fresh money in case Rosoff decided to cash in. He put in a hurry call to Stoneham, who opened the wall safe in his home, removed $300,000 and rushed it to the Brook. When the money reached Rothstein, Rosoff was $100,000 behind.

What made Rosoff so great a risk, in addition to his unpredictability, was that he could "tap out" Rothstein. With the limit off, he could use his bankroll, so much bigger than Rothstein's, and take loss after loss and still come back for more. He gambled the percentage his bankroll gave him against the percentage the house had running for it.

Another type of gambler, a type whom Rothstein wanted as customer, was Nick Dandalos, "Nick the Greek." Nick made his first big success as a gambler in Canada, where he beat the bookmakers for more than $250,000. Nick felt he had served his apprenticeship and was ready to take on the biggest gamblers. He picked Rothstein as his target.

The game Nick chose was his best game—poker. They played table stakes. And Rothstein cleaned out Dandalos. The end of the game found Nick rising from the table, waving a good-by and announcing "I'll be back."

He did return. Again he had a stake in six figures. Again Rothstein broke him.

Rothstein said it wasn't luck but percentage. He didn't claim to be a better poker player than Nick. It was just that his bankroll was so much bigger. He could afford to lose more bets than Nick.

And, ultimately, he was bound to win one. Nick could tap him out —as far as money on the table went—and Rothstein could dig down in his pocket and come up with another bankroll. Nick didn't have the reserves and he was bound to lose once. That was enough.

Nick knew the percentage was running against him, but he was a gambler, whereas Rothstein was a businessman. Nick delighted— still delights—in bucking the percentage. And the percentage defeated him against Rothstein.

As long as the Brook operated, Nick was a welcome visitor.

Not so, however, Colonel Henry Simms, who lost $60,000 of his oil millions at the Brook. Simms felt this gave him the right to brag. After all, how many men could afford to lose $60,000?

Rothstein disliked such talk. It was bad for business. He liked the advertising that came from men talking about their winnings, not that which came from telling of losses.

Encountering Simms in the clubhouse of the race track, Rothstein maneuvered him into a group that included Stoneham, Hildreth and some others. "Colonel," Rothstein said, "I hear you're telling people that you're a gambling man. How come you only play for chicken feed when you come to the Brook?"

Simms sputtered, "What—what do you call $60,000?"

"Chicken feed," Rothstein replied. He took a roll of bills from a pocket. "If you want real action, I have a hundred thousand here. You match it and we'll toss a coin for the money."

Simms managed to get sufficient voice to say, "I never heard of such a thing."

Rothstein pointed toward the stables. "Next time you want to gamble, Colonel, try there. They match pennies every day."

Simms, his face sunburst red, turned and walked from the clubhouse. He never again talked publicly of his "heavy" losses.

Rothstein operated the Brook Club through the 1922 season. There was a municipal election in Saratoga that year and, despite large contributions to the clique in power, the reform candidate beat the friend of the gamblers and bookmakers.

Rothstein was in New York by that time, of course, the racing season long over. A few days after the election a man called on him, identifying himself as an emissary of the newly elected administration. "The Mayor," he announced, "is willing to forget some of the promises he made."

Rothstein asked, "How much?"

"You can take care of it for $60,000."

"You go back," Rothstein said, "and tell him to go to hell. Anyone who'd sell out a whole town wouldn't hesitate to double-cross one man."

Rothstein put the Brook on the market, and it was sold soon after.

While he no longer operated his own show place, Rothstein did remain part of the gambling picture in Saratoga until his death. He bankrolled a game operated by Jules Formel and "Gold Tooth" Moore and was one of the partners in the downtown "Chicago Club." This was probably the biggest money-maker in the entire history of Saratoga gambling.

After Rothstein's death, the Chicago Club became the sole property of the syndicate of mobsters headed by Lucky Luciano.

Actually, it was neither moral principle nor fear of being double-crossed that decided Rothstein to sell the Brook. Many other factors were behind that decision. By 1923 Rothstein had achieved an unwelcome notoriety.

He had been accused of fixing the 1919 World Series.

He had been involved in a number of racing coups.

He had become *persona non grata* at the race tracks.

He had so many other business ventures going that the operation of a gambling club, even one as profitable as the Brook, was a liability.

After all, why should he spend time, take risks, front for his own gambling game, when he could make more money in two minutes by betting on a race than he could make in two years of operating a gambling game?

Chapter **10** *Six Seconds—Three Firsts*

Horse racing, the "sport of kings," has also been acclaimed the most democratic of sports because "On the turf and under it, all men are equal."

Horse racing was a part of British culture that was taken over bodily by the United States. George Washington was one of its earliest enthusiasts. Andrew Jackson liked to wager that one horse could run faster than another.

There were races in Virginia and Kentucky, in New York and even in Puritan New England, almost from their beginnings.

While there were some who owned and raced horses for sport's sake alone, the majority of those involved in racing were in it because it was a socially accepted form of gambling. The wager was nearly always the thing.

Bookmakers—pool operators—came into existence early. They were the merchants in the gambling market place. Sometimes bookmaking was legal. More often it was extralegal. Most often it was held to be illegal and its practitioners subject to fine and imprisonment.

Bookmakers were believers in rugged individualism, in private enterprise. They were men who backed their judgment with their pocketbooks. Sometimes they lost, but more often they won. They were unorganized in their dealings except when it came to purchasing protection from the law. Then they frequently acted in concert.

It was Arnold Rothstein who made a big business out of bookmaking.

116

Arnold Rothstein, in his last photo, and one of the few ever taken of him, not long before he was murdered.

Carolyn Rothstein Behar wrote a book called *Now I'll Tell*, but she did not tell very much that was new or important about her husband's life or death.

Lieutenant Charles Becker went to the chair for hiring the killers of Herman Rosenthal. Becker's place in politics and crime was taken by Rothstein.

Herman (Beansy) Rosenthal disobeyed the first rule of the underworld, "Thou shalt not squeal." He talked and died.

Lillian Lorraine combined a career as show girl and steerer for Rothstein. Her name was linked with Rothstein's, but their relationship was purely a business one.

Abe Attell, former boxing champion, was Rothstein's bodyguard and later was named in the "fixing" of the 1919 World Series.

Nicky Arnstein and Fannie Brice were happier in this photo than they were later when Nicky was charged with masterminding the multi-million-dollar bond robberies. (Said Fannie: "He couldn't mastermind an electric bulb into a socket.")

Charles F. Murphy (left), last of the great Irish
leaders of Tammany Hall, in one of the St. Patrick's
Day parades. With him are Eugene Wood and Mrs. Wood.

Herbert Bayard Swope (right)
with Dudley Field Malone
going to the World War I Peace
Conference.

James J. Hines, with his protégé
and attorney, Joseph Shalleck.
Hines later went to jail for his
relations with Dutch Schultz.

Big Tim Sullivan, bow-tie, was always available to his constituents. At right, his step-brother, Larry Mulligan.

Peggy Hopkins Joyce showed off an orchid georgette negligee with ostrich plumes in 1925. When she brought suckers to Rothstein's gambling houses, her dress was more formal.

William J. Fallon (right), the "Great Mouthpiece," had John J. Curtin as his attorney of record when he successfully defended himself against a charge that stemmed from his employment by Rothstein.

The beginning of the end, as the coffin containing Arnold Rothstein's body is carried from the funeral parlor to the hearse.

The end of the end, as Rothstein's coffin is lowered into an open grave. There were only a few mourners, a group of sensation-seekers and a squad of police, hoping to get some clues to Rothstein's murder at his funeral.

George McManus was
unworried during his trial
for the murder of
Arnold Rothstein.
He had good reason,
for the case was
dismissed, and his
Chesterfield coat,
found in room 349
of the Park Central,
was returned to him.

Charles Evans Hughes
looked out from a portrait
as Frank Costello took the
oath as a witness
before the Senate Crime
Investigating Committee.
If Hughes' own Republican
party had backed his
anti-bookmaking bills,
Rothstein might never have
built up the gambling
empire which Costello
took over.

As early as 1914 Arnold Rothstein became a bookmaker for bookmakers. He opened a discount house for wagering.

To understand how this happened it is necessary to explain how bookmakers operated.

Each bookmaker employed the services of handicappers and timers. Employees caught early-morning workouts of horses, listened to stable gossip, tried to get as much inside information as possible. On the basis of all these reports the bookmakers listed their "overnight line." These were the opening odds on each race.

Since different bookmakers had different sources of information and different handicappers, there was usually a slight divergence in the odds against each horse in a race. A careful bettor—like a careful shopper who reads the ads in the newspapers—would look for bargains; that is, he would try to find the longest odds on the horse of his choice.

Bookmakers used to set up odds which gave them from eight to fifteen per cent the best of it, with the general average about ten per cent. The bookmakers, like the gambling houses, figured their profit on turnover.

However, a bookmaker would frequently find that he had too much money bet on one horse and not enough on others in the same race. He would then try to lay off the bets with other bookmakers. However, it rarely happened that he could, for if there was a heavy play on one horse that play was not limited to one bookmaker, but was spread among all of them.

Under such circumstances many bookmakers would be forced to wipe the odds against the heavily played horse from their slates. The word "Out" would appear in the odds line.

This was bad for business. It alienated many customers who felt that the bookmaker should take all bets. Nevertheless, this was a common practice at the track when it was impossible to lay off bets.

In 1914 Arnold Rothstein let it be known that he would take all such lay-off bets. However, he discounted them, as a bank discounts notes. If the odds the bookmaker had given was 3 to 1, Rothstein would offer the bookmaker 5 to 2. He would give 8 to 5 against a horse where the slate odds had been 2 to 1.

He had the bookmakers over a barrel. They either took his odds, where the best they could do was break even if the horse lost, or they took a gamble, which could tap them out. Bookmaking being a hazardous business, the bookmakers more often than not took the odds Rothstein offered. They were paying for insurance against going broke. They paid a high premium, but they couldn't buy that insurance anyplace else.

It was not long before word spread throughout the gambling world that Rothstein would take any amount of lay-off, or "comeback," money. The long-distance wires and the telegraph wires were kept busy by such gamblers as "Sport" Sullivan in Boston, "Smiley" Daniels in Kansas City, and Danny Kling in Chicago, who were anxious to protect themselves.

In this manner Rothstein had a far better percentage going for him than the average of ten per cent the ordinary bookmakers had. And he had a far larger turnover out of which to grind that percentage.

In the beginning he had taken only a few such bets. As time went on, he was taking bets that amounted to tens, then hundreds, of thousands each day. He had a crew of men working around the clock, first on Forty-sixth Street and later in the various offices he had, both in downtown New York and on West Fifty-seventh Street.

He was to continue as the biggest source for lay-off bets in the country until he was killed. And then his empire would be taken over by Frank Erickson, who would be forced to share it with the syndicate headed by Lucky Luciano and then Frank Costello.

Bitter as the bookmakers were about the high "premiums" which Rothstein extorted, they were even more bitter about the way he frequently pulled betting coups on them. They even formed a loose organization to try to beat him, but they never succeeded. And in the meanwhile Rothstein pulled off three of the biggest killings in the history of race-track gambling.

Omar Khayyam, owned by Wilfred Viau, won the Kentucky Derby of 1917. Later, Omar Khayyam defeated Hourless, owned by August Belmont and trained by Sam Hildreth, in two races, one of them the Lawrence Realization Stakes at Belmont Park. That race was one of the weirdest ever run.

The jockey on Hourless lost his whip at the break. He hand-rode the colt the rest of the way, looked like the winner until he got pocketed in the run down the stretch and had to pull up and go far outside. A horse running into a pocket is not unusual in a large field and this is accepted as a part of racing luck. However, in this race just three horses ran and how Hourless could get pocketed in a three-horse field was something few people, including Hildreth, could understand.

Immediately after the race Hildreth asked for a chance to prove Hourless was the better horse.

There have been few better trainers in the history of racing than Hildreth. And few bigger gamblers. He came from the West, had grown up in rugged, frontier country. He had gambled from the time he was a boy and there was no game he wouldn't try. For years he was one of the biggest faro players in the country.

Sam Hildreth was not in racing for the sport. He was in it for the gamble. He had few illusions about his fellow trainers and owners. And even fewer about jockeys. When Hildreth watched Omar Khayyam beat Hourless in the Lawrence, he took it as part of the game. This was one time he had been outsmarted.

He let it be known that it wouldn't happen again.

The late Colonel Matt Winn was manager of the Laurel race track in 1917 and he offered to put up a purse for a match race between Omar Khayyam and Hourless. Hildreth and Belmont immediately accepted and, after a time, Viau and his trainer agreed to the race. It was set for October 18, after the New York season closed.

The whole metropolitan bookmaking contingent reached Baltimore well before the race. Among those who made the trip was Rothstein.

The day before the race Hourless was established as an odds-on, 3 to 4 favorite. That meant the bettor had to put up $4 to win $3. Rothstein tried to bet $240,000 against $180,000 at that price. He could find no takers for a bet of that size.

He left word around that he was still looking for such a bet and went to bed. When he awakened in the morning he received a call from a Baltimore bookmaker. He was told that a syndicate had been formed and was ready to book any bet Rothstein might want to make. "What limit?" Rothstein asked.

"No limit."

Rothstein hedged. "I'll be down about noon."

Rothstein felt that there was something crooked in the air. Or that the bookmakers had information about the condition of Hourless that he did not know. He immediately dispatched some members of his entourage to the track. "Let me know anything you learn right away."

He got a quick report from the track. Hourless appeared in fine shape. The stableman who had taken him out for his morning walk and the groom who had gone along both attested to this.

That left only the first possibility. Sometime during the night the local bookmakers had learned "something" or made some sort of deal. They certainly had not reached Belmont. And Hildreth had made this match a matter of pride. In addition, Rothstein knew that Hildreth had bet a lot of money on Hourless. He had booked some of it.

Rothstein recalled the running of the Realization and the peculiarities in that race. He decided to take steps.

Edwin C. Hill, later known as a radio reporter and commentator, but then a fine reporter for the New York *Sun,* gave this story of what followed:

"Rothstein thought he knew precisely what had happened, so he did a bold and clever thing. He called Hildreth, Hourless' trainer, on the phone.

" 'Mr. Hildreth,' he said, 'you don't know me, but my name is Arnold Rothstein and I am a gambler. I am not asking anything from you, of course, but I have something to tell you that you ought to know, not only in the interest of Mr. Belmont, but in the interest of racing.'

"Then he told the story of the bookmakers' change of mind, exactly as the incident occurred. Hildreth listened, thanked Rothstein, and hung up without volunteering any information whatsoever. But, when the right time came, he did something.

"In the meantime, Rothstein shrewdly figured he was safe—as

safe as any man ever is on a gambling proposition—in making a tremendous bet, so he telephoned the bookmaker and in rather a hesitating voice, as if doubtful and even fearful—his whole tone and manner indicating uncertainty—told the bookmaker that he would take the bet. Was it a go: $400,000 against $300,000 on Hourless to win? It certainly was and the word was passed that sealed the bet.

"Mr. Hildreth said nothing until ten minutes before the horses were to go to the post. Then he called Frank S. Hackett, his assistant, aside.

" 'Frank,' he said, 'go over to the jockey house and tell Frankie Robinson that he is going to pilot Hourless in this race.'

"He wanted Robinson, since a substitution of jockeys was necessary, because the boy was cool-headed, with a fine pair of hands and good judgment of pace. He had been riding Harry Payne Whitney's horses.

"When Robinson's name was posted instead of the name of Hourless' regular jockey, the crowd was dumbfounded and you could read a bookful in the faces of the ordinarily stone-faced gamblers. But it was too late to do anything about it and in a minute or two the horses were leaping forward to run the greatest race Hildreth says he ever saw. At the end of it, Hourless was in front by a clear length. . . ."

The major facts were as Hill recounted them. Rothstein did call Sam Hildreth and Hildreth did order the change of jockeys moments before the bugles blew for the parade to the post. And Rothstein did win $300,000 on the race.

A number of vital details, however, were not quite as Hill reported them. To start with, Rothstein and Hildreth knew each other quite well. When Rothstein telephoned, it was not a stranger who spoke to the trainer, but a man with whom Hildreth had gambled quite often and a man, moreover, who, Hildreth knew, had the best sources of information in the world of gambling.

Rothstein gave a better picture of what he had said to Carolyn, who was in Baltimore with him. "I told Sam the word was out that his horse was going to lose unless he made some changes. He told me he would make them."

That was enough for Rothstein. He knew Hildreth would protect his employer, his horse and himself. He could be assured he would get none the worst of it when the race was run.

This big wager was another index of how high Rothstein stood in the gambling world. He had placed a bet of $400,000 over the telephone and it was accepted. He did not put up a penny in cash, but the men with whom he had bet were willing to take his word for so large an amount.

The man who used to be able to count all his worldly wealth in minutes would not have time for anything else if he attempted to do that now.

There is an interesting sidelight to this bet. Shortly afterward Rothstein became a member of a syndicate which included many of the same local bookmakers from whom he had won the $300,000. This group then built Havre de Grace race track. Given little chance to succeed, the track became a big money-maker. The local gamblers went to Rothstein and made him an offer for his interest. He refused to sell.

Using their Maryland connections, the local group then had a bill enacted in the state legislature limiting the amount of stock a nonresident of the state could hold in any race track to seventy-five shares. Rothstein had to sell or fight the constitutionality of the law through the courts. Fallon, who was then his attorney, advised Rothstein to make the fight, assuring him that he would win. Rothstein, however, wanted no part of a court fight. He sold his stock for $50 a share.

The stock finally went to more than $400 a share and the seventy-five shares he retained brought $33,000 to his estate.

Rothstein shrugged off what had happened. He repeated an apothegm he had uttered many times before: "The hardest thing in the world to find is an honest partner in a skin game."

The bet which Rothstein had won on Hourless was the largest he had won on a race track up to that time. He would top it only twice, both times in 1921. By then he owned a racing stable.

There was nothing illegal, nothing unethical, about any of his big winnings. In the Hourless race he was sure that the edge was not against him. In the two later races he would be able to have the edge going for him. The highest morality of the race track—idealists aside—is to win your bet. In this respect, if in no other, Rothstein was moral. And smart.

He was no innovator in this respect. When The Allen closed his Square Deal Club, he gave an interview to a reporter for the *World*. The reporter asked Allen if he didn't think he had led a sinful life. Allen's answer was a succinct "Right is when you get away with it. Wrong is when you get caught."

To Rothstein, as to all gamblers, there was nothing wrong in doing what he could to help himself. "You're always alone," he told Carolyn. "You're always against everyone else and they're always trying to outsmart you. You mustn't let them and you have to find a way to outsmart them. If a man is willing to be paid off, I'll pay him off. If I don't, someone else will."

In 1921, when Rothstein won $1,350,000 on two races, he paid no one off. In the view of the gamblers he did no wrong—except to win money from them, which they always regarded as unpardonable.

In the period when Rothstein operated on the race track, purses were small and expenses high. There were no $100,000 and $200,000 purses. And there was also relatively little policing of the tracks. No saliva tests were given, no scientific examinations made of the sputum and urine of winning horses. Jockeys, trainers and some owners used their horses purely as gambling instruments.

And yet it was not by doctoring horses but by outsmarting the other gamblers that Rothstein made his biggest killings.

The other gamblers watched every move Rothstein made. They tried to bribe—and sometimes succeeded—his stable help and people who worked in his offices. They had the co-operation of some guards who worked for the race tracks. The Jockey Club long sought a way of barring Rothstein from the turf.

When it was known that Rothstein was betting a horse the odds were shaved. Often the horses were wiped off the slates. And yet Rothstein could not be stopped.

The first coup, which took place at Aqueduct, was unplanned. It resulted from a hunch Rothstein played, plus an assessment of all the factors involved. It was a lightning decision, reached in a matter of minutes. It succeeded by the margin of six ticks of a watch.

The date was July 4, 1921. This was the second big day of the racing season. The first was Memorial Day and the third was Labor Day. On only those three days of the racing season were the tracks thronged. On only those days were the crowds so large that they filled the clubhouse and overflowed the big betting shed in the grandstand. The crowd played an important part in helping Rothstein.

The horse by means of which Rothstein won $850,000 was named Sidereal, a two-year-old by Star Shoot out of Milky Way. Herbert Bayard Swope had picked the fortuitous and fitting name for the colt. Though it was owned by Rothstein, it was registered in the name of Max Hirsch, now an elder statesman of the turf but then Rothstein's trainer.

The Rothsteins arrived at the track shortly after noon and went to the table that Rothstein always had reserved in the clubhouse restaurant. While Carolyn ate, Rothstein attended to business.

The table resembled an anthill, with a continual parade of people moving to and from it. These were a motley group. Clockers and trainers. Men who were settling the losses of yesterday or collecting their winnings. Stage stars and producers. Big-time politicians. Betting commissioners. Touts and would-be borrowers.

After a time Rothstein left the table and went toward the stable area with Hirsch. They had to muscle their way through the thick crowds.

The clubhouse bookmaking section was a solid mass of people, all trying to get down their bets. Under the grandstand thousands were surrounding the bookmakers who had their stands there. Rothstein said, "They're so busy, they don't have a chance to think. This would be a day to put a horse over. By the time they got wise they'd be paying off."

He did not like the idea of losing so rare an opportunity. He was not certain that another would arise soon. Hopefully he asked Hirsch, "Do you know anything?"

Hirsch shook his head. "Nothing. The only horse we were going to run today was Sidereal. I'm going to scratch him for a race on Friday."

Rothstein's head jerked up. "What shape is he in?"

"He's sharp." Hirsch looked at his program. "I think he could beat these other horses."

"Then run him." Rothstein was eager, scenting the chance of a big winning.

"I didn't van him in. He's in the stable at Belmont." That was three miles away. Hirsch looked at his watch. "I can get him here in time, though, if you want to run him." Getting the horse there "in time" meant twenty minutes before the horses went to the post.

"We'll never get another chance like this," Rothstein said. "Get the horse here." He walked away from Hirsch.

Now Rothstein had to make his plans. His own employees and betting commissioners were known to every bookmaker. If any of these started making bets of any size, the bookmakers would immediately scent trouble. Not even the size of the crowd would prevent that.

Rothstein's first step, therefore, was to ask a number of people if they would mind his using their commissioners during the day. He made the request casually. "I don't figure on betting today, but I may change my mind. I gave Nat [Evans] and the boys a day off."

Those whom he asked had no choice but to grant permission. You didn't refuse Arnold Rothstein a slight favor; you never knew when you might need a large one.

Rothstein immediately hunted up the various commissioners. He told all of them he might be using them during the afternoon. He added, "If I do use you, don't tell anyone for whom you're betting; bookmakers know I'm playing a horse, they'll shave the odds on a five-dollar bet." The commissioners knew that this was true. And, like their principals, they were only too eager to do a favor for Rothstein.

There were two races to be run before that in which Sidereal was entered. At the track, betting was primarily from race to race. It would be some time before the prices went up on Sidereal's race. However, the "overnight" line had Sidereal at prices ranging from

25 to 1 to 40 to 1. He was the outsider, his form unknown, in the figures.

Rothstein now went looking for Hirsch to see how arrangements were going. He located him at a telephone, sweat running down his face. The trainer had been unable to get anyone at Belmont to answer the phone. It was a holiday and no one was in the track office.

He told this to Rothstein quickly.

Rothstein's lips thinned. He wasn't going to have his plans upset. "Come with me," he said, and hurried back to the table where Carolyn was sitting.

Of course, if the horse couldn't be vanned to Aqueduct in time, Rothstein would lose nothing. But he was already counting his potential winnings and these had attained a reality to him. In addition, there was his ego to satisfy. He had to make chumps of the bookmakers.

Carolyn caught his signal, rose from the table and joined Rothstein and Hirsch.

"Tell her what she has to do," Rothstein said. "Tom Farley's out in the car and he can run her over."

Hirsch grasped at this. He lived close to Belmont and his wife was at home. "Pick her up," he said, "and go to the stables with her. Tell her to have the horse's plates changed and then put him into a van and get him over here. Tell her and the foreman we don't have any time to waste."

This was literally true. One race had been run. The horses were being saddled for the next. And Sidereal was entered in the race after that. Hirsch, not having scratched the horse, was responsible for its being in the stable area in time to run. If the horse was not there, Hirsch could be fined and suspended.

Carolyn rushed from the track. Farley drove her to the Hirsch home, where Mrs. Hirsch was picked up. On the way to Belmont, Carolyn explained what was to be done.

She knew something big was happening and was caught up in the excitement of it. This was one of the few times when she shared anything with Rothstein. She didn't want to fail him.

The car pulled up in front of the stable where Rothstein's horses were quartered. A stableboy was sent to find the foreman. When he appeared, Mrs. Hirsch told him what had to be done. He said, "You'll never make it."

"We have to," Carolyn said.

The foreman shrugged. "I'll see what I can do." He sent the stableboy to find a van and driver. No blacksmith being available, he changed the shoes on the horse himself. As he worked, the stableboy returned. He had found a driver. The van would be on its way soon.

Carolyn looked at her watch. Time was going fast.

Time was also going fast at the track.

Rothstein had begun his betting campaign. He had given cash to some of the commissioners, told others to bet in the names of their regular employers. His orders were simple. "Get as much as you can down, but make all your bets small. Use anyone you need to help you."

The opening price on Sidereal was 30 to 1. At this price, a bookmaker might take a $100 bet in the clubhouse, a $50 bet in the grandstand. However, after taking the bet, the bookmakers would probably cut the price. It was up to the agents, and their agents, to protect the price as long as possible.

Normally, if one bookmaker cut a price, others received a report quickly and, even though not carrying any bets, they would cut their price too. This day, however, most bookmakers were so busy they could hardly keep track of their own books, let alone keep watch on the competition. This was what Rothstein was banking on.

He had forty men placing bets for him, placing bets at the same time. The bets were relatively small, but they started adding up. The odds dropped from 30 to 25, and then to 20.

Now some bookmakers began to wonder what was going on. They dispatched men to seek Rothstein out and observe what he was doing. These spies returned to say Rothstein was sitting in a box with friends and apparently totally unconcerned with the wagering.

Since none of the bets had been placed by men who worked for Rothstein, it was plausible that he had nothing to do with the wagering. The race track was filled with many amateur gamblers on this holiday and most of these were long-shot players. That was why holidays were red-letter days to bookmakers. These were the days when they got the sucker play.

Nonetheless, the price on Sidereal dropped steadily as the bookmakers sought to keep their ledgers in balance.

Meanwhile, Hirsch was waiting at the gate. He had virtually no leeway left. It was five minutes to saddling time, five minutes until the horse had to be in the saddling area or Sidereal would automatically be scratched.

Jimmy McLaughlin, the paddock judge, began to verify the presence of the horses. He saw Sidereal's stall was empty. Hunting for Hirsch, he found him at the gate.

"Where's your horse, Max?"

"On the way" was all Hirsch could say. He was staring down the dirt road. He wondered if that was a dust cloud he saw.

McLaughlin looked at his watch. "Two minutes, Max."

"I know." Hirsch kept peering and was sure that it was a dust cloud.

Then it was one minute. McLaughlin said, "I'll have to notify the stewards, Max. Sorry." He started to turn.

As he did so the dust cloud lifted. A van was rolling up to the gate. It came to a stop. It wasn't enough that the horse was on the track; it had to be in the paddock.

Hirsch ran and opened the tail gate. The ramp went up. Hirsch jumped into the van, led the horse down, brought him into the paddock.

McLaughlin looked at his watch. "You sure drew it fine, Max. You beat the gun by six seconds."

Hirsch had no time for McLaughlin. He was rubbing the horse down, quieting him. Grooms and stableboys went to work on Sidereal. The jockey, who had been standing about, joined them.

Carolyn Rothstein drove up while this was going on. She got out of the car. "Were we in time?"

"Yes," Hirsch said.

Carolyn went back to the clubhouse. Walking through it, she

saw Rothstein. Casually, she stepped into the box. Rothstein gave her a quick look. Her nod was almost imperceptible. So was Rothstein's smile.

The saddling bell sounded. Then the bugle for the parade to the post. The horses came out slowly, led by the outrider.

Rothstein got word to the commissioners. "Take any price."

Now the money was poured in. The price kept dropping and dropping. To 15 to 1, to 12, to 10, to 8, to 5, to 4.

There is a contagion, a hysteria, at a race track. Word spreads without a word being spoken. Five people, fifty, five hundred—five thousand—suddenly become aware of the same thing at the same moment. That happened at Aqueduct. It seemed as though everyone at the track simultaneously decided to bet on Sidereal.

Professional bettors, casual visitors and touts. The innocents and the smart money. All of them wanted to get in on this. It was the same at every book, clubhouse or grandstand. Price meant nothing.

The books did the only thing they could. They marked "OUT" opposite the name of Sidereal, boosted the odds on every other horse in the race, hoping, somehow, to balance their sheets.

The horses were nearing the post. Marshall Cassidy, the starter, and his assistants were at the barrier. And still Rothstein sat in the clubhouse box, chatting and smiling.

But the bookmakers were no longer fooled. They knew that they had been hoodwinked, outsmarted. And there wasn't anything they could do about it. There was no place—no one—to which they could turn and try to lay off the bets they had taken. The man who had made those bets was the only place open for laying them off.

Some did try, however. And, surprisingly, Rothstein was willing to take back some of the bets. But at "closing" odds. That meant the last price that had been posted against Sidereal, 8 to 5. He accepted bets amounting to $125,000 at those odds.

Why? Because it meant that, no matter what happened in the race, he had to be a winner. He was playing with the bookmakers' money. If Sidereal won, even after paying out $200,000, he would still be $850,000 ahead. If Sidereal lost, he would be about $40,000 winner. Not bad for an afternoon.

Of all the gamblers at the track he was the only one who could relax and watch the race. He had taken advantage of every bit of percentage. The odds were working for him. This was the gambler's dream, the sure thing. That is, if the gambler was Arnold Rothstein.

Sidereal was a golden chestnut with a glistening coat. He was a handsome horse, thick in the withers. There was a full field in the race—thirteen horses—but the crowd was interested in only one. Sidereal.

Cassidy and his assistants lined up the horses. This was before the starting gate was in use, and the horses ranged behind a barrier. It took time to steady the horses, to have them get over their nervousness. But Sidereal appeared without nerves. The horse stood ready, poised to break when the barrier went up. Its jockey, Billy Kelsay, was crouched low.

The chart on the race reports: "Start good." The horses broke almost in a straight line. Kelsay broke Sidereal fast so as to avoid trouble at the first turn. Sidereal was fourth as the horses went around the bend. Ultimo, owned by Charles Stoneham, was in the lead, with Northcliffe, owned by Thomas Fortune Ryan, the traction magnate, second, and Harry Payne Whitney's Brainstorm running third.

The horses ran in that position up the backstretch, made the turn and then came around again into the stretch, with a quarter mile to go. Here Kelsay made his move. He loosed his grip on the reins, slapped the horse. Sidereal passed Brainstorm and ranged up alongside Northcliffe. A half dozen strides and Sidereal was second, a length behind Ultimo.

The boy on Ultimo started using his whip. The roar that was thundering out of the stands told him something was moving up behind him. Ultimo gave his best, but it was not enough. He was a tired horse and a hundred yards from the finish he began to bear out slightly. Kelsay had racing room, went inside Ultimo. He was a neck in front, a half length, and then a full length.

The chart reported: "Won driving. Place same." The margin of Sidereal's victory was a length and a half.

The time for the race was 1:11 2/5. Good time, but not sensational. But in that short time Arnold Rothstein had won more money than most people earned in all their lives.

He appeared to give no sign of strain, of pleasure. But Carolyn Rothstein knew how much emotion he felt because, when he spoke to her, there was a quiver in his voice. It was the only time she ever heard the quiver when he was a winner. All the other times it was present was when he was a loser.

There is one thing about a horse race. A man—a thousand men —live a lifetime in a space counted in seconds. The life begins when the flag falls, ends when the first horse crosses the finish line. A thousand dreams, a thousand hopes, a thousand ambitions have been realized or destroyed. But there will be more dreams, more hopes, more ambitions in a few minutes. There will be another race.

There is not even time to bury the dead dreams, no time for mourning.

With the end of the race won by Sidereal came the birth of a new race. The bookmakers, many of them knowing they were in debt to —and some beyond—the limit of their resources, had their slates up again. The bettors began to place fresh wagers.

Rothstein had made a killing, but done nothing dishonest. Sidereal was a two-year-old maiden, a nonwinner in the three races in which he had started. Two-year-olds were permitted, by racing custom and racing law, to "qualify" in their first few races. That meant that owners and trainers did not run them to win, but to "educate" them.

In this manner a horse's true form and ability were concealed by its owner. This was part of the game. The one rule of the betting ring was "Caveat omnes." Let everyone beware.

The "qualifying" rule still holds. However, the pari-mutuel machines prevent any such killing as Rothstein made. A horse can open at 100 to 1 but the final price on the board determines the pay-off. And the more money bet on a horse in a race the smaller the pay-off.

Rothstein sat through two more races and then he and Carolyn were driven back to New York. He did not tell her the amount of his winnings, saying only, "I won a big piece. A very big piece."

After a time he said, "This is my lucky day. I feel it in my bones. I think I'll find a game tonight. Do you mind if I don't take you to dinner?"

For the first time in their marriage, Carolyn lost her temper. "Damned right, I do," she said. "We're eating together tonight."

Taken aback, Rothstein said, "All right. All right." He tried to appease her in the one way he knew. He took out his bankroll, peeled off a number of bills. "Buy yourself something with this. You earned it." It was $5,000.

They had dinner at Delmonico's. All evening men came to their table. Some came to congratulate Rothstein on his killing; the word had spread very quickly. Others were bookmakers, come to negotiate a settlement with Rothstein. Some means of having him carry their debt to him. He acceded to some of the requests. At six per cent.

It was almost eleven o'clock when Rothstein brought Carolyn home. He went inside with her, checked his telephone messages, and then went out. Still looking for a game.

She went upstairs, read awhile, and then went to bed.

It would appear highly unlikely that the bookmakers, still seeking to win their way back to solvency after the debacle of July 4, would lay themselves open to another betting coup a few weeks later.

They did.

The race was the Travers Stakes, oldest of American stake races, for three-year-olds. It looked as though the 1921 running of the race was a "lock"—a sure thing—for Harry Payne Whitney's great mare Prudery. So much of a certainty that the day before the race it appeared that Prudery's only competition would come from one of Rothstein's horses, Sporting Blood.

Sporting Blood was a good horse, but even Rothstein was aware that he was not in Prudery's class. However, the purse for second money was not to be sneezed at. Why pass up a chance to win a few thousands when there was no risk?

The race was run on August 20. As late as the afternoon of August 19, Rothstein had no plans for betting on his horse. About four that afternoon, however, one of Rothstein's agents brought him word that Prudery appeared "off her feed."

Rothstein immediately double- and triple-checked this report. The word came back that it was true. A stableman, for ten dollars, added that Prudery had not been worked out for the race.

A veterinarian, one who worked for Rothstein as well as Whitney, brought the information that he had examined the mare, found nothing seriously wrong with her, but that she was disturbed. He said there was a chance that she might come around before race time, but he did not feel she would be at her best.

Under ordinary circumstances a sportsman like Whitney would have scratched his horse. However, that would have made the race a walkover, "no contest." It would have been the first in the long history of the Travers. As much to uphold tradition as for any other reason, Whitney and his trainer decided to run Prudery unless the mare's condition worsened. Besides, they felt that, even off form, Prudery would beat Sporting Blood.

What they did not know—but what both Rothstein and Hirsch knew—was that Sporting Blood was going into the race sharper than ever before in his life. Hirsch had conditioned the horse carefully and felt that it had improved four or five lengths over any past performance. This would not be enough to beat a Prudery in good shape. It might be enough to beat a Prudery that was off form. Hirsch told Rothstein that he felt Sporting Blood, under the conditions, was a good bet.

Rothstein, however, made no decision on betting on his horse until the morning of the 20th. That morning he learned that Prudery showed no improvement.

The morning line on the race had Prudery at 1 to 4, odds on. And Sporting Blood at 5 to 2. Still, Rothstein made no move.

Then late in the morning Sam Hildreth announced that he was going to run Grey Lag in the Travers. By this time Hildreth was training for Harry Sinclair and Grey Lag was one of the finest horses that Sinclair ever owned. He was the money-winning champion of his year, a great handicap horse.

To racing people it looked as though this made it a two-horse race, between Grey Lag and Prudery, with Sporting Blood now running for third money instead of second.

Rothstein, however, had different ideas. He began to bet on Sporting Blood, through his agents, with bookmakers throughout the country. In this manner he placed about $100,000 at an average price of about 3 to 1. To bookmakers this looked like an outright steal. Sporting Blood, which, to their minds, had little chance against Prudery, certainly had no chance against Prudery and Grey Lag.

Meanwhile Rothstein placed another $100,000 with the race track bookmakers. They, too, felt as though they had been given a key to the vaults at the Federal Reserve Bank.

Now, in a stake race, a horse can be "declared" up until thirty minutes before post time. ("Declaring" is stakes language for scratching a horse.) A trainer had the right to make such a withdrawal without explanation. Just at the deadline, Hildreth told the stewards that Grey Lag was not going to run.

This made it a two-horse race again and the bookmakers adjusted their prices, reverting to the morning line. With Grey Lag out of the race, a lot of people began throwing their money on Prudery. They felt that no competition remained for the mare.

And, further to lull the bookmakers into a feeling of complacency, there was no rush of money for Sporting Blood at the track. This information went out over the long-distance phone to handbook operators, who were puzzled over Hildreth's maneuvering with Grey Lag and wanted to know what was going on.

Again Kelsay rode for Rothstein.

At the break, Prudery went to the front and Sporting Blood was lapped on her. They ran this way for three-quarters of a mile and then Prudery's jockey made his move. The crowd expected to see the mare pull away. But Sporting Blood moved with Prudery, stayed just a half length off. These were their positions as the two horses passed the mile mark and headed down the stretch for the last quarter mile.

Now the pace and lack of condition began to tell on Prudery. Her stride shortened and became uneven. She had given her best, but it was far from enough. Sporting Blood passed her and, as the colt crossed the finish line, Kelsay still had a snug hold and was looking back over his shoulder at the mare.

Once again Rothstein had put one over. This time, however, he had used more chicanery than in his two other big winnings. Chicanery and shrewdness.

First, the shrewdness. All bookmakers employed spies to keep an eye on everything that occurred at a race track. It was important for them to know when a stable was betting, when a horse was being primed for a race. However, in this instance they had felt secure. After all, Prudery was a Whitney horse. And Whitney was a sportsman. He was not in competition with the bookmakers for dollars.

But Rothstein, holding Whitney in the same esteem, nevertheless kept constant watch on the Whitney stable. And he was rewarded.

And he also rewarded those who provided him with information. In addition to those he employed there were dozens of volunteers who rushed to him with information. He never refused to listen. Nor, for that matter, did he ever take this information without a handful of salt. He always verified it.

When it was good, he paid for it. Paid for it in proportion to its value. No man, he knew, ever went broke taking a profit.

There were hundreds in Saratoga who curried his favor. They believed that he was the man who ran Saratoga during the month of August. This was not quite true, but he did have influence with those who ran the town. Why not? Didn't he pay out some $40,000 —a pool raised by all the bookmakers but which he controlled—for protection?

That was why Whitney's own employees came to Rothstein with their information. That was why the veterinarian told Rothstein, before he told Whitney's own trainer, the results of his examination of Prudery.

As always, he sought to copper his bets. There was the possibility, until the last moment, that word would get out of Prudery's condition. Few people sold their information exclusively; the men who had come to him might well go to others with what they knew. Should that happen, the odds against Sporting Blood would be cut deeply.

Rothstein didn't want that to happen. He had to create another element in the race which would help him. That element was provided when Hildreth announced that he intended to run Grey Lag.

Hildreth's activities in first announcing Grey Lag would run and then withdrawing the horse were not treated too censoriously by the sports writers who covered racing. No matter what they might have thought, none of them wrote that Hildreth acted in concert with Rothstein. That would have been knocking their own racket.

Racing writers lead a pleasant life, with winters in California and Florida and summers spent in the shade of the different press boxes throughout the country. Many were then, as they are now, more interested in protecting their own way of life than in protecting the public. The race tracks never like public airing of dirty linen and they have ways of reprisal against sports writers who speak out.

So no writer said, after the race, though many suspected, that Hildreth had arranged an "accommodation" for Rothstein. "Accommodation" is a synonym for "favor," but more euphemistic. Hildreth, bluntly, had acted in concert with Rothstein and shared the profits of the winning wagers with Rothstein.

Once again, this was not illegal. Right, as The Allen had remarked, was what you got away with.

Neither Rothstein nor Hildreth cashed all the bets he ever made. Both of them had their losing days. As an instance, Rothstein lost more than $270,000 on a race in the fall of 1921 at Aqueduct. Sporting Blood went off at 1 to 4, a prohibitive favorite in a three-horse race. He finished second.

Rothstein paid off even though he knew that the race was not truly run.

It is interesting to note that such diverse persons as Carolyn Rothstein, Herbert Bayard Swope and Max Hirsch all maintain that Rothstein ran an honest stable.

Swope said, "I believe that his horses all ran honestly. He took every possible advantage of the rules, but he did not break them.

Even if he had wanted to, Hirsch would not have been a party to it."

"Arnold never was mixed up in a crooked race," Mrs. Rothstein said. "He made his big winnings on races where he had superior information. He used every possible trick to find out more than anyone else and get the best odds. Everyone did in those days, including millionaires who headed great corporations and kept stud books on their families as well as on their horses to make sure the blood stayed blue.

"He won and he lost big bets. Of course he won more than he lost. Just the same, no one ever charged him with running a crooked stable. Not even the men who ran the Jockey Club—which is really the outfit that runs racing. They didn't want him to own horses or to appear at the track because he was so well known and so was his business. But they never said he was crooked."

One of those who did not want Rothstein as a steady visitor at the track or as an owner was August Belmont. At the end of the 1921 season Belmont stopped by one day when Carolyn was alone in the Rothstein box.

"I wish," he said, "that you would ask your husband to limit his bets. If he doesn't, it may be necessary for the Jockey Club to act to prevent his making a daily appearance at the track."

"I think you should tell him that, Mr. Belmont, not me."

"I would, but I thought you might have more influence with him."

Belmont did go to Rothstein. After all, the two men knew each other quite well. They had been in the Delmonico with Charley Murphy many times. Rothstein had acted as a messenger between the two men dozens of times.

"You know your reputation," Belmont said. "It hurts racing to have you such a conspicuous figure."

Rothstein's eyes narrowed. "What are you trying to say?"

Belmont averted his own eyes. "You know what people are saying, Arnold. And what they're thinking. Half the country believes you were the man who fixed the World Series."

Chapter **11** *The Man Who Fixed the Series*

"Who is he, anyhow, an actor?"
"No."
"A dentist?"
*"Meyer Wolfsheim? No, he's a gambler." Gatsby hesitated, then
added coolly: "He's the man who fixed the World's Series back in
1919."*
"Fixed the World's Series?" I repeated.
*The idea staggered me. I remembered, of course, that the World's
Series had been fixed in 1919, but if I had thought of it at all I would
have thought of it as a thing that merely* happened, *the end of some
inevitable chain. It never occurred to me that one man could start to
play with the faith of fifty million people—with the singlemindedness of a burglar blowing a safe.*
"How did he happen to do that?" I asked after a minute.
"He just saw the opportunity."
"Why isn't he in jail?"
"They can't get him, old sport. He's a smart man."
—F. SCOTT FITZGERALD, *The Great Gatsby**

Fitzgerald, in Nick Carraway's interior monologue, came closer
to the truth of the 1919 World Series than most. The fix did happen
as the end of an inevitable chain of events.

The world in which Arnold Rothstein lived is now long gone. Far
more deserving men than he have been forgotten. But not Rothstein.

* Published by Charles Scribner's Sons.

138

His memory is disinterred each autumn when World Series time rolls around. He is the legendary figure, the "man who fixed the Series."

He did not fix the Series.

The Series, however, could not have been fixed had there been no Arnold Rothstein.

These statements are not contradictory, but complementary. Rothstein's name, his reputation, and his reputed wealth were all used to influence the crooked baseball players. But Rothstein, knowing this, kept apart from the actual fix. He just let it happen.

The story of the fix is the story of a flock of lambs who appealed to a wolf to protect them. What happened thereafter was inevitable.

Looking back almost four decades, it is hard to find one adjective which would describe the actions of the ballplayers. They were inept. They were naïve. They were stupid. They did everything wrong and, in the end, were cheated of their promised reward.

The gamblers who were let in on a sure thing, whether amateurs, like Bill Burns and Billy Maharg, or professionals, like Rothstein and Sport Sullivan, never realized on the potential that lay before them.

From beginning to end—and even beyond the end—there was no logic to what happened. There were confessions and these were recanted. There were affidavits and these disappeared from the locked files of the authorities. There were indictments and most of these were dismissed. There was a trial and it never went to the jury.

The records of the Series show that some of the fixers played better than had been expected. Some players, beyond suspicion, made the damaging errors on the field, failed to hit at the plate. It was a Greek tragedy that was played as a farce.

The Chicago White Sox team of 1919 was one of the great baseball teams of all time. It had the potential to rank with Connie Mack's Philadelphia Athletics with its "Million-Dollar Infield." It was a team on the way up.

Charles Comiskey, the "Old Roman," owned the team. (His heirs still control it.) Comiskey, a great baseball man, was one of the founders of the American League. He was the type of employer who believed that labor should be bought as cheaply as possible. His reasoning was blunt and simple. "If they don't play for me, they can't play for anyone."

He was, of course, correct. Baseball's reserve clause, which bound a player to one team so long as that team desired his services, was in effect then as it is now. A ballplayer had no freedom of choice, could play only for the team with which he had originally signed.

Comiskey, more than any other team owner, used this power to keep wages low. Some of his better players were paid less than $4,500, others were paid the big league minimum of $2,500. True, this was before the era of Babe Ruth and his $80,000 salary, but Comiskey paid bottom wages even by 1919 standards.

In the middle of the 1919 season the players staged a mild revolt. Their first step was orderly.

A group of them asked William ("Kid") Gleason, their manager, to intercede with Comiskey to get them raises. Gleason, whose sympathies were with the players, did go to Comiskey with the request. He returned with Comiskey's answer, a blunt "No."

The players sulked, but won ball games. They clinched the pennant early on their last Eastern swing. And during that swing, they —not all, but a sizable group—conceived the idea of throwing the World Series.

The ring leader, as he later admitted, was Eddie Cicotte, the team's leading pitcher. Chick Gandil, the first baseman, has written that he connived with Cicotte from the start.

The World Series was always one of the big gambling events of the year. Adult males took their baseball partisanship as seriously as their political partisanship, and were more likely to back up the baseball loyalty with cash. It looked, to the scheming ballplayers, as though they could not miss making large fortunes. All they needed to assure this was a gambler to work with them.

Their choice was Joseph ("Sport") Sullivan, of Boston. Sullivan was the biggest gambler in New England. Cicotte laid the proposition on the line for Sullivan.

The White Sox would deliberately lose to Cincinnati, the National League pennant winner, if Sullivan would pay $10,000 to each of the players who would be involved in the plot. Cicotte thought it would require ten men to assure certainty. His price for throwing the Series was set, in round figures, at $100,000, payable in advance.

Sullivan agreed the deal had merit. However, he explained, there was one drawback. He didn't have $100,000. But there was one gambler to whom that kind of money was ordinary—Arnold Rothstein. "I'll talk to 'A.R.,' " Sullivan told Cicotte and Gandil, who were the two players present at this meeting. He expressed certainty that Rothstein would provide the bribe money.

Gandil and Cicotte regarded the deal as good as arranged. Their next step was to enlist other players in their cabal. It was later charged there were eight players involved. These were Cicotte and Gandil, the ringleaders; Claude Williams, second-best pitcher on the team; Swede Risberg, shortstop; Buck Weaver, third baseman; Joe Jackson (next to Ty Cobb the best hitter in the league) and Happy Felsch, outfielders; and Fred McMullin, utility infielder.

The group included five of the eight regular starters, the team's two best pitchers, and, in McMullin, the player who would "scout" the Cincinnati team.

Of this group, Cicotte, Jackson and Williams confessed their part in the plot to a Cook County (Chicago) Grand Jury. Felsch and Gandil gave signed confessions to newspapers. Weaver denied complicity in the plot and neither McMullin nor Risberg ever made any statement. All eight, however, were indicted for throwing the Series.

The plot was all arranged, but no word had come from Sullivan. When Cicotte, growing anxious, sought to telephone him, Sullivan could not be reached.

Cicotte sought another gambler to implement the scheme. He chose Bill Burns, a former baseball player who had grown wealthy in the oil business but who gambled heavily on the side.

Burns, like Sullivan, agreed this was a foolproof way to make a fortune. However, like Sullivan, he pleaded inability to raise $100,000 in cash and, to continue the parallel, he suggested Rothstein as the best source for that much money. He said he did not know Rothstein, but he did have "connections" through whom he could reach him.

Cicotte told Burns to try.

The middleman whom Burns chose was a former boxer and petty gambler, William Maharg, of Philadelphia.

What then ensued was told in the testimony which Maharg gave at the trial of the ballplayers late in 1920. Here is a portion of his testimony:

"In the autumn of last year," Maharg told the jury, "I received a call from Burns from New York. I hopped a train and met Bill at the Ansonia. . . .

"He said a group of the most prominent players of the White Sox would be willing to throw the coming World Series if a syndicate of gamblers would give them $100,000 the morning of the first game. Burns said, 'Do you know any gamblers who would be interested in the proposition?'

"I said I would go back to Philadelphia and see what I could do. Burns said he would have to go to Montreal to close an oil deal and that he would wire me about the progress of the [baseball] deal. That explains a telegram sent to me from Montreal, when he wired:—'What have you done about the ball games?'

"I saw some gamblers in Philadelphia. They told me it was too big a proposition for them to handle, and they recommended me to Arnold Rothstein a well-known and wealthy New York gambler.

"When Burns returned from Montreal, I went over to New York and joined him. Through my Philadelphia connections, I made an appointment with Rothstein. We met Rothstein by appointment in the Astor and put the proposition to him. He declined to get into it. He said he did not think such a frame-up would be possible.

"We left Rothstein and I hung around a while in New York. Then I returned to Philadelphia, thinking everything was off until I received the following wire from Bill Burns:—'Arnold R. has gone through with everything. Got eight [players] in. Leaving for Cincinnati at 4:30. Bill Burns.' This was only a few days before the Series.

"I went to Cincinnati the next day and joined Burns. He said that after I had left New York he ran into Abe Attell, the fighter, who had gone to Rothstein and fixed things. Burns added that Rothstein had 'laid off' us because he didn't know us, but was very willing to talk turkey with Attell whom he knew.

"Attell was in Cincinnati, quartered in a large suite in the Sinton Hotel. He had a gang of about twenty-five gamblers with him. He said they were all working for Rothstein.

"Their work was very raw. They stood in the lobby of the Sinton and buttonholed everybody who came in. They accepted bets right and left and it was nothing to see $1,000 bills wagered.

"I had my first suspicion on the morning of the first game when Burns and I visited Attell. We asked for the $100,000 to turn over to the White Sox players for this part of the deal. [This was the sum Burns had promised Cicotte, rather than the original $10,000 per man.] Attell refused to turn over the $100,000, saying that they needed the money to make bets.

"He made a counterproposition that $20,000 would be handed the players at the end of each losing game. [In 1919 the Series was played until one team won five games.] Burns went to the Sox players and told them and they seemed satisfied with the new arrangements.

"We all bet on Cincinnati the first day and won. The next day, Burns and I went around again to Attell at his headquarters. I never saw so much money in my life. Stacks of bills were being counted on dressers and tables. I asked for the money for the players and Attell said that he would pay them at the end of the Series. I said they wanted their money now.

"When Attell refused to pay the money that he had promised the players, Burns said I should go to New York and talk to Rothstein. I went to New York and called on Rothstein."

Here Maharg's testimony concluded. The defense objected that details of the meeting—if there had been a meeting—were not relevant. The judge upheld the objection.

This was the last time that Rothstein's name appeared in any official proceeding resulting from the fixed Series. The coupling of his name and the 1919 Series, a coupling that began with the plotting, has continued to today.

The first person to accuse Rothstein directly of fixing the Series

was Ban Johnson, president of the American League. Johnson, on
the basis of widespread rumors that the Series had been crooked,
hired private detectives to make an investigation before the last
game of the Series was over. In September, 1920, Johnson announced the results of that investigation. He stated categorically
that the Series had been deliberately lost by the White Sox and
added:

"The man behind the fixing of the Series was Arnold Rothstein."

Rothstein issued an immediate denial, the first of many. He said,
"There is not a word of truth in the report that I had anything to do
with the World Series of last fall. I do not know if it was fixed. . . .
My only connection was to refuse to do business with some men
who said they could fix it. . . . I intend to sue Ban Johnson for
libel. . . ."

Rothstein, of course, did not sue. Perhaps he had in mind Tim
Sullivan's old warning: "Never sue. They might prove it."

Johnson's charges set off an official investigation in Chicago.
State's Attorney Maclay Hoyne began presenting evidence to a
Grand Jury. The three players made their confessions. And, in every
report of what was happening, Rothstein's name led all the rest.

Rothstein, asked for a statement, announced that he was "sick
and tired" of rumors and allegations. To put an end to them, he was
going to make a voluntary appearance before the Grand Jury.

Rothstein had a prepared statement ready. He read part of it to
newspapermen before he went in to testify.

"Attell did the fixing.

"I've come here to vindicate myself. If I wasn't sure I was going
to be vindicated, I would have stayed home. As far as my story is
concerned, I've already told most of it, but I guess you [the Grand
Jury] want it on the official record.

"The whole thing started when Attell and some other cheap gamblers decided to frame the Series and make a killing. The world
knows I was asked in on the deal and my friends know how I turned
it down flat. I don't doubt that Attell used my name to put it over.
That's been done by smarter men than Abe. But I wasn't in on it,
wouldn't have gone into it under any circumstances and didn't bet a

cent on the Series after I found out what was under way. My idea was that whatever way things turned out, it would be a crooked Series anyhow and that only a sucker would bet on it.

"I'm not going to hold anything back from you [the jury]. I'm here to clear myself and I expect to get out of here with a clean bill of health."

After Rothstein testified, State's Attorney Hoyne told reporters that Rothstein's statement had been read to the Grand Jury exactly as Rothstein had read it to the reporters. "It's part of the record," he said.

The reporters asked Hoyne for his reaction to Rothstein's appearance and testimony.

"I don't think Rothstein was involved in it [the fix]."

Alfred Austrian, attorney for Comiskey and the White Sox, said to the same reporters, "Rothstein, in his testimony today, proved himself guiltless."

Obviously the Grand Jury also believed Rothstein. At the end of its deliberations it returned indictments against the eight players, Attell, Sullivan and Rachel Brown. Mrs. Brown was Rothstein's chief bookkeeper. She had been in Cincinnati and Chicago with Attell and had kept the records of all the bets.

Sometime between the Grand Jury hearings and the following September a peculiar happening occurred. All the records and minutes of the Grand Jury hearings disappeared. So, too, did the signed confessions of Cicotte, Williams and Jackson.

When the case went to trial, Attell was not present; he had gone to Canada, where he successfully resisted extradition.

The state, virtually all of its evidence gone, sought to get the players to repeat their confessions on the stand. This they refused to do, citing the Fifth Amendment. To talk would "tend to incriminate or degrade them." This was a new tactic in the Chicago court, but not new in New York. It was a favorite device of William J. Fallon's.

The state was left with only Maharg's testimony. Since he was one of the conspirators, his testimony required corroboration before it could be used as evidence. When no corroboration was forthcoming, the judge had to dismiss the case.

Thus, on the official record and on the basis of Hoyne's statement, Rothstein was never involved in the fixing of the Series. Also, on the official record, it was never proved that the Series had been fixed.

Nick Carraway was right. It just happened.

Nevertheless, trial or no trial, Grand Jury or no Grand Jury, Rothstein was fixed in the public mind, in history, as the man who fixed the Series. That judgment is fair enough. By reason of his being what he was, he was responsible for the crooked Series.

Here is the record of his involvement:

Immediately after Sullivan talked with Cicotte he went to New York, where he offered the deal to Rothstein.

"I don't want any part of it," Rothstein said. "It's too raw. Besides, you can't get away with it."

Sullivan pressed Rothstein, suggesting he at least look into it. "Not for my $100,000," Rothstein said. "You might be able to fix a game, but not the Series. You'd get lynched if it ever came out."

To Rothstein, as to millions of others, baseball ranked with love of mother and respect for the flag as untouchable. It was the "Great American Game." Its stars were among the folk heroes of the age. A man who would trifle with the honor of the game was a Benedict Arnold.

But, much as he respected baseball, Rothstein loved money more. It was hard to pass up the chance for so big a winning. He might have decided to play along with Sullivan had not Burns and Maharg appeared on the scene. They impressed him as amateurs and bunglers.

What bothered Rothstein most was that the deal was being peddled. His eleven times eleven progression had reached an astronomical total. To succeed, a fix should be a secret, not public property.

But one thought gnawed at him. Maybe it could be done. Maybe, despite all the stupidity involved, the fix could be brought off.

If there really was a sure thing going, he could make hundreds of thousands of dollars. He had to find out. For this purpose, he used

Attell. He told him to maintain contact with Burns and Maharg. "I think they're puffing a pipe," he said, "but keep an eye on them."

Burns knew that Attell worked for Rothstein. He had no hesitancy about repeating his story. He added that he felt the deal could be made firm by a down payment of $10,000. Attell reported this back to Rothstein.

Now Rothstein discussed the Series with Nat Evans. He trusted Evans' judgment as he did that of few others. Evans, like Rothstein, was not too impressed. However, also like Rothstein, he felt there was too much risk in not knowing what was happening.

The $10,000 was a small sum to pay for "insurance." The money was given to Burns, its source not specified.

A few days before the Series opened, Evans went to Cincinnati, taking Attell and Rachel Brown with him. There, Evans again met with Burns and, after the meeting, he telephoned Rothstein and said, "I talked with Burns and some of the players. They're in so deep, they've got to throw the Series even if it don't mean a dime to them."

Rothstein still hesitated, but he knew time was growing short. He was taking bets on both teams, shaving the odds, of course, in his own favor. He could keep his books in balance and assure himself of a profit no matter which team won. Or he could start betting on Cincinnati.

His decision, reached twenty-four hours before the first game, was to accept Evans' judgment. But he coppered even that bet. "We'll play the Reds from game to game," he told Evans. "There's always the chance of a double-cross."

The situation was ironic. Rothstein could no longer doubt that the Series was fixed, yet he was unwilling to accept that as reality. He was certain the players were going to throw the Series, but he refused to bet on his own certainty. Bet, that is, to the limit.

And, though he had not fixed the Series, he was aware that already a gambler as well known as Honest John Kelly was announcing to would-be bettors that he would not take any bets on the Series because, "Everybody knows Arnold Rothstein has fixed it."

Rothstein took some steps to protect himself. He made a number of public wagers on the White Sox. He let it drop that he had heard the rumors but that they were untrue. And he stated, emphatically, that he would never have a part in anything as dirty as fixing a Series.

He was certain that the story would someday break. He wanted to have as good an alibi as possible when that day came.

The end result was that, while Rothstein won the Series, he won a small sum. He always maintained it was less than $100,000. It actually was about $350,000. It could have been much—very much —more. It wasn't because Rothstein chickened out. A World Series fix was too good to be true—even if it was true.

The Series resulted in an end to Rothstein's association with Attell. The latter had done what Rothstein had paid him to do. Nothing more. But Rothstein decided to make Attell the goat for the entire fix and his testimony, as much as anything, resulted in Attell's indictment.

After the trial, Attell cut himself off from Rothstein. The former featherweight champion found different fields in which to operate and, only a few years ago, was honored by the Boxing Writers of New York.

Rothstein confidently expected that his appearance and exoneration would close the matter. He said, "I went there to shut everybody up. I was tired of seeing my name in the papers."

His expectations were not fulfilled. The "Black Sox" story stayed on the front pages for a year. And every time anything was written Rothstein's name was mentioned. No one really believed in his innocence, only in his cleverness.

At one time that would have been enough for Rothstein. Now it was not. He was no longer the brash young gambler in search of identity, but a man of wealth and importance and one who would prefer to stay out of the limelight. Publicity was bad for business— and Rothstein had a lot of businesses.

He met with Fallon, with Tom Foley, and with other friends. They all agreed that he would have to take some drastic step.

The end result was that, late in 1921, Arnold Rothstein made an announcement which hit the front pages all over the country.

Chapter **12** *The Record Is Barren*

On September 7, 1921, the New York *Mail* carried a sensational story on its front page. It was headed:

ROTHSTEIN RETIRES
AS GAMBLING KING

The newspaper reported, in the body of the story, that Rothstein was through with gambling. It printed a statement he had issued, which concluded:

"From now on, I shall devote most of my attention to my racing stables and my real estate business. It is not pleasant to be, what some call, a 'social outcast.' For the sake of my family and friends, I am glad that chapter of my life is over."

All other papers picked up the story and commented on it.

"Arnold Rothstein," the *Tribune* said, "was one of the greatest plungers in the history of the American turf. . . . His gambling establishments in the Tenderloin flourished like the green bay tree." Then, waxing lyrical, the writer characterized Rothstein as "The Merry Monarch of Dame Fortune's realm." The story closed with an estimate of Rothstein's wealth, placing it as somewhere between three and four millions.

The *World*, too, estimated his holdings at that figure and said, "Rothstein has long been known as one of the heaviest bettors in

149

America, even more so, if less spectacular, than Davy Johnson and John W. Gates."

The staid *Times* treated Rothstein kindly. "He has many business interests, but betting, gambling and speculation in Wall Street brought Rothstein the greater part of his wealth." The newspaper then listed some of Rothstein's real estate holdings, most of them on Fifty-seventh Street, just west of Fifth Avenue. "His major business interests," the *Times* concluded, "include the Arnold Rothstein Realty Corporation and the insurance firm of A. L. Libman, Inc., of which Mr. Rothstein is president."

The *American* printed a character sketch. "For straight, undiluted gambling, the risking of money on sheer chance, Rothstein is unrivalled. . . . He will bet on anything, any time. . . . He does not pretend to be exceptionally skillful nor even lucky. He seems to bet because an inner force propels him. . . ."

It was George Daley, writing in the *World,* who came closest to explaining the real reason why Rothstein had made his announcement. "Rothstein," Daley wrote, "has been much in the public eye the last two or three years, far more than he has liked and in ways not pleasant to him. He has faced many charges, some of which were born in malice, but has stood to his guns and not once has any charge, legally made against him, been sustained."

Rothstein had truly been much in the public eye, in ways not always pleasant to him. The whole world knew who he was and knew him as himself, not as the son of Abraham nor as the brother of Harry. This need—this inner compulsion—had been satisfied. But it had entailed a price. Arnold Rothstein had identity, but it was an identity that had liabilities as well as assets.

His was the type of life that found sustenance in the dark. Sunlight—publicity—seared it.

The announcement was an effort to turn back the clock. It was an attempt to regain anonymity. It had not come easily.

It meant that he had to make sacrifices. He had to give some things away. Every one of them had cost him a price. Discarding them went hard against all his basic beliefs. But it had to be done.

He ceased direct ownership of gambling houses.

Despite his statement that he would devote himself to his racing interests, he ultimately sold these out.

No longer did he stand in doorways, whispering the site of a floating game.

Thus he gave the semblance of truth to his statement, a statement which the newspapers had apparently accepted without questioning. But it was semblance only.

He was still the great bookmaker. His office handled tens of thousands of dollars each day in lay-off money, in come-back money. Clockers and handicappers and spies and price-makers worked for him, providing him with the information that was his stock in trade. He took big bets and, as the record shows, he made big bets.

His money was behind bookmakers who operated in the clubhouses and the grandstands of New York tracks.

As a player, he sat at a card table and threw dice.

The *Times* had mentioned his "speculations in Wall Street," but had not enumerated them. Rothstein, in Wall Street as elsewhere, did not speculate; he played sure things. His percentage in his Wall Street ventures was quite high and that was the way he liked it. The people with whom he dealt had almost no chance.

He had other businesses about which he wanted no publicity. They were far more vicious, far more illegal than gambling. These were jeopardized every time his name appeared in the papers.

The Black Sox scandal was not the first, but the latest, in a series of incidents which had caused his name to appear on front pages. And each time his name was printed a little more had been revealed about him.

This was especially true of the incidents involving Albert ("Killer") Johnson and Inspector Dominic Henry of the New York police department. Both had evolved from floating crap games.

The first, the Johnson incident, occurred on May 16, 1917, at the Hotel St. Francis on West Forty-seventh Street. Rothstein had taken a suite in the hotel for his game.

There were extra locks and bolts, even a peephole. There was no fire escape by which intruders might enter the suite. The help at the hotel were all paid off. This included the doorman, house detective, elevator operator (who doubled as bellboy), and the night clerk, who also worked the hotel phone switchboard.

These precautions were necessary because gangs of free-lance holdup men were operating boldly. They made a specialty of sticking up crap games and poker games, on the theory that the operators of such enterprises could hardly ask for help from the police.

On this occasion about thirty players were crowded around the dice table. Among the participants were a stockbroker, two doctors, some actors, a theater owner, two attorneys, a poultry merchant, a silk manufacturer, an editor, and a number whose only profession was gambling.

One of these latter had a bad reputation. It stemmed from his having been present at a number of gambling games which had been robbed. Too many, the more cynical felt, for it to have been purely coincidental. Rothstein was aware of the man's reputation, but he also knew the man had a hefty bankroll. Weighing these, he decided in favor of the bankroll.

The game had been in progress about four hours when, at two in the morning, a group of men entered the hotel. One detached himself and made a beeline for the desk clerk. When the clerk looked up, he found himself staring down the barrel of a gun.

A second man headed for the house detective, who was also acting as downstairs lookout. The detective made a grab for his gun, but stopped. He was too late, already covered.

The remaining three men went to the elevator and surrounded the operator. They, too, were armed.

The leader of the group, one of the men at the elevator, said no one was going to be hurt provided no one sought to be a hero. He knew, he said, that there were frequent calls from the Rothstein suite for cigars or mineral water or food. When the next call came he and his two companions intended to make the delivery.

The gunmen rode upstairs with the elevator operator. When the car stopped, they marched the boy down the hall. They flattened themselves against a wall as the boy knocked at the door, and called, as he had been told, "Got your order."

The peephole was opened. Only the boy, tray in hand, was visible. The door was unbolted and opened. The boy was thrown through it, as a shield, and the gunmen moved in behind him.

Rothstein, with a sixth sense, reacted as the men came into the room. He flipped his bankroll out of his pocket to the floor and kicked it under a rug. Even as he did, his eyes were fixed on the suspected finger man.

Telling of this, Herbert Bayard Swope said, "Rothstein always reacted faster than any other man I ever knew. This was as good an example of his reaction time as you could want. There were only a few seconds for him to figure out what was happening. He didn't need more than one or two. But hiding the roll was only part of what he had to do. He had to make certain the tipster didn't tell the holdup men where the bankroll was.

"His eyes were on that man from the moment the door swung open. He kept him under constant watch all the time the holdup was going on."

The three gunmen began a systematic collection of cash and jewelry. They swept up all the money on the table, then two of them searched the pockets of all the men in the room. As they searched the tipster, he looked at Rothstein. His face was pale and sweat was running down his face. He couldn't take his eyes away from Rothstein's.

The searchers reached Rothstein and went through his pockets. He was searched twice, for they refused to believe that all the money he carried was the $2,600 that they found in his watch pocket. Disgusted, one of them removed the diamond stickpin Rothstein was wearing.

The man said, "I'll send you the pawn ticket, A.R."

"Don't bother," Rothstein said. "I'll have it back before the mail arrives tomorrow morning."

Rothstein at no time had removed his eyes from the suspected tipster. When the holdup men left, after the usual warning not to try to follow them, Rothstein still stared at him. Finally he dropped his eyes, bent down and turned over the rug. He picked up the thick bankroll and put it back in his pocket. Later he said it amounted to $20,000. Swope maintained that there was more than $60,000 in the wallet.

"I rarely saw him when he wasn't carrying close to $100,000," Swope said.

The game, of course, broke up. The players started to leave, but Rothstein beckoned to the man he felt had set up the robbery. "Let's you and me and Abe [Attell] go get a cup of coffee." The man broke into a heavy sweat, but he didn't say anything.

The last three to leave the suite were Rothstein, Attell and the gambler. Rothstein explained this to Swope. "I thought the bastards might be waiting for me outside and, if they were, I was going to make sure that fellow got what was coming to him."

However, there was no one downstairs. Rothstein sent the man on his way.

The next afternoon Swope encountered Rothstein and asked, "What are you going to do about the stickup?"

"I'll take care of it," Rothstein left no doubt that he intended to do so.

"The police know about it."

Rothstein shrugged. "So what?"

"Arthur Woods [the Police Commissioner] says you're too yellow to report this."

"People know better. I never take my troubles to the cops." He laughed, touched the tiepin he was wearing. "Why do I need them? The fence got this back to me before breakfast."

Swope hit at Rothstein's weakest spot, his vanity. "They're laughing at you, Arnold. The word is out that you're buffaloed."

Rothstein rose to the lure. "I'll show them who's buffaloed. No one can laugh at me."

Accompanied by Swope, he went to the old West Side station and made a formal report of the robbery. From there he went downtown and examined files of pictures in the Rogues' Gallery. He identified two, one of Gene Price, a small-time crook, the other of Killer Johnson. His long record included two murder charges and the notation that he was a drug addict.

The police found the pair and arrested them. They were arraigned and held for trial.

Shortly before the date set for the trial of the two men Swope paid another visit to Rothstein. He said he had been with Woods and the Commissioner had offered to bet that Rothstein would not repeat his identification at the trial. "Woods says you've got cold feet."

"Tell him I'll take any bets he wants to lay."

On August 22, 1917, wearing the stickpin that had been stolen from him, Rothstein for the first time—and the only time—in his life appeared in court as a state's witness. Looking directly at the two men, he said they had participated in the holdup.

Johnson, a big, red-faced, red-haired man pulled himself out of the restraining hands of a policeman and shouted, "I'll get you for this. No jail can hold me."

The pair were convicted and sent to Sing Sing. Two months afterward Johnson made good one part of his threat: he escaped from jail.

His cellmate told the warden that Johnson had said his first act would be to kill Rothstein.

Even Swope was worried. He called Carolyn Rothstein and told her that she ought to get her husband to go out of town somewhere until the police recaptured Johnson. "You know Arnold," she said. "He wouldn't run away and have people say he was scared."

Swope warned Rothstein personally. "As long as you walk along Broadway you're an easy target for Johnson."

"I wasn't afraid of him before and I'm not afraid now."

This bravery—it was really bravado—was part of the public Rothstein. At home, alone with Carolyn, he was not so brave. "If I ran away," he said, "people would know that I was buffaloed. I'd be finished. I have to stay here."

"I'd rather you were buffaloed than dead," Carolyn said.

"It's the same thing," he answered her. "A man who backs down is finished. Well, I won't be finished that way. I'll just have to take the chance that they'll catch Johnson before he shoots or, if they don't, that he'll miss when he does shoot."

"Then you are afraid?"

He nodded. "I'm afraid, all right. There are only two people who know that, though. You and me. We're the only two people in the world I trust enough to let them know it."

So Rothstein continued his normal activities, walking the streets, going to his office, going to Reuben's restaurant. He seemed casual, self-assured. He knew that the Broadway crowd admired him, that they were saying, "One thing about A.R., he's got nerve." That was the accolade he wanted. It justified his making a target of himself.

Some weeks after Johnson made his escape Rothstein was awakened one noon by a call from a friendly police officer. "Just wanted to tell you Johnson was killed in a bank stickup in Detroit. I thought you might want to know."

Later the details came out. Johnson had apparently changed his mind after his prison escape. Knowing the police would be waiting for him to return to New York, he had, instead, gone to Chicago. There he had joined a mob of safecrackers. The gang had attempted a robbery in Detroit and Johnson had been killed by a bank guard.

The Johnson story had received a great deal of publicity. As a result, it had strengthened a minor part of the Rothstein legend. Because of it, he had become known as a man of iron nerve.

The Dominic Henry incident occurred on January 19, 1919. Again it stemmed from a floating crap game, this one taking place at 301 West Fifty-seventh Street.

On this night there was a peremptory knock on the door of the suite. Then a shout, "Open up, before we bust in."

The response was a fusillade of bullets fired from inside the suite.

Someone outside shouted, "This isn't a stickup, it's the police. This is John Walsh and you've hit me."

Most of the dice players knew Walsh. He was a member of the mid-town detective squad commanded by Inspector Henry.

Someone unlatched the door and the raiders moved into the room. Three of them had been hit by the gunfire from within the room, Walsh, John McLaughlin and Dick Oliver. A bullet had "creased" Walsh's right arm, barely touching his flesh. McLaughlin's shoulder was seared by a bullet. Oliver, it developed, had escaped any real injury, the bullet going through his left sleeve and leaving only a scratch.

The twenty men inside the room stood about the table, their hands raised over their heads. Among these was Abe Attell. But there was no sign of Rothstein.

While the injured men checked their wounds, the other raiders searched the rest of the suite. They found no gun.

Someone put in a call for a patrol wagon, and while it was on its way the detectives tried to find out who had done the shooting and what had happened to the gun. They learned nothing.

When the wagon arrived, the men were hustled out of the gambling place, taken downstairs and placed in the wagon. The whole matter might have ended there had it not been for the inevitable innocent bystander. He approached one of the detectives and said, "There's someone on the fire escape."

Looking up, the detective saw a huddled figure on the second floor, where the fire escape ended. While one man stood guard below, another went up to the second floor, made his way to the fire escape and arrested the man who was hiding there. It was Rothstein.

He was taken downstairs. By this time the wagon was gone. Rothstein, concerned about the wounded men, offered to drive them to the hospital in his car. Sometime during that ride the police obtained from Rothstein a revolver for which he had a permit. At the hospital the wounds were treated and dressed and then Rothstein chauffeured the three men to the station house.

Once there, he was booked on a charge of assault. This came after a protracted period, during which an uncertain lieutenant did not want to make any booking until he had talked with certain of his superiors. The decision to charge Rothstein with a crime was made by Inspector Henry.

All the others who had been arrested were placed in a detention pen, but Rothstein remained in the police station until it was time to go to court.

The magistrate listened to the story told by the police and decided there was enough evidence to hold all who had been arrested, including Rothstein, on a charge of felonious assault. He set bail at $1,000 for each of the twenty-one persons involved.

Rothstein provided the bail from his "walk-around money," his traveling bankroll. A neat pile of exactly twenty-one $1,000 bills. He and the rest were then free until the Grand Jury acted.

The newspapers leaped on the story. Once again the name Rothstein was headlined. However, only one newspaper, the New York *American,* named Rothstein as the man who had fired the shots which struck the three detectives. This surprised no one. The *American,* a Hearst paper, was then carrying on a war against Murphy and Foley. And in its stories it said that "Rothstein has long been known as a lieutenant of Tom Foley."

No other gun was ever found. However, there was no proof that the gun Rothstein had turned over to the police was the gun which had been used in firing through the door.

There was a unanimity of opinion among Rothstein's friends, of whom there were a few, and his enemies, of whom there were many, that Rothstein had fired the shots. However, both friends and enemies felt that he had been in his rights in blasting away. Until the police had identified themselves, it was reasonable for Rothstein to believe that he was being held up. He had a right to protect both himself and his bankroll.

The police, it was agreed, had made a tactical error by failing to announce themselves at once. One of the wounded detectives, Oliver, said as much to a reporter for the *World.*

On this basis it was felt that the men would probably be fined for gambling and the shooting would be glossed over.

This might well have happened except for two men, Inspector Henry and Assistant District Attorney James E. Smith.

No matter how tight the control of the politicians on the police force, there are always some policemen who are regarded as unreachable. Usually such officers find themselves in Staten Island or handling traffic in the Bronx. Only rarely do they become, as Henry became, heads of borough detective squads.

Henry did not like Rothstein. He had an even greater dislike of men who fired at his officers. He reasoned, with logic, that if one man could make targets of raiding officers, others could do the same. Therefore he pressed for some action against Rothstein. In Smith he found someone who was willing to go along with him.

Smith was a career man in the District Attorney's office. He was an expert lawyer, a man on whom fell much of the detail of the office and little of the glory. He knew that the man who convicted Rothstein would receive a great deal of newspaper publicity, all of it favorable. So he, along with Henry, followed up the Rothstein case.

Smith announced that he was taking the case to the Grand Jury. He said the law made it a felony to shoot a policeman in the pursuit of his duties. In this instance, three policemen had been shot.

While the Grand Jury investigated, the twenty-one were arraigned in Magistrate's Court. Charges against twenty of them were dismissed by Magistrate McQuade, Rothstein's good friend. But Rothstein was held until the Grand Jury completed its investigation. His bail was continued at $1,000. Rothstein picked up the other $20,000 from the court clerk.

The Grand Jury questioned the gamblers and the police who had been involved in the shooting. Some of the gamblers revealed the trend of questioning. Each had been asked if Rothstein had fired the shots. And each of the twenty, testifying under oath, had denied any knowledge of just who had done the shooting. A number of the gamblers had even sworn they believed that the shooting had taken place outside the room and that the detectives had been wounded by their overzealous fellows.

Nevertheless, and much to the surprise of Broadway, the Grand Jury handed down an indictment on June 5, 1919, charging Rothstein with two counts of felonious assault. A warrant was immediately issued for Rothstein's arrest and detectives were dispatched to his home and to Belmont race track on the theory that, if he was not at the one place, he was sure to be at the other.

Rothstein did not suffer the indignity of being arrested. Instead, informed somehow that he was being sought, he had his chauffeur drive him to the District Attorney's office, where he surrendered.

Rothstein went back and forth across the "Bridge of Sighs" which connected the Tombs with the old Criminal Courts Building. He was booked and then taken to General Sessions Court, where he entered a plea of "Not Guilty." He was permitted to go free on the same $1,000 bail that had been in effect since the day after the shooting.

The courtroom was crowded when Judge John F. McIntyre called the case. The audience was composed of gamblers, police officers and an abnormal complement of curiosity seekers.

Rothstein sat with two attorneys, Emil Fuchs, who had been a magistrate, was to buy the Boston National League Baseball Club, and was a sachem of Tammany Hall, and William J. Fallon. As usual, someone else was going to handle the law in the case and Fallon was kept in reserve for courtroom histrionics.

On this day Fallon's services would not be needed.

As soon as Judge McIntyre called the case, Fuchs moved that the indictments be dismissed on the basis that there was no evidence to justify them.

Judge McIntyre then handed down judgment. He said, in part:

"The record is barren of any evidence tending directly or indirectly to connect the defendant with the commission of any crime. Much time was spent and, doubtless, much public money expended, in an effort to fasten the crime on the defendant, and, I might add, that in the Court's judgment, the time was uselessly spent. Not a word of evidence appears in the Grand Jury minutes showing that the defendant committed an assault upon anybody. All that is disclosed is as follows:

"Q.   'Do you know who did the shooting?'
"A.   'No.'
"Q.   'Did you see Rothstein have a gun, or did you see him do the shooting?'
"A.   'No.'
"Q.   'Well, who in your opinion did the shooting? Give us your best opinion.'
"A.   'From reading the papers, my opinion is that it was Rothstein.'

"This appears to be the only evidence that in any way relates to Rothstein.

"Under our system of jurisprudence, fortunately, a surmise, a conjecture, or a guess can have no place as evidentiary of the commission of a crime. Why the Grand Jury ordered an indictment in this case is incomprehensible. It should not have been voted. It was idle to do so. The motion to dismiss is granted."

Well, this was no more than had been expected by the cynics. A certain public showing had been made by which the authorities had saved face. But the result, as far as these were concerned, had been the inevitable.

Rothstein, freed of one of the two indictments ever brought against him, made another visit to the court clerk and was returned his $1,000.

This should have been the end of the incident, but it was not. The *American* continued to press for some sort of action against Rothstein. It reported that there was more than had been revealed to the public in the dismissal of the indictment. It went even further and printed: "It is believed that Rothstein's bankroll is now some $32,000 lighter than it was when he was placed under arrest."

No direct charge of bribery was made, but it was implied that this money might well have ended in the pockets of certain officials of both the police department and the District Attorney's office.

Mayor John F. Hylan owed his election to the Hearst press. He had been discovered by Hearst in Brooklyn, publicized by him and, according to Nat J. Ferber, an outstanding reporter for the *American,* the man who first put Hylan's name in the newspaper: "Hearst, the most hated publisher in New York City, was able, singlehanded, to elect Hylan."

No wonder then that Hylan, requested to do so by the *American,* wrote a letter to Police Commissioner Richard Enright, in which he called Enright's attention to these rumors and asked that they be investigated. Hylan even gave Enright a lead to follow. He suggested it would be advisable to discover if it had not been Herbert Bayard Swope who handled the dispensing of the $32,000.

This suggestion must have been a pleasant one for Hylan to

offer. Swope, by then, was executive editor of the *World* and the *World* was bitterly anti-Hylan. As an addendum, Hylan mentioned that "it is common knowledge that Swope knows Rothstein and has long been friendly with him."

Enright did as directed. He ordered an investigation. And requested a written report from Inspector Henry.

The inspector not only prepared a report but swore to an affidavit which he wrote himself. The language was hardly diplomatic and some persons concluded from it that he was making a series of nasty charges against Assistant District Attorney Smith.

District Attorney Edward Swann then took over the investigation. Swann was an amiable gentleman, with the right connections to get a Tammany nomination for district attorney. His personal honesty was never attacked, but his capabilities for his important office were. Certainly he was no better and no worse than other district attorneys who appointed assistants sponsored by Tammany district leaders.

At any rate, when Swann began to lay the charges before the Grand Jury, it was a pretty good bet that nothing would come of them. Certainly nothing that would be harmful to Rothstein, close friend of Swann's Tammany sponsors, or to Swope, the powerful editor of the powerful *World*.

And when the Grand Jury brought in its findings, those who had bet that way collected. The charges against Swope were held to be ridiculous. He had been in Paris at the time of the shooting and during the period when Rothstein was indicted and brought to trial.

As to Rothstein, the jury reported there was no evidence of any kind to show that his case had been improperly presented or that there had been any bribery of any law official.

However, the Grand Jury did bring in an indictment. It charged Inspector Henry with perjury!

Broadway, the underworld, chortled. This was what happened to anyone who tangled with Arnold Rothstein.

Only the *American* came to Henry's defense. Here was a police officer with a fine reputation, a man who had risked his life in the line of duty, charged with a major crime while "a gambler, a friend of Tammany politicians, goes free."

Henry was bewildered at the turn of events. "I have done nothing except perform my duties," he told the *Tribune*. "I have every confidence I will be vindicated if this flimsy charge against me is brought to trial."

Henry was honest. Henry was a good policeman. But he was out of his depth. He was caught in the middle in a fight between the Hearst press and Tammany. He had taken no sides, but that was of no consequence.

At his trial Henry was his own principal witness. Without guile, apparently still unaware that he was a pawn, he told his story. And that story was not good enough. The jury found him guilty. He was sentenced to five years' imprisonment.

Now Broadway really rocked. Rothstein had been discharged without a trial, but Henry had had the book thrown at him. If ever there had been need to show the power, the influence, of Rothstein, that need no longer existed.

Henry remained free on bail pending his request for a new trial, suspended from the police department, his pay discontinued.

Two and a half years after he was convicted, that conviction was reversed by the Appellate Division. By that time Henry had spent all the money he had and all that he could borrow. For almost thirty months he had been stigmatized as a criminal, a convicted perjurer. Vindication had finally come, but it had come very late. And most people had forgotten about him and the reason for his troubles. Nor were all of these over.

With his record cleared, Henry now applied for reinstatement in the police department. He made formal petition for a return to duty, and this was approved. There was nothing else the department could do; the law was explicit on that point. Henry also requested that he be paid for the period of his suspension, plus the money he had spent to obtain exoneration. Normally this would have been routine. There were dozens of precedents. But this was not a normal situation.

Much time had passed since the story was front-page news. But the man behind the fight on Henry had grown more powerful in that time. The city had to make a choice. It chose to withhold payment from Henry. He had to return to court and sue.

This case, too, went through the entire court system until, at long last in 1924, Dominic Henry won a final victory. He got his money.

The Henry case revealed Rothstein's power. It had impressed police officers that there was no point in sticking out their necks. It had shown others, anxious to joust for power with Rothstein, that the time had not yet come when they could safely make such a challenge.

But it had also revealed Rothstein's power publicly. The mass of the people of New York paid little attention. But those to whom such knowledge was important heeded it. And some others reacted to it.

These people were unhappy about the publicity, publicity which continued over the years. True, it was primarily in the Hearst papers and the *American,* but the Hearst papers had a lot of readers. And Hearst editors and reporters, whatever their motives, were not going to let up their attack on Rothstein.

Not when Rothstein was close to Foley and Foley close to Murphy. And Murphy—and Al Smith—were constant targets for Hearst.

The Henry case had backfired, but the *American* was ready with new ammunition. It was preparing to break its exposé of the bucket shops in New York and their connections throughout the country. Its primary targets were Murphy and Foley. Before the exposé was completed, it was directed at Rothstein and Fallon. At the end, on Fallon alone.

But, always, Rothstein was involved in it.

Chapter **13** *Mr. Arnold*

Arnold Rothstein made a great deal of money out of, but not in, Wall Street.

He made it by peculation and not, as the *Times* had reported, "by speculation."

He played the market only once in his life. That was on a tip from his friends, Joe and Nick Schenck, who advised him to get in on the ground floor when they, and others, formed Loew's, Inc., parent company of M-G-M pictures. Rothstein bought some Loew's stock, held it for seven months. He profited by about $40,000.

However, much of Rothstein's bankroll came from Wall Street. He was involved in the ownership, operation and protection of bucket shops. He also served as a lobbyist and public relations man for the bucketing industry. He was their bondsman and their fixer.

A bucket-shop was an ostensibly legal brokerage firm. Some of these firms operated within the law. Others did not. The latter cheated their customers, stole from them, misused their customers' money. It was this second type that needed Rothstein.

He acted as "fence" for many of these crooked firms. He took valuable securities off their hands—securities to which they had no right—and found a way to dispose of them.

When the bucketeers required legal counsel they got it through Rothstein. For much of the time that counsel was William J. Fallon, dubbed "The Great Mouthpiece."

Fallon was one of the two men who figured most prominently in Rothstein's Wall Street operations. The other was that extraordinary citizen of the world, Nicky Arnstein. Telling the story of Rothstein's financial operations requires telling the stories of both Fallon and Arnstein.

When Rothstein began his gambling career his office was under his hat and his safe-deposit box in his pants pocket. He could prepare a profit-and-loss statement by counting his bankroll at the end of each day. He didn't need a ledger for simple addition—or, as sometimes happened—simple subtraction.

But when his activities grew more complex and his bankroll larger he needed an actual office and had to keep physical records. His first office was in his home on West Forty-sixth Street. And his first ledger was a small, black book that he kept in a code of his own devising. He used that code for the rest of his life and, according to the investigators who went through his records after his death, they were never able to break that code.

From 1914 on, Rothstein always had an outside office in a building he owned. This office was primarily used in his bookmaking operations, for these required the listing of many details.

But for his other activities Rothstein still sought to keep his own books. And he used his residence—or part of it—as an office.

A chronology of these residences gives a good picture of Rothstein's rise.

He moved from Forty-sixth Street to a larger apartment on the corner of Broadway and Fifty-second Street. Then he bought a house for $35,000 at 355 West Eighty-fourth Street and lived there for a time. His next home was a duplex suite in the Ritz-Carlton. And from there Rothstein went to 912 Fifth Avenue. This was his legal residence when he died.

In each residence Rothstein had an office. In each he kept records in his private code in his little black books.

He found early that, in addition to books and records and political influence, he needed a lawyer.

His first lawyer was George Young Bauchle. Others followed, among them Hyman Turchin, Isaiah Lebow, Emil Fuchs, Joseph Shalleck, George Morton Levy, George Z. Medalie and, at the end,

Maurice Cantor. From about 1919 until 1924 Fallon was the brightest star of Rothstein's legal galaxy.

Rothstein held lawyers in peculiar esteem. He delighted in being with them, in listening to tales of legal brilliance. Over the years he collected them as J. P. Morgan collected porcelains and paintings.

The prize of the collection was also the gadfly. With some of his lawyers Rothstein attained an intimacy. He gambled and played with Bauchle and Turchin. With others, like Fuchs and Shalleck, he had a political connection. George Morton Levy and George Z. Medalie represented him, but kept him at a distance.

His relationship with Fallon was a duel. It was a case of two egos in conflict.

Fallon was a shooting star, brilliant for a time and then fizzling out. He was more actor than lawyer, with a flair for self-dramatization. Nowhere was this more marked than in the courtroom, where he referred to himself in the third person. "Fallon," he told a judge and jury, "does not have his back to the wall."

He lived fast and drank hard. He could have been a great lawyer, but that demanded an inner strength, an inner belief in himself, that he did not possess. It was easier to play a part, with the courtroom his stage. Unfortunately, the man who would be Hamlet ended as Charlie McCarthy to his partner, Gene McGee, who played Edgar Bergen.

His friends, his admirers and his apologists have all blamed whisky for Fallon's downfall. They have refused to see that the weakness was in the man, not in the bottle. These same friends created a fantasy Fallon and this fantasy was exploited by them, by Fallon himself and by the newspapers. The fantasy was larger than the man, demanded too much of him. When Fallon found this out he took to drinking too much. Drunk, at least he did not have to see himself clear.

There came a time when the impossible was expected of him and he tried to live up to the impossible. He was "The Great Mouthpiece," "The Jail Robber," the man whose clients were never convicted. To live up to the legend he had to stoop far down. In the end he had to defend himself against a charge of bribing jurors. He was acquitted, but as he left the courtroom he told reporter Nat Ferber, "I promise you I'll never bribe a juror again." That wasn't irony; that was fear.

It was in that trial that Fallon came closest to living up to the myth, the fantasy. He was, for once, truly the "jail robber."

It is hard to tell whether the twenties produced the individuals who made it so remarkable a decade or whether it was the characters who made the decade so memorable. Those were flamboyant years, loud, roisterous, bibulous, hedonistic. Some few individuals stood out so much from the mass that they became known by their nicknames. "Lucky Lindy." "Scarface." "The Manassa Mauler." "The Bambino." "The Brain." "The Boy Wonder of Wall Street." "The Great Mouthpiece."

Yes, Fallon was included among these. There was a short period when it seemed he would be the heir of William F. Howe and Abraham Hummel, those twisted lawyers who were as much a part of the underworld as their clients in the Mauve Decade. But Fallon never truly was. He merely represented the same type of clients. Fallon was a peacock and the others had been vultures.

And, where Howe and Hummel were always their own bosses, Fallon worked for Rothstein. He was paid by Rothstein to do Rothstein's bidding. He resented this, took out his resentment in bitterness and sarcasm, like a small boy drawing caricatures of the teacher on the school blackboard. He got under Rothstein's skin, of course. But, then, Rothstein dug deep into Fallon also.

The two men never liked each other. Nor were two men ever such opposites. Rothstein liked the shadows. He felt the cardinal sin would be to undress his emotions and reveal them publicly to the world. Fallon pawned his soul for another drink.

Gene McGee said of Fallon, "He lived as if he were afraid the light would go out any minute and he wouldn't have another quarter to put into the meter."

The basic difference between the two men was that Rothstein believed in, and respected, himself. Fallon had no self-respect and sobriety showed him he could not believe in himself. Fallon pursued a course of denigration, of self-destruction. He lied. He cheated his clients. He was personally unclean.

Fallon came to Manhattan from Westchester, where he had been successful as both prosecutor and defense lawyer. Handsome, a good-sized man, he early began to dominate the courtrooms in which he appeared. He took to Broadway and Broadway took to him.

He went to work for Rothstein because Rothstein paid him—or arranged for others to pay him. Fallon had no respect for money, only a great need for it. That was his weakness and Rothstein exploited it.

The first time that Fallon appeared in court in behalf of Rothstein was during the Inspector Henry case. There was no need for his services; Rothstein had seen to that, but, as always, had coppered his bet. He was willing to pay a little extra for the edge.

Fallon never did appear as attorney of record for Rothstein during the years in which they were associated. But he did appear for those who were connected with Rothstein.

For Abe Attell, in the baseball scandal. For "Curly" Bennett, panderer and member of Tom Foley's Downtown Tammany Club. For "Ratsy" Tourbillon, better known as "Dapper Dan" Collins, the confidence man whom Rothstein banked in endeavors ranging from shakedowns to rumrunning. For Philip ("Dandy Phil") Kastel, small-time gambler, "badger-game" operator and bucketeer, who rose to become one of the overlords of the underworld in partnership with Frank Costello. For Nicky Arnstein, when Arnstein was accused of masterminding bond thefts of $5,000,000. And for Edward M. Fuller and William F. McGee, the bucket-shop operators.

Over the years Rothstein and Fallon fell out frequently. Usually it was because Fallon had gone on a bender. Rothstein told Fallon often, "I can't trust a drunk."

Carolyn Rothstein gave a good sidelight on their relationship. She said, "Fallon was the only lawyer who ever worked for Arnold who was not named as executor in at least one of the wills Arnold was always drawing up."

But Rothstein kept Fallon on the payroll for a long time. He was instrumental in reconciling Fallon and McGee after their first big disagreement. McGee asked him, "Why do you want us together again?"

"For insurance," Rothstein said.

And certainly Fallon was insurance in the cases involving Nicky Arnstein, and the $5,000,000 bond thefts, and Fuller and McGee (no relation to Gene McGee), the bucket-shop operators who mulcted their customers of another $5,000,000.

The Arnstein case came first, in 1921.

Nicky Arnstein was—is—a charming man. Tall, lean, aristocratic in mien and bearing, he creates confidence on sight. That has been both his greatest asset and the cause of his downfall.

He is well-educated and self-educated. During his prison terms in Sing Sing and Leavenworth, he was prison librarian and the best-read man in both institutions.

He has—no, had for those days are far beyond him—a long record as confidence man, gambler, swindler and heartbreaker. He made the gentle art of separating a fool and his money not only painless but a pleasure. The late Assistant Chief Inspector John J. Sullivan once tried to warn a victim away from Nicky. "Don't you know he's a card sharp?" Sullivan asked.

"Of course I know it," the man replied, "but he's better company than the honest men on board this ship."

Nicky could discourse on art and literature and beautiful women and foreign places. He knew members of the nobility as well as fellow Sing Sing alumni.

Nicky is a long man. He is long-faced, long-nosed, long-chinned, long-waisted and long-armed. His hands are long and delicate, as are his fingers. He can palm a card—or a full deck of cards—in those beautifully kept long hands.

Nicky worked the transatlantic steamers before World War I. He gambled all over the world. He was involved with the Gondorf brothers in a wire-tapping swindle that brought him many thousands and his first term in prison.

In 1920, one prison term behind him, Nicky was happily married to Fannie Brice. Happily, that was, for him. He lived in luxury, had an adoring wife, mingled with the best people and talked of his plans. Nicky always had wonderful plans.

Also in 1920, and for some eighteen months earlier, various Wall Street security houses had been the victims of robberies in which the total loot was between four and five million dollars in securities, primarily highly negotiable Liberty Bonds.

The pattern of these robberies was simple. A messenger would be dispatched with an envelope containing some thousands of dollars in securities. On his way to a brokerage house or a bank he would be held up, slugged and robbed. And the bonds, like the girl in the magician's act, would disappear into thin air.

Looking back, it is obvious that the security houses were as criminal in their negligence as the thieves in their robberies. No guards were provided the messengers and no extra precautions taken, even after the robberies became epidemic. Of course the real losers were not the security houses, but the bonding companies which insured the brokers.

The robberies were frequent and successful. And no one was apprehended over a long period. The police said this was because they were all being engineered by a supercriminal, a Mastermind.

And it was whispered, though never openly charged, that this mastermind was Arnold Rothstein.

This was the situation on February 6, 1920, when the police arrested seven men and charged them with stealing $2,500 in securities from a messenger employed by Parrish and Company, of 115 Broadway. Among these seven was one Joe Gluck.

Gluck had a long record, which included robbery, assault and other assorted crimes. When he was arrested and first questioned, he told the police, "I'm not talking. My lawyer will talk for me." He expressed confidence that both attorney and bondsman would appear as soon as they learned of his difficulty.

However, something apparently went wrong. Gluck was arraigned and he had no lawyer. He entered his own "Not Guilty" plea and bail was set at $5,000. And now there was no bondsman.

Gluck sat in the Tombs for ten days and waited with surprising patience. But at the end of that period his patience gave out. He asked one of his keepers to inform the District Attorney's office that he might have something to say if offered the proper inducement. Something like a suspended sentence.

Assistant District Attorney James Dooling had a talk with Gluck. And with Nick Cohn, another of the arrested seven who was still in jail. Dooling made no promises, something to which he was to swear in a court hearing, but did agree to ask for leniency for Gluck if the information Gluck provided proved of value.

What Gluck then told him was most startling. According to Gluck, the bond thefts were, as the police had been saying all along, the work of a "Mastermind." It was he who had organized and planned and recruited underworld characters to carry out the actual robberies.

Gluck said he was only an underling and had never met the Mastermind. However, he added, the Mastermind had been pointed out to him in a restaurant and he was a man of such striking appearance and individuality that Gluck was certain he could identify him from a picture.

The Mastermind, Gluck said, was known to him only as "Mr. Arnold"!

Gluck then explained how he had happened to see Mr. Arnold. He said Mr. Nick Cohn had recruited him for the organization. He, and a few others whose names he could not remember, had been told to make friends with messengers for the different security companies and gain their confidence.

According to Gluck, a good share of the messenger boys were willing to enter the scheme. However, a number of them wanted further assurance that they were really being taken into a ring.

Gluck reported this to William Furey, who was his superior in the chain of command, and Furey in turn reported this to Cohn. The latter said the best proof that he could offer the boys was the sight of the man behind the robberies, the boss himself. Mr. Arnold. Mr. Arnold, of course, was not to be bothered or spoken to, merely put on display.

Cohn was informed that this was agreeable to the boys. Cohn then called Nicky Arnstein at his home and said there was a matter of business which he would like to discuss with him. Since Arnstein had at one time had a business connection with Cohn which had proved profitable, he agreed to meet Cohn at a restaurant only a short distance from where he lived. "Remember," Nicky said, "I am on the square now."

"This proposition," Cohn said, "is strictly on the level, Nicky. You know me."

It was that very knowledge which made Nicky doubt the statement but, always the gentleman, he said the best time for the meeting was about six.

Cohn arrived early and found a table near the window facing the street. When Nicky arrived, he joined Cohn. He was, as usual, dressed in Bond Street fashion and looked as though he had been made for the clothes and not the clothes for him.

Cohn conducted a desultory conversation with Nicky. At the same time a half dozen young men pressed their noses against the restaurant window and peered into the room. All of them had earlier met Cohn. Now, they were told, they were seeing Cohn with "Mr. Arnold."

Better men—and smarter—had been impressed by Nicky's appearance.

At any rate, the group needed no further convincing. And they proceeded to commit their larcenies until the unfortunate instance when the messenger for Parrish and Company, a young man of honesty and courage, fought back and managed to get the attention of the police, who arrested the group of seven.

When Assistant District Attorney Dooling heard the name "Mr. Arnold," he started the wheels moving as a rapid rate.

Within minutes, Dooling gathered up all available pictures of Arnold Rothstein and showed them to Gluck. He looked at them and shook his head. This definitely was not "Mr. Arnold." He lacked the class, the polish of "Mr. Arnold."

Dooling then asked Gluck to describe "Mr. Arnold" as best he could. Gluck said he was tall, slender, handsome, distinguished, and with a dashing moustache.

This description was passed on to the Bureau of Identification at police headquarters. Police sifted the photos in the Rogues' Gallery and found a dozen that fitted the description. These would be shown to Gluck the next day.

That evening Rothstein was approached by a detective he knew. Rothstein was told of Gluck's confession, his naming a "Mr. Arnold," who, it had turned out, was not Arnold Rothstein. Rothstein was further informed that Gluck would be shown other pictures the next day, among them a full-face and a side view of Nicky Arnstein.

Rothstein at once telephoned Arnstein and told him what he had learned. When Rothstein mentioned Nick Cohn's name, Arnstein at once recalled the hitherto pointless restaurant meeting, a meeting which now took on point.

"Get out of town," Rothstein advised Nicky. "Hide out."

Nicky immediately began to pack. He knew where he would head, a city in Ohio which was a "safe" town. That meant certain local officials had an agreement with the underworld that they would provide sanctuary for wanted men at a price. In return, crooks, hoodlums and lawbreakers of different kinds agreed not to ply their trade locally. As a result, such towns rank among the most law-abiding in the United States.

It was proved early the next day that Nicky's flight had been a necessary precaution. Gluck, riffling through the pictures as though they were playing cards, brought Nicky's to the top and said, "That's him. That's 'Mr. Arnold.' "

Furey and Nick Cohn also identified the picture as that of "Mr. Arnold."

The police, of course, knew Nicky, knew he had often used the alias "Jules Arnold." Just the same, they were doubtful. And it was because they knew Nicky.

Without disparaging Nicky's intelligence and background, the police still found it difficult to believe that he could organize an operation like the bond thefts. They knew that Nicky had been much in the public eye since his release from prison and marriage to Fannie Brice. There had been a number of casual interviews with him by detectives. These interviews had convinced the authorities that Nicky was not involved in anything nefarious.

However, here were witnesses who had identified Nicky and were prepared to testify against him. Here was a chance for the police and the District Attorney to get a conviction in a matter that had long been on the front page. If Nicky was innocent he would have his day in court to prove it.

An alarm was sent out for Nicky. A story was released to the newspapers. The Mastermind behind the bond thefts had been identified. He was Nicky Arnstein!

When Fannie Brice heard this her reaction was: "Mastermind! Nicky couldn't mastermind an electric bulb into a socket."

Arnstein stayed in his hideout for a little more than two months. Meanwhile, the police, the District Attorney, and special investigators employed by the National Surety Company tried to get further information from Gluck. He insisted doggedly he had told all he knew.

Rothstein's friends in the various investigating agencies kept him informed of what was going on. He was aware that continuing efforts were being made to implicate him and that these efforts were futile.

Meanwhile Rothstein alerted Fallon and McGee that they would be counsel for Nicky when he finally gave himself up. Nicky had demanded this.

Nicky, in his hideout, knew he was innocent, but he also knew that Gluck's testimony, plus further corroboration from Furey, might be sufficient to put him in jail. He needed the best legal help he could get and that meant Fallon and McGee. And Rothstein was the man who could get him such counsel.

Nicky also made one other demand. That, before giving himself up, bail arrangements should be set and bail money should be ready. Nicky did not like the food and accommodations normally provided prisoners in the Tombs.

Rothstein, in the background, waited while Fallon argued the bail amount with the District Attorney's office. The first figure named was $100,000 and Fallon maintained this was too high. Later a figure of $60,000 was agreed upon.

The next step was up to Arnstein. He agreed to surrender, but insisted that he be allowed to do so on his own terms. He would not permit himself to be returned to New York in handcuffs.

Shortly afterward, Rothstein told Fallon to go to Mamaroneck, in Westchester County, Fallon's home grounds. "Arnstein will meet you there."

At the same time Rothstein notified his old friend Herbert Bayard Swope that Arnstein was going to surrender the next day and that if Swope assigned a reporter to stay with Fallon for twenty-four hours the *World* would have an exclusive story. Swope immediately gave the assignment to Donald Henderson Clarke, then one of his star reporters, later a well-known novelist.

Fallon didn't want to waste twenty-four hours waiting for Arnstein. Not when there was so much whisky to drink and so many beautiful women about. So he and Clarke went on a bender. Fallon showed he was in better condition than Clarke by lasting through the day and night. Clarke, early in the morning, knew when he was beaten and managed to get a message to his editor that he would be unable to carry through on the assignment. Swope then had George Boothby, another fine newspaperman, take Clarke's place.

There are a number of versions as to Arnstein's actual surrender. Gene Fowler, Fallon's biographer, has it that Fallon and Arnstein came into New York from Westchester together and were met by Miss Brice and the reporter on upper Broadway and the group then drove downtown. On the way they found themselves caught up in New York's annual police parade and drove the length of Fifth Avenue as part of the parade.

Miss Brice, according to her biographer, met Fallon that morning in New York and went with him to upper Broadway, where they met Arnstein. They, too, were reported to have been accompanied by Boothby.

Whichever story is more factual, the basic story is true. Arnstein rode in the police parade with his entourage to the District Attorney's office and there surrendered.

When he was arraigned, however, there was a change in plans. The judge set bail at $100,000, rather than the $60,000 agreed upon and which had been provided by Rothstein. Nicky had to wait in the Tombs while someone went to get extra collateral from Rothstein.

An incident then occurred which was related by Clarke in his book, *In the Reign of Rothstein.* It reveals the potency of Rothstein's name and influence.

To while away time during the wait, Clarke wrote, Miss Brice, Fallon, Harold Norris, of the National Surety Company, and Clarke went to a nearby speakeasy. Fallon and Clarke were well known to the proprietor.

While the group drank and waited, Miss Brice's new Cadillac landaulet was stolen from its parking place outside the speakeasy. Fallon and Norris, working on the thesis that the proprietor knew the persons who had stolen it, demanded that he have the car returned. The proprietor told them to "tell it to the cops."

Clarke then took the proprietor aside. He said it was not important that it was Miss Brice's car, but the thieves ought to know that Miss Brice was under the protection of Arnold Rothstein, who was even then providing bail for Nicky Arnstein, a member of their union.

This put an entirely different face on the theft. The proprietor hurried to a wall phone, put in a call to a number he did not have to look up in the phone book, and returned minutes later to say that the car would be right back, without even a dent in a fender.

It was not a quarter of an hour before four men, one of them Monk Eastman, were back with the car. Eastman, their spokesman, was full of apologies. The boys had not known to whom the car belonged and, even more important, that it belonged to a "friend of A.R."

"The proximity of the District Attorney's office," Clarke wrote, "did not prevent Monk Eastman and his followers from stealing the car. Mere mention of Arnold Rothstein's name got it back."

A short time later the deficiency in collateral arrived. It was in Liberty Bonds!

In addition to providing Arnstein's bond, Rothstein paid all the expenses of his defense. It was not friendship that caused Rothstein to aid Nicky, but self-preservation. Rothstein told his wife, "They're not after Nicky, they're after me. A lot of people would like to tie me into this and some of them think they can get Arnstein to say something that would lead them to me."

A lot of people did think so. When Arnstein was being questioned by detectives and members of the District Attorney's office, he was told repeatedly that if he would tell the full story of the bond thefts and name the man behind them he would be treated most leniently. Time after time he was asked directly what he knew of Rothstein's connections with the bond thefts.

"I know nothing," Nicky said, "of any relevance about any thefts of any kind. I am an innocent man."

Even Clarke, the reporter, was questioned about Rothstein and his connections with the bond thefts. In his book, *Man of the World,* Clarke told how two FBI men transported him to Washington for questioning. They wanted, Clarke wrote, "proof that A.R. was the Man Higher Up."

Clarke said he knew no more than the authorities. He added that he was not a police or law official and it was not his job to investigate rumors or whispers. Besides, if he did know anything, it was part of the confidential relationship which existed between a newspaperman and his source of information.

This did not stop the authorities. For more than a decade, long after Rothstein's death, they continued their hunt for the bonds.

They did not recover them, of course.

Some of the bonds went to England, Scotland, Canada and Cuba in payment for bootleg whisky.

Others were sent to Belgium, France and Switzerland and were used to pay for shipments of narcotics.

Many of them were scattered around the country, among both bucket shops and legitimate brokerage houses. They were turned into cash by a series of maneuvers, and the cash sent to Rothstein.

There has never been any evidence that Rothstein was the "Mastermind." It is quite possible that he had nothing to do with the actual thefts. However, it was because he was available to act as "fence" that the thefts were profitable. The thieves would have had difficulty finding places to dispose of their loot without him.

He did not ask for a pedigree when the bonds were offered to him at a discount. Why should he, when it was almost like buying legal tender for half its face value?

Many times the suspicion was voiced in court that the bonds used by Rothstein in his business activities were stolen. However, no evidence was ever introduced—not by lawyers for surety companies, not by referees in bankruptcy, not by the police—that would prove the charge, give foundation to these suspicions.

Nor could Nicky Arnstein have given truthful evidence which would have linked Rothstein with the thefts.

Rothstein did his best to reward Nicky's "stand-up" performance. It was almost enough to get Nicky out of trouble. It might have been enough had not Fallon fallen in love, head over heels—"like a schoolboy," to quote Nicky—with Gertrude Vanderbilt.

It was a pity that Fallon, after beginning one of his most brilliant defenses, should have failed to stay the limit in the case. As long as he was in the courtroom, Nicky's chances were good.

Fallon "made law" in his defense of Nicky. McGee and he told Nicky to refuse to answer questions asked of him by resorting to the provisions of the Fifth Amendment to the Constitution. Arnstein was held in contempt by the court for this.

Fallon then argued the case in the United States Supreme Court, where he maintained, before the nine black-robed justices, that no man should be deprived of his constitutional rights. "He does not have to give answers that 'might tend to incriminate or degrade him.'" The justices found for Arnstein—and Fallon.

It is this decision which still holds in the cases of all those witnesses who have "taken the Fifth."

Fallon also pleaded that Arnstein's case be tried in Washington, in a federal court, rather than in a New York court. The penalty, in New York, for the crime with which Arnstein was charged, was twenty-five years. The federal penalty was only two years.

The New York charges, no matter what the federal court verdict, had to be dropped. Trying Arnstein on them would have violated the "double jeopardy" provision of the Constitution.

The result of Arnstein's first trial was a hung jury. This, despite the fact that Arnstein did not take the witness stand in his own defense. The combination of McGee's legal knowledge and Fallon's courtroom brilliance overcame this.

It was after this trial, and before the retrial, that Fallon lost all sense of proportion because of a woman. There had been many women in his life, but lovely Gertrude Vanderbilt was "the woman." Because of her he broke with McGee, broke with Arnstein, and even broke with Rothstein.

McGee, far superior in knowledge of the law than Fallon, handled Arnstein's defense in the second trial. He lacked his partner's brilliance, his ability to sell himself to at least one person in the jury box. Nicky was found guilty and sentenced to the federal penitentiary.

Where Fallon had created some doubt in the jury's mind by his cross-examination of the state's witnesses, McGee failed. He could lead witnesses into the same traps, but he could not produce Fallon's effect upon them.

Nicky Arnstein is now long past recriminations. He is living a quiet, semiretired life in California, his only vice trying to dope out three-horse parlays at Hollywood Park or Santa Anita race track. "They needed a fall guy," he said, "and I turned out to be it. I don't hate Fallon and I'm not bitter about him. How can you hate, or be bitter about, a dead man? He let me down, but that was long ago.

"Arnold [Rothstein] went all out to help me. Don't ask me his reasons. I'm not sure that I know them. There have been stories that he collected a lot of money for helping me. Those stories aren't true. Arnold backed my play all the way and there wasn't any charge."

Was Rothstein the "Mastermind" behind the bond thefts?

"If I answered that, I'd be admitting I knew something about the bond thefts and I never did."

Rothstein resented Fallon's desertion of Arnstein. He was not so resentful, however, that he did not reconcile with him and then bring Fallon and McGee together again. He set them up in a new office, provided them with cash.

"Use some of this," he said, giving money to Fallon, "for a haircut and a clean shirt."

"Yes, massa," Fallon replied.

Chapter **14** *He Popped Up Everywhere*

f George Graham Rice did not coin the phrase "You can't kill a sucker" he certainly proved it. Rice, originally Jacob Simon Herzig, was one of the most successful bucket-shop operators in history. He must have had a sense of humor for, after swindling investors of hundreds of thousands of dollars and serving a jail term, he wrote a book titled *My Adventures with Your Money,* and then returned to bucketeering for twenty more "successful" years.

Watson Washburn and Edmund DeLong, in their book, *High and Low Financiers,* expressed much the same conviction as Rice when they wrote, "The sucker is the eternal optimist." They used official records to substantiate their case.

The word "sucker" identified customers of bucket shops in both instances.

No official total of bucket-shop "take" has ever been compiled. Nat J. Ferber, the New York *American* reporter who did more to expose bucketeers and their activities than any other newspaperman, estimated the take in his book, *I Found Out* as $6,000,000,000. His figures, however, included both cash extracted from suckers and the "value" of the securities they supposedly owned.

This much is on the record. In New York State, in one five-year period, bucket shops went into bankruptcy owing their customers more than $212,000,000!

The bucket shop derives its name from those ancient markets

181

where flour and grain were sold in buckets to the poor and needy. The wealthy could buy in larger amounts.

Bucket shops operated in all parts of the United States. They had their beginnings soon after the Civil War when railroad stocks were placed on the market and sold to thousands of investors. Such financiers as Daniel Drew, Jay Gould and Jim Fisk early set the standard for the bucketeers. They created artificial markets, issued public proclamations concerning the value of their stocks, unloaded them at the same time they were doing this, and printed fresh stock as long as there was a demand.

This was larceny—but legal larceny.

By the turn of the century the bucket shops had become firmly entrenched. And they found themselves under attack not from the public but from more respectable brokerage houses. Many of these had started as bucket shops but, having prospered and found religion, the new converts got after their heathen brothers.

It took a third of a century for the legitimate brokerage houses, the New York Stock Exchange, and the big bankers who had connections with security houses to put the bucketeers out of business. When they did so, as the Black Committee which investigated Wall Street revealed, it was not a victory for the righteous over the wicked but for the stronger over the weaker.

The heyday of the bucketeers came during two periods, from about 1900 to 1907 and from 1917 until 1929. The bucketeers operated as successfully outside New York City as in it. The most successful had branch offices throughout the country.

The bucket shop was a cut-rate, bargain-basement securities supermarket. It operated on the layaway, or installment, plan, with very little down. Purchasers of stocks could buy on a margin as low as one point. That meant that by paying just $10 a man could "purchase" ten shares of stock. He owed the balance of the purchase price to the broker and technically was required to pay interest on this indebtedness. In most instances this was disregarded. The customers never did hold the stocks long enough to build up any debt for interest.

Having bought stock on a point margin, the customer actually had only three-quarters of a point leeway, for the other quarter was the bucketeers' commission. If the stock fell more than three-quarters of a point, the broker would sell out the customer at the market. If there was a deficiency, the customer was called on to pay it. Some did.

The bucket shop was a brokerage house. It had the normal complement of tickers and a board on which prices were posted as they came over the tickers. In their early days the bucket shops were straight gambling houses. Their commission was their "vigorish." The customers bet on the numbers that would next appear on the tape.

Each customer would, on purchase, get a slip of paper giving the details of his transaction. A "buy" slip would be blue, a "sell" slip would be white. He could go "long" on the market, that is, buy on the premise that the stock would rise, or go "short," betting that the stock would fall.

Like the operator of a gambling house, the bucket-shop operator had the percentage always running for him. He was getting bets on both sides of the ticker tape and collecting percentages all the time.

Even with the odds against the speculators so high, there were a few who did make a profit in these bucket shops. Probably the most famous of such speculators was the late Jesse L. Livermore, who was known as the "Boy Plunger of Wall Street." Livermore got his start as a speculator in Boston. There he "played the tape" and made his first big stake. Later he went to New York, where he continued to trade in bucket shops.

Livermore told Richard D. Wyckoff, publisher of the *Magazine of Wall Street*, "I had ten years' experience in bucket shops before I began trading in regular brokerage houses. One of the reasons why this form of speculating was valuable to me was because it practically forced me to trade with a 'stop.' [A "stop" was an order to buy or sell at a certain price.] I had to put up only two points margin in a bucket shop and, of course, if it went against me one and three-quarters I was wiped out of that trade. But it was good training for me because it limited my risk and got me in the habit of letting my profits run."

The early type of bucket shop went out of business with the panic of 1907. For the next few years there was virtually no money available for speculation. However, with the First World War this changed. And the public sale of Liberty Bonds resulted in the public once again becoming interested in investments and securities. And the booming economy produced excess cash.

The hustlers and thieves began operations to get this cash. As a result, a new type of bucket shop was born, a bucket shop that marked the difference that a score of years had made.

These new places were lush, provided with a good front. Some of them were far more lavishly furnished than legitimate brokerage houses. The ticker and blackboard were still there, but a number of new features had been added. These included high-pressure salesmen, customers' men and a "boiler room." This latter was an inner office, equipped with banks of telephones, at which salesmen sat. All day, six days a week, these salesmen called potential suckers. The lists they used were the names of men and women who had subscribed to tipster services of various kinds. George Graham Rice, for instance, used the list of customers from his horse-racing tipster sheets.

The foundation upon which the bucketeers built was the Consolidated Stock Exchange, originally located on the corner of Broad and Beaver Streets. Its president was Jacob ("Jakey") Fields, a dynamic little man who suffered from insomnia and gambling fever.

The Consolidated had a long history. It was originally called the Consolidated Stock and Petroleum Exchange and included among its members such illustrious persons as John D. Rockefeller, Henry H. Rogers and all the early oil tycoons. There was a period when transactions in oil stocks, according to Wyckoff, were greater than those in railroad shares.

However, this phase of the Exchange's activities ended when Standard Oil decided to end competition in the industry. It did this by leaving a standing order on the floor to buy and sell at fifty cents a barrel any quantity of oil. Since the heart of speculation is fluctuation, it killed oil speculation at the source.

The Consolidated members dealt in odd lots of stock in multiples of ten shares, but not as many as a hundred. The Big Board would take no orders for less than 100-share lots and that left a large group of customers for Consolidated. However, it wasn't because of odd-lot deals that the bucket shops depended upon the Consolidated. It was because they could list their "house" stocks on that exchange, deal in them, and have available quotations.

The best way to demonstrate the workings of a bucket shop is to give the case history of George Graham Rice and Idaho Copper stock. This will also demonstrate Rothstein's unique contributions to this multimillion larceny. Rothstein's relations with Rice were much the same as they were with many others in the field.

Rice was, according to Washburn and DeLong, the "most audacious, plausible and successful swindler" in this country's history. In his early days—he was born in New York, on the lower East Side, of hard-working, honest parents—he was a petty thief and forger. He went to Sing Sing and Elmira for prison terms.

On his release from prison, about 1900, he became the first mail-order racing tipster in the country.

His success was instantaneous when the first horse he publicly advertised won at long odds. Realizing there was nothing like success to breed profits, he spent a great deal of money to get the best information obtainable for his clients. Once he had ingratiated himself with these, he started to cheat. He would give a number of horses in the same race to his clients and the winners always came back for more. The losers, recalling earlier profits, also would return for more.

Over a three-year period, according to the United States Attorney's office, which closed him up in 1903, he averaged a profit of about $1,000,000 annually.

After this experience Rice went to Tonopah and Goldfield, in Nevada, scene of a big mining strike. He now became interested in mining stocks. He also became a partner in two banks, and in a number of mines which did not pan out. Like so many others who lived off the gullibility of suckers, he was a sucker himself. He was taken in by promoters who outsmarted him and he went broke.

He returned to New York, where he started to promote a stock known as Rawhide Coalition. He succeeded in getting this listed on the Curb Exchange and, using flamboyant advertisements and "endorsements" from prominent figures like the late Broadway favorite Nat C. Goodwin, he sold a great deal of this stock. However, this venture ended when the Curb investigated the value of the stock and, finding it had none, removed it from its board.

One stock was as good as another to him and one corporate entity no different from another. So he organized B. H. Sheftels and Company and established branch offices in Chicago, Philadelphia, Boston and Detroit. This time he did not bother to list his stock on any exchange, but used his boiler rooms, his financial newsletter and his outside salesmen to peddle the valueless stock. His take was close to $1,000,000—again according to the federal government.

Rice had made the mistake of writing to some of his prospective victims and this had resulted in a mail fraud charge against him.

Rice went to jail for ten months, convicted in a federal court. There were no state laws under which he was liable.

He next attained newsworthiness in 1920, when he was arrested on a charge of grand larceny involving money received for securities. He was found guilty and sentenced to Sing Sing. He immediately changed lawyers and his new counsel obtained his freedom on a technicality. He was ordered retried, but the case never came up. His new lawyers were William J. Fallon and Eugene McGee.

He was now ready to launch his biggest coup. It yielded him $25,000,000!

His preparation was thorough. To start the ball rolling, he began to print a financial newspaper called the *Iconoclast*. His editorial policy was twofold. On the one hand, it was bitter in its attacks on the financial powers of the country. It blamed "Wall Street" for all the ills that affected the people. It charged that multimillionaires and insiders were using the Stock Exchange to mulct hundreds of thousands of innocents of millions of dollars. On the other hand, he promised his subscribers his own "private" information.

This was a very popular campaign, so popular that the daily circulation of the *Iconoclast*, which had a national distribution, was soon over 300,000.

He soon had the biggest sucker list in America. He sold off parts of his list to other bucket shops, but only after he had first mulcted the persons on the list.

This was immaterial to the purchasers. Like Rice, they believed that old suckers never died. There was always a little more loot, even in lists that had already been exploited.

Once Rice had set up his suckers he started to work on them. His medium was a corporation he called the Colombia Emerald Company. According to the stories in the *Iconoclast*, a Colombian priest had discovered an ancient map which led him to a mine abandoned by the Incas when Pizarro conquered the Inca kingdom. The mine had been located and was now operating, producing emeralds valued in the millions.

There were, even then, few come-ons that were older or more exploited. Just the same, the suckers bit. They took the bait to the tune of a half million dollars. However, this was so flagrant a larceny that it did not last long. The authorities issued an injunction restraining further sales of the stock. They also threatened criminal prosecution.

When Rice appeared at the office of the United States Attorney, Gene McGee was with him. McGee quoted the law. So long as there actually was a mine in South America—and Rice, acting on his attorney's instructions had purchased such a mine for $800—Rice was not liable to criminal prosecution. There was no prosecution.

The *Iconoclast* played up the story of the injunction. This was just another of the tricks of Wall Street, intended to prevent the little man from becoming a millionaire. But Rice was too smart for these powerful interests. He had discovered another mine—this one a copper mine—that would yield a golden return.

On the front page of the *Iconoclast* there appeared, in large-size type, boxed on the front page:

SELL ANY STOCK YOU OWN AND BUY IDAHO COPPER, NOW ON THE BOSTON CURB. WE KNOW WHAT THIS LANGUAGE MEANS AND WE MEAN IT.

Rice owned some 1,300,000 shares of Idaho Copper, for which he had paid $10,000, approximately eight cents a share. The mine had not been worked for more than twenty years. The stock had two big assets. It was listed on the Boston Curb Exchange and it actually existed.

When Rice began his campaign the stock was listed at about ten cents a share. Shortly after his advice first appeared in the *Iconoclast* it began to spurt. It went to $6.25 a share, as thousands of suckers rushed to get in on the ground floor. After all, had not Rice tipped the stock when it could be bought for pennies?

"Idaho Copper goes to 6¼—sky rocketing move to $25 now forecast as result of ore disclosures!" This was the headline in the *Iconoclast*. And the repeated exhortation: BUY! BUY! BUY!

Of course, wherever there was a buyer there had to be a seller. In this case it was Rice, unloading his 1,300,000 shares of stock.

Once again the federal authorities stepped in. Once again Rice was enjoined from selling a stock—in this case Idaho Copper. And, once again, Gene McGee appeared with Rice in the courtroom. For the first time the Bureau of Securities of the State Attorney General's office took action. It quickly found that it had no jurisdiction—as McGee had maintained in his brief.

Idaho Copper fell to ten cents a share. So Rice announced in the *Iconoclast* that there had been a tremendous new strike! In addition, Idaho Copper had bought the properties of the Idaho Copper Company, Ltd.

The Boston Curb Exchange ordered that stock of the Idaho Copper Corporation be withdrawn from sale and its listing canceled. At the same time the Boston Exchange permitted Rice to substitute Idaho Copper Company, Ltd., stock on the listing.

Rice reported this to his faithful readers. Once again, he told them, they and he had been the victims of the predatory interests, but he had already moved to circumvent the villains. A page-one story in the *Iconoclast* told the suckers that they could now exchange one share of the old stock for one of the new.

If the investors were wise, the story said, they would not only convert their old stock, but would load up on the new.

So much business poured into Rice's office that he had to move from the suite he occupied at 28 West Fifty-seventh Street to a loft building on East Seventeenth Street, which he occupied from basement to roof.

Both the former office and the new one were in buildings which Rothstein owned. Rice paid Rothstein a high rent, but he got more than office space for it. How high a "rent" was revealed when he was back in court some time later.

The federal government continued its investigation of Rice. He called it "harassment" in the *Iconoclast*. Engineers from the Bureau of Mines were sent from Washington to examine and appraise both the old mining properties and new ones. They reported the original mines were abandoned, worthless and completely flooded.

The new properties were only half flooded and did contain copper ore. However, this ore was of such low grade that it was unprofitable to mine it.

Rice was again indicted, charged with using the mails to defraud.

A court order was issued, placing the company in receivership, and the receiver was told to seek out all Rice's assets and place them in escrow for the benefit of the stockholders.

After searching office safes, bank boxes and Rice's suite in the Hotel Chatham, the only assets discovered were a $100 Liberty Bond, a copper penny, and thousands of certificates for stock in Rice's many enterprises.

Rice's books were examined. These records were almost valueless. However, the auditors found a record of loans made to Rice by Arnold Rothstein. These totaled $262,800!

Rothstein was questioned about these loans. He said Rice had come to him for money, that he had lent the money to Rice, and that Rice had posted collateral to secure the loans. The collateral? Liberty Bonds, of course. Rothstein would hardly have taken copper stock.

Where was the collateral? Sold. Rice had defaulted on his loans and Rothstein, as was his legal right, had sold the bonds.

Both Rice and Rothstein held to this story. It was illogical on its face. Rice was daily receiving tens of thousands of dollars in cash.

He probably had more cash than Rothstein at any given moment. Why, then, should he borrow money from Rothstein? For that matter, Rice could very easily have cashed in the Liberty Bonds if he was temporarily short of cash. Why make the loan, then?

The answer is that Rice did not make any loan. The story was a fiction. Rice had paid Rothstein for protection. This was the "rent" Rothstein had collected. Rice, for some unknown reason, had entered this transaction in his books, called it a loan.

After Rothstein's death, Rice altered his story of the loan. He sued the administrators of Rothstein's estate for return of some $70,000, maintaining this was due him from "business transactions" with Rothstein. These transactions, his plea for subpoenaing the Rothstein records declared, had resulted in his giving Rothstein the Liberty Bonds in the amount of $262,800.

Federal Judge Bryant heard Rice's plea and denied it. He said there was no evidence to back Rice and he refused to issue the subpoenas. Rice dropped the suit.

As a result of the copper company bucketeering, Rice was sent to jail. When he was freed, Rothstein was dead and the boom days of the bucket shop were gone forever. For the record, Fallon and McGee were not Rice's counsel when he was convicted.

The story of George Graham Rice, interesting though it is, is important only because of Rice's connections with Rothstein and the firm of Fallon and McGee.

No matter how much he differed from other bucketeers, in this respect Rice was like most of the big, successful brethren in the field. Some of his take went directly to Rothstein, directly to Fallon and McGee. In Rice's case, it was disguised as a loan. Other bucketeers called their pay-off money by different names.

The law firm was involved because it was "house counsel" to Rothstein. He, in turn, arranged protection for Rice. That protection included the best legal talent available. That was as necessary as a bondsman, in case of arrest, a "connection" with Tammany, in order to do business.

Rothstein was the principal here. Once again, he was the necessary man.

Bucketeering was big, profitable and crooked. If it required less financing than other rackets, it required even more protection and influence.

The biggest need was protection from interference by the law. This danger was diverse. It came from the police, who might move on a complaint, or from the District Attorney's office, which might take some action. Rothstein had friends in both places.

But the danger also stemmed from another source. There was always the possibility that the state legislature would pass some kind of regulatory law. Someone was needed to exert influence to prevent enactment of any such law. Someone whose connections went all the way to Albany.

Here Rothstein fitted peculiarly, in a way no one else did. He could act individually. He could act through Tom Foley. He could use his influence with Murphy. Murphy, in turn, made "suggestions" to Democratic legislators in Albany. Of course, "suggestions" were made by other persons to the Republican legislators as well.

Rothstein collected from the bucketeers and turned over funds to district leaders and campaign treasurers. Such always are in need of "contributions," and they rarely forget their friends.

When, as did happen, some bucketeer became involved with the law, Rothstein was ready with help. He posted bail bonds. He provided counsel. He interceded with his friends in the District Attorney's office, with his friends in the police department. There were judges with whom he was most friendly.

The function which Rothstein performed in New York was performed by others in most major cities throughout the country. Everywhere that bucketeers operated, someone was acting for them in fighting legislation, in buying protection, in safeguarding their activities. It did not matter who controlled the state administrations —Democrats or Republicans. There were always some crooked legislators and crooked politicians with their hands out.

Rothstein was the overseer in New York. Ferber reported, at the end of his investigation: "Rothstein popped up everywhere. . . .

In my . . . investigations of bucketeers or their aides, I found that
with very few exceptions all had had some dealings with [him].
. . . He had helped one get a ticker wire; he had lined up a high-
priced lawyer for another; he had gotten a third an interview with
a big Tammany leader. Rothstein, more than any one or five politicians, was in on the birth or death of many bucket shops."

There was a good reason for this omnipresence. Ferber referred
to Rothstein as an "underworld busybody." He was. That was his
business.

He maintained a close relationship with Jakey Fields, head of
the Consolidated Exchange. He gambled with Fields. He traded his
Liberty Bonds and other securities through the Consolidated. His
insurance firm carried all the insurance on the Exchange and much
of Fields's personal insurance.

No wonder Rothstein could get a ticker wire or arrange for his
friend, Phil Kastel, to get membership in the Consolidated.

And, as to lining up a "high-priced lawyer," all he had to do was
tell Fallon and McGee he wanted them to defend some individual
temporarily in legal trouble because of bucket-shop activities.

Rothstein's closest associate in bucketeering was Charles A.
Stoneham.

Born in Jersey City, New Jersey, Stoneham had left school early
and gone to work in the New York financial district while still in
short pants. He served a long apprenticeship as stock salesman and,
later as a "dynamiter" in a boiler room. A dynamiter was the super-
visor of the boiler room, the man who was called on to close the
deals. Later Stoneham became a floor partner for various bucket
shops and then went into business for himself.

Stoneham was a man who put on weight early in life. By the time
he was in his middle thirties he was a walking mass of blubber.
But, if his body was flabby, his mind was keen. He, more than anyone else, was responsible for transforming the old-fashioned bucket
shop into the sleek, mechanized operation that it became during
World War I.

He was able to operate and grow rich in this field, not because
he broke the law but because, for a long period of time, there were

no laws to break. When such laws were passed, Stoneham was shrewd enough to get out of the bucket-shop business. His activities did not go unnoticed by the law, for he was indicted for both perjury and income tax evasion. But, like Rothstein, he was not found guilty of any crime.

Again like Rothstein, he was a big gambler and very interested in sports. They met even before Stoneham went into business for himself. They gambled together. Stoneham bet with Rothstein on horses and gambled in his gambling houses. When Stoneham became head of the gambling syndicate which took over the casino and race track in Havana, Cuba, Rothstein was one of his partners.

It was Rothstein who acted as middleman in the deal whereby Stoneham, John McGraw and Judge McQuade purchased the New York Giants baseball team from Tammany sachem Andrew Freedman.

Stoneham, the poor boy from Jersey City, became a millionaire, most of his wealth tracing to his bucket-shop profits. Ferber called him "the godfather of the bucket shops," who initiated their chain-store type of operation.

"The largest bucketeers in the country," Ferber wrote, "seemed to stem from the Chicago and New York offices of Stoneham and Co. Bill Jones, of Jones and Baker, was a Stoneham graduate, as were a dozen others. And these others, in turn, fathered the entire band of thieves which quartered in the three-million-dollar shelter known as the 'Consolidated Stock Exchange.' "

In every investigation of bucket shops the names of Rothstein, Stoneham, Fallon and McGee were important. In bankruptcies and trials these same names occurred time after time.

Chapter **15** *File #77*

In 1921 Charles A. Stoneham, grown wealthy, the
owner of a championship baseball team and with
major interests in Havana, closed his numerous brokerage firms.

Customers, whose holdings aggregated more than $4,000,000, were
listed in his books.

When Stoneham retired from the bucketing field he sold his ac-
counts and goodwill to a number of other firms. Among these were
E. M. Fuller and Company, E. H. Clarke and Company, Dillon and
Company (a name which for a generation has plagued those legiti-
mate firms with the name "Dillon" in their titles), and E. D. Dier and
Company. Among the operators of these successor firms were Phil
Kastel, Ross Robinson, Harold Sonking and—especially—Edward M.
Fuller and William McGee.

On retiring, Stoneham sent a form letter to all his customers, telling them that the companies which were taking over his brokerage
accounts had a good moral and financial standing. He could recom-
mend all of them most highly.

Almost all his customers then began to trade through these successor firms.

In the next two years every one of these firms went into bankruptcy.

Some went into bankruptcy voluntarily. Most were forced into it
by action of the authorities, primarily federal authorities. The total
loss to customers of these firms was more than $20,000,000.

In most instances no criminal action was taken against the various

194

members of the different firms. They could be forced out of business but they could not be charged, under existing law, with any crime.

The Hearst newspapers were deeply interested in the bucket-shop cases. They had long campaigned against bucket shops and had gathered much of the evidence which was used in forcing some of them out of business.

That interest began at the top—with William Randolph Hearst. And it went back to Hearst's short-lived political career. The reasons for the interest were rumors and suspicions that Tom Foley and Arnold Rothstein were deeply involved in the Fuller-McGee case.

Hearst had never forgiven Foley, now a man past seventy, for his defeats in 1905 and 1906. If it were not for Foley, he felt, he might well have been elected mayor, then governor. And what would there have been to stop him if he sought the Presidency afterward?

Hearst had still another political ax to grind. He was engaged in a feud with Governor Alfred E. Smith, a Foley protégé.

Foley was of the mold that had formed Croker, Sullivan and Murphy. He had been born in Williamsburg, now a part of Brooklyn, but had remedied that error by moving to Manhattan just before his twenty-first birthday, in 1873. He had gone into the saloon and gambling house business almost at once and had, of course, prospered.

A few years later he bought a saloon on the East Side and was elected a district leader. Next he opened a new saloon at Centre and Franklin Streets, across from the Criminal Courts Building and the Tombs. This became a meeting place for politicians, lawyers, judges and gamblers.

From operating saloons and gambling houses Foley decided he had the qualifications to hold public office. He was elected to the City Council, then to its successor, the Board of Aldermen. In 1907 he was elected sheriff of Manhattan. With this office he had attained the height of his ambitions. He served one term, then was content to become a private citizen again.

He was leader of the Second District, close friend of Murphy, and successor to Big Tim Sullivan in the councils of Tammany. In addition to his other activities he operated a real estate and bail-bond business next door to his Centre Street saloon. He and Arnold Rothstein were closely connected in both fields, sharing many commissions.

If Hearst disliked Foley, Foley disliked Hearst as much. In 1923 Foley was seeking to unseat John F. Hylan, the Hearst candidate, as mayor of New York.

This background was known to Nat Ferber when he was given orders by his editor to investigate the bucket-shop mess. He was not surprised when he was told, "Get Foley." This was, as all concerned knew, no easy task. But, in a way, Ferber succeeded.

Among the firms which Ferber investigated was that of Fuller and McGee. This company went into forced bankruptcy, its customers losing some $5,000,000. An investigation revealed enough evidence to warrant the two partners being indicted. They could not be found. It might be that the police did not know where to look.

Arthur Garfield Hays, in his book, *City Lawyer*, revealed how he learned their whereabouts. Hays had been retained by the firm some time previous to their bankruptcy. He wrote:

"After the bankruptcy of E. M. Fuller and Company, the assets, Fuller, and McGee all vanished. A few weeks later a telephone call summoned me to a brownstone house on the upper West Side. I asked who lived there. 'Arnold Rothstein.' . . . Fuller and McGee were comfortably living in Rothstein's home, waiting for the storm to subside. They were expecting Bill Fallon that afternoon."

The two men gave themselves up shortly thereafter. They were tried twice, defended by Fallon and McGee, and each time there was a hung jury. When Ferber began his investigation they were awaiting a third trial.

Ferber received permission from the District Attorney to examine the records of the firm. These, as he quickly discovered, were incomplete, assembled without order, badly kept and out of balance. It was obvious that someone had been at these records before Ferber.

However, among the myriad papers, Ferber discovered "File

#77." Inside that file was a canceled check for $10,000, made out to, and endorsed by, Tom Foley. Also in the file were a number of checks which totaled $353,000.

These checks had all been made out to Arnold Rothstein.

While Ferber was making his painstaking investigation the partners were tried a third time and, again, there was a hung jury. One of the jurors in this case was Charles W. Rendigs.

The District Attorney's office was preparing to drop the case when Ferber appeared with his evidence. The District Attorney had no choice now but to order a new trial.

As soon as the checks, made out to Rothstein, were discovered, Rothstein was inescapably tied into the case. He was immediately subpoenaed and began a series of appearances in various courtrooms and referees' chambers that were to continue to the time of his death.

He was forced to produce books and give evidence. He was indicted by a state court for perjury and by a federal court for income tax evasion. Stoneham, too, was brought into the case and indicted with Rothstein on one count.

Of primary interest to various courts, to a number of surety companies, and to receivers for the bankrupt company was where the millions poured into Fuller and McGee's company had gone. All of these felt that Rothstein could give them at least a partial answer. They had the mass of checks for a third of a million dollars.

Rothstein and his attorneys fought to keep out of court. They fought against producing books and records. Usually it was a losing fight.

However, when Rothstein did appear, lugging his books and records, these proved of little help to the inquiring attorneys. Rothstein's records were what he said they were; they were indecipherable to anyone else. He admitted they were sketchily kept, saying blandly he had a "good head for figures and did not have to write anything down."

The "good head" was no help to the frustrated examiners. "When I wipe out a deal in my head, I forget all about it," he said repeatedly.

His appearance belied a real nervousness. The first time he testified he suffered an attack of dysentery. Later appearances frequently
brought on the same disability.

Yet, in a perverse way, he enjoyed his appearances. It was a continuing battle of wits and he delighted in the contest. He jousted
with the lawyers, waving off his own attorney. He spouted legal
gibberish which he had learned from years of contact with many
lawyers.

He acted as though it was his show and others involved were only
spear carriers. He would sit, seemingly relaxed, in the witness chair,
hands in his lap, legs crossed. He made a good witness for himself.
He rarely let either vanity or anger trip him.

He avoided direct answers when he could. Made his own deci-
sions as to whether a question was "irrelevant and immaterial."

In one instance he announced, "This hearing is illegal and I am
going into the United States District Court and ask to have the proceedings certified."

Referee Coffin, one of the many to preside at such hearings, first
appeared baffled and then said tartly, "You have used the wrong
term. I do the certifying here."

Unruffled, Rothstein answered, "Then do something about it."

From the start Rothstein had a set answer for any question that
he felt might be dangerous or entangling. He said, "I refuse to answer that question on the ground that my answer might tend to
degrade or incriminate me." Fallon had taught this to him, just as he
had earlier taught it to Arnstein.

There is no doubt that his interrogators were allowed great leeway. In 1923 William M. Chadbourne, a distinguished attorney, represented the receivers. He put Rothstein through the most severe
grilling the man ever faced. He delved deeply into Rothstein's past,
with special emphasis on the 1919 World Series.

From the outset Rothstein admitted he had received all the checks
which bore his endorsement. However, he claimed that these were
merely evidence of an "accommodation." He had advanced money
to Fuller and the checks had been repayment of these advances, not,

as Chadbourne and others claimed, payment of Fuller's gambling losses. (Fuller was a gambler, but his partner was not.)

Pressed as to whether he had ever gambled with Fuller, Rothstein finally admitted that he had, but he said, "I lose," in the gambler's vernacular. He maintained that Fuller was one of the few who beat him on wagers.

Chadbourne, seeking to lay a foundation for later questions, asked, "Did you wager on the 1919 World Series?"

"I object," Rothstein answered, "on the ground that the question is irrelevant and immaterial."

Referee Coffin asked Chadbourne if he could sustain the question.

"I am seeking to prove," Chadbourne said, "that the witness had full knowledge that the Series was fixed and that, with this knowledge, he won various wagers including some from Mr. Fuller." His further contention was that any such wagers won by Rothstein were criminal and that Rothstein should be forced to return such money to the receivers for distribution to the creditors.

Rothstein broke in and said, "This baseball thing has been the sore spot of my career. I faced a Grand Jury and was vindicated."

Coffin, however, agreed to Chadbourne's pursuing the line of questioning he had begun. Rothstein said, "I object and I want this objection in the record."

Chadbourne ignored this and asked, "Didn't you hire counsel to appear in your behalf in the investigation?"

Rothstein snapped, "You ought to be ashamed to ask me that. This is no place to ask that kind of question. You ought to be ashamed. Before I'd be a tool like you, I'd jump into the Hudson River."

"Strike that remark from the record," Coffin told the stenographer.

"You know that isn't fair," Rothstein said.

"Strike that remark from the record also," the referee ordered.

Chadbourne's next question was, "Didn't you hire Attorney William J. Fallon to defend Abraham Attell and Joseph J. Sullivan after they were indicted by a Cook County Grand Jury?"

"Absolutely not," Rothstein answered, blandly perjuring himself.

He turned again to the referee and announced, "I'm not going to answer any more questions like that."

The referee told him that he had better answer the questions or face a citation for contempt.

Rothstein shrugged, looked at his attorney, who nodded. He turned to Chadbourne. "Go ahead." He was a potentate granting a supplicant permission to speak.

"Did you bet with Fuller on the 1919 Series?"

"I made a lot of bets. It's a long time. I'm not sure I remember."

"Check your records," Coffin suggested.

Rothstein opened one of the pile of books resting beside him. Finally he said, "Yes."

"How much did you bet with Fuller?" Chadbourne pressed.

"The bet was $25,000."

"Then you won $25,000 from Fuller on a Series that was fixed," Chadbourne exulted.

Here Rothstein threw his bombshell. "I didn't win," he said. "I lost." And, as Chadbourne stood deflated before him, Rothstein grandiloquently waved a canceled check in the air. "I happen to have with me the check with which I paid." He handed it to Chadbourne, who had no choice but to accept it and, on the motion of Rothstein's counsel, to have it marked as an exhibit.

At the next session Chadbourne opened up a new line of questioning. A check of the Fuller and McGee books had revealed that Rothstein had borrowed $172,358 from the firm, giving Liberty Bonds as collateral. This followed earlier revelations that Rothstein had borrowed some $407,000 from Dillon and Company, Phil Kastel's bucket shop, using Liberty Bonds as collateral for that loan. In neither case did Rothstein ever pay the loan, permitting the lenders to take over the collateral.

An interested observer at this hearing, as he had been at earlier hearings, was Abraham Meyers of the National Surety Company. Meyers had said that he hoped some evidence might be forthcoming linking these Liberty Bonds with those stolen during the preceding years from the Wall Street messengers.

Rothstein admitted making the loan from Fuller and McGee and then Chadbourne asked, "Where did you get those bonds?"

Rothstein immediately appealed to the referee. "There's some double meaning in that question," he said. "I don't want to answer it. Mr. Chadbourne has an ulterior motive in asking it that I get but you don't. I can't compete against Mr. Chadbourne. He's a lawyer. He's too full of tricks. He's trying to force me to tell untruths."

Coffin told Rothstein that he would have to answer the question. "You have an attorney who will safeguard your interest."

Chadbourne repeated his question and the answer was unsatisfactory. Now Chadbourne appealed to Coffin, asking that Rothstein be forced to give a more satisfactory reply.

Rothstein told Coffin, "I answered that way to keep from going into details." Then he added, "Besides, your questions don't make sense."

Chadbourne and Coffin absorbed this forerunner of double-talk and Coffin advised Chadbourne to rephrase the question.

"I will ask my questions simply," Chadbourne said, "and I will ask the referee to direct that the witness give forthright answers. Where did you buy the Liberty Bonds, or, if you did not buy them, where did you procure them?"

"Now," Rothstein said, "that's a question I can answer. I can't remember. I racked my brains and looked over every paper in my office, but I can't remember."

Chadbourne could not control his temper. "It is perfectly obvious," he snapped, "that the witness is not only being evasive, he is being untruthful."

Of course, Rothstein was lying. He perjured himself time after time all during the five years when he was questioned about Fuller and McGee. But he was not the only liar. Fuller, seeking to alleviate the punishment he faced, lied too. Both of them were engaged in a battle for self-preservation.

Their testimony was diametrically opposed. Rothstein, for instance, said his records showed that he had made but two bets with Fuller over the years. One of these was on the 1919 Series and the other on the 1920 Kentucky Derby. What was more, Rothstein said, Fuller won both of those bets.

Fuller, on the other hand, swore he had gambled with Rothstein over a long period of years, wagering on anything from whether the license number of the next auto that passed ended in an odd or an even number to which cube of sugar a fly would first alight on. What was more, Fuller said wryly, he never won a single bet.

George Z. Medalie, Rothstein's attorney at the hearing where Fuller made this statement, said, "It is the most remarkable situation in the history of gambling that Fuller could have made something more than sixty bets on various types of sporting events and have lost every single one of these bets."

Justice Gibbs, of the New York State Supreme Court, before whom Fuller testified, heard Fuller's testimony, heard McGee corroborate that testimony, and then heard Rothstein swear to a completely opposite set of facts. The justice said, "Someone is obviously lying." He was right and wrong. All the principals were lying.

Like so many other investigations in which politicians were concerned, this one, too, was hardly thorough. Bitter as were the personal attacks on Rothstein, counsel were always careful to avoid getting to the relationship between Rothstein and Foley, between Rothstein and Murphy. This was a no man's land that both sides agreed to ignore.

The big campaign against Foley petered out. The evidence of the check was there, but it was never really followed up. Foley, almost senile, was a target that aroused pity. Appearing on the witness stand, he created sympathy for himself. A slashing attack on him would only have hurt the attackers. So, instead of Hearst's using Foley as a wedge to show the relationship between bucketeering and politics, he had to be content with a one-day sensation.

Eventually the prime targets of the investigation became Rothstein and Fallon.

Rothstein stayed under attack until 1928. He last appeared in a courtroom on June 23 of that year, and once again it was in an attempt by the receivers to recover money from him for the creditors of Fuller and McGee. By this time George C. Sprague was receiver and it was he who questioned Rothstein. Sprague spent a lot of time trying to prove what the whole world believed, that Rothstein was a gambler.

And Rothstein tried desperately to avoid giving a direct answer.

"What is your business?" Sprague asked.

"I am in the insurance business."

"Has that always been your business?"

"No."

"In what other business have you been engaged?"

"I've done a lot of things."

"I don't doubt that," Sprague said, "but I will rephrase my question. Have you ever been a bookmaker?"

Rothstein asked the judge, "Do I have to answer that?"

"It's an easy question to answer," the judge replied. "Yes or no."

"Well," Rothstein said to Sprague, "yes and no. In 1914 and 1915 I was a betting commissioner."

"Didn't you operate gambling houses between 1913 and 1922?"

"I was interested in some clubs," Rothstein said. "I had some partners."

Sprague asked that the witness be forced to give more responsive answers and the judge told Rothstein to answer the questions.

"That's what I'm doing," Rothstein said. "I can't help it if he don't like the answers."

"Those clubs you mentioned," Sprague said, "were really gambling houses, were they not?"

"I suppose you would call them that."

"I do call them that. You took the profits of these gambling houses, did you not?"

"I had partners in the gambling houses—" Rothstein caught himself up. "In the clubs, I mean. If we won, we divided the money. If we lost, we made up the bankroll."

"That last didn't happen," Sprague said.

"You'd be surprised how often," Rothstein said.

Sprague sought to get testimony about Rothstein's reputation from Joseph F. Levins, who described himself as a "betting commissioner." "What," Sprague asked, "would you know about Mr. Rothstein's activities as a gambler?"

"He'll bet on anything," Levins said. "Everybody knows he's the biggest gambler in the country."

This last part of Levins' answer was stricken from the record as based on hearsay.

Rothstein was then recalled to the stand and Sprague asked him, "Would you agree with Mr. Levins that you would gamble on anything?"

"Absolutely not," Rothstein responded. "I don't bet on football or boxing."

This was about as true as the majority of the answers Rothstein had given.

In 1924 Rothstein was indicted for perjury, as was Fuller. The charge was that they had lied about a business deal involving Fuller's Rolls-Royce automobile. In this instance both had given the same testimony. They swore that Fuller had borrowed $6,000 from Rothstein in 1922 and given the car as collateral for the loan. They both maintained that this transaction took place before Fuller filed a bankruptcy petition and before his firm was found insolvent.

Rothstein and Fuller also agreed in their testimony that Fuller had not repaid the loan and that Rothstein had then sold the car for $5,000.

The Grand Jury accepted one part of the testimony—that Fuller had given the car to Rothstein and that the latter had sold it—but decided both men had lied about the date of the transaction. On that basis, the perjury indictment declared that they had both lied in order to conceal an asset of a bankrupt from the courts.

This perjury indictment never came to trial. Nor, for that matter, did another indictment that arose from the trial. This was one for income tax evasion.

In 1922 Rothstein filed an income tax return which showed a gross income of $31,544.48 and a net of $7,257.29, for the preceding year. The government, on the basis of an examination of the books of Fuller and McGee, charged that Rothstein's gross income had been at least $70,227.88, and that his net was $45,490.29, on which he owed a tax of $4,795.32. This was considerably more than the check for $35.25 which Rothstein had dutifully sent to the Bureau of Internal Revenue on March 15, 1922.

This indictment, like perjury indictments against Fuller and Charles Stoneham, just died.

The one indictment that did come to trial was that of William J. Fallon on a charge of jury bribing.

It was noted earlier that a juror named Charles W. Rendigs had sat in one of the trials of Fuller and McGee, a trial which had resulted in a hung jury. Now when Rendigs was being questioned, before acceptance, he was asked if he knew any of the principals in the case or their counsel. He had sworn that he did not.

The *American*, checking jury records, discovered that Rendigs lied. He had served as a juror in a federal court case involving another brokerage house—Durrell, Gregory—and that trial had also resulted in a hung jury.

Immediately the newspaper went to the authorities. Here was the chance to prove what had so long been suspected—that Fallon didn't win cases on the law and his eloquence alone.

Rendigs was indicted and, as soon as he was, he began to talk. He not only admitted that he had lied, but he also swore that Fallon had paid him $1,000 to hang the Durrell, Gregory jury.

About this time Fallon had a falling out with one of his employees, a 300-pound, woman-crazy investigator named Ernie Eidlitz. He fired Eidlitz, charging Eidlitz with forging his name to some checks. Eidlitz, bitter at losing his job, turned on Fallon by going to the *American* and offering to give the newspaper the lowdown on Fallon's activities. He speedily agreed to corroborate Rendigs' testimony.

And, simultaneously, the United States Attorney's office and other law-enforcement agencies were told that Fuller and McGee, tired of moving in and out of jail, were ready to turn state's evidence, plead guilty to one of the various counts against them, and put an end to the uncertainty in which they lived.

However, neither Fuller nor McGee offered any evidence against

Foley, Rothstein or Stoneham. Removed from jail, established in more pleasant surroundings, permitted visits from their wives, they paid off solely with evidence against Fallon. And so, at the end of the long case, Fallon became the lone target.

Fallon, during this period, was almost constantly drunk. He neglected his practice, fought with his friends. His one interest was Miss Vanderbilt. It undoubtedly was whisky which caused him, when he heard that he was indicted, to hide from the police. Ultimately he was found, and he said he had hidden out only because he was attempting to raise bail. Once that had been arranged, he said, he would have surrendered.

It was a weak excuse, made even weaker when Rothstein provided Fallon's bail minutes after Fallon was arraigned. But there was nothing weak about the defense Fallon offered for the most important client in his career, himself.

The evidence against Fallon appeared to be unbeatable. Rendigs was ready to testify that he had been bribed. There was the check which Fallon was supposed to have paid to Rendigs. Eidlitz was prepared to tell of his part in the bribery. Fuller and McGee were going to add their testimony, corroborate Rendigs' statement that he had met with Fallon in the office of the two brokers.

No wonder that Federal Judge McClintic, trying the case, remarked that "Fallon has his back to the wall."

Fallon seized on the phrase, threw it back at the judge. "Fallon's back is not to the wall. He is in the front line. Fallon is the victim of a gigantic conspiracy." Fallon had finally found the starring part for which he had been searching so many years. He could dramatize not only his cause but himself.

His defense was built on his charge that he was the victim of a conspiracy. A conspiracy formulated and directed by William Randolph Hearst himself. And what was the reason for that conspiracy?

Fallon gave the answer when he summed up before the jury. He placed a hand over his breast pocket and paused a long instant, then he said, his voice rising with each syllable, "I have here in court the actual birth certificates of the illegitimate children of a motion-picture actress!"

This was his bombshell. Hearst had been linked with an actress for years. Everyone knew her name. And now, according to Fallon, he had proof of offspring of that liaison. Certainly this was sufficient reason for a conspiracy against him.

Then Fallon added a postscript to his charge that he was the victim of a conspiracy. And not he alone. He told the jury, "I now say to you publicly that I don't know anything about anybody—about any big politician or any big gambler—that would ever put them in jail."

This was more than a plea for his acquittal. It was his way of telling the world that mattered to him that he had not talked, did not intend to talk. It was his way of saying that he had resisted all the pressure brought to bear on him to give evidence against Foley and Murphy—and Rothstein.

At the end Fallon dropped his eyes, dropped his shoulders. "All that the world means to me," he said, "I now leave in your hands."

Some hours later the jury brought in its verdict. Foreman Rosing looked not at the judge but at Fallon as he uttered it. "Not guilty on both counts."

Fallon rose and walked to the box to thank the jurors, then he turned and walked back to where Nat Ferber sat, Ferber whose investigation into the bucket shops had ended in this trial. "Nat," Fallon said, "I promise you I'll never bribe another juror."

His voice had been loud, loud enough for judge and jury and a good share of spectators to hear his words. It was a great curtain line, one he must have rehearsed many times.

Fallon's acquittal ended the more spectacular phases of the bucket-shop investigation.

The investigation failed of its primary purpose. It never proved a relationship existed between the bucketeers and the politicians, with Rothstein in the middle. However, if it did not prove it it certainly implied it and implied it publicly, day after day, in the newspapers.

If no one else went to jail, the president of the Consolidated Stock Exchange, William H. Silkworth, did. Silkworth had succeeded

Jakey Fields. The Consolidated Exchange itself was razed. The heyday of the bucketeer was at its end.

It was not so much because of the revelations as because of politics that legal steps were taken to destroy the bucket shops. Investors were voters. Something had to be done to show that the politicians had their interest at heart. So something was done. Laws were passed, others strengthened, to protect the investors. Candidates could say they had seen their duty and they had done it.

None of the millions lost by the suckers was ever recovered. That money was irrevocably gone. The investors could charge it off to experience.

Where did the money go?

Some evidence came out of the Fuller and McGee case. Accountants decided that Rothstein had received a minimum of $425,000.

Out of this money Rothstein paid legal fees to Fallon and McGee for the services they rendered the bucketeers, but the lawyers got only a small part of it. This did not surprise them. Fallon said bitterly to Ferber, "If Watson [managing editor of the *American*] had any brains, he would have known that the wise guy—Rothstein—paid the fees in half the bucket-shop cases in this town."

Fuller told Ferber, "We paid him [Fallon] his fee and Rothstein gave him some money too."

Ferber asked Fuller, "Why did you give him [Rothstein] anything?"

"We didn't give him anything. He got his hooks into everything lying around."

Rothstein—and Fallon, too—got money from the different bucket shops which Phil Kastel ran.

Rothstein got money from Stoneham and Company.

He got money from many other bucketeers.

And he kept some and passed some on. That was his function. It was as ridiculous to imagine that all the politicians got was the $10,000 check for Foley as to accept at face value the charge, some fifteen years later, that all Jimmy Hines got for protecting "Dutch" Schultz and his two-million-a-week policy racket was $500 a week.

A lot of people got the money, but none of them were the victims of the racket.

Looking back one senses an aura of fantasy about all the charges, the court proceedings, the publicity, that surrounded the end of the bucket shops. On the surface these were desperate battles, filled with gougings, kneeings, shrieks of pain, like the wrestling matches that delight television fans. But there is a question if they were any more legitimate than those same wrestling matches.

There was great care taken to keep the names of important politicians out of the records of the proceedings. The *American* could charge and fulminate, but it could not ever produce evidence that a court would allow. Actually, the various prosecutors ducked this issue. They were not interested in offering it to juries.

Tom Foley got some publicity. But Tom Foley was an old man and his story was accepted, albeit with some grains of salt.

Charley Murphy's name was never mentioned in any of the cases. Nor, for that matter, did anyone mention Tammany Hall or the Republican organization which had, for so long, worked with Tammany to prevent passage of regulatory legislation.

Rothstein, of course, was held up before the public as a mystery man. His name was mentioned continually. But the connection between Rothstein and Tammany Hall was never entered into the record.

The various indictments were nothing but window dressing. They were either dismissed or allowed to gather dust.

Fuller's attacks on Rothstein sounded good, but a look behind the scenes makes them suspect. Fuller, free on bail, spent many of his evenings, and much of his money, in the Silver Slipper and the Rendezvous, night clubs in which Rothstein had an interest and where he made frequent appearances. In two instances Rothstein cashed checks for Fuller at the Silver Slipper.

There was even some doubt about Chadbourne's attacks on Rothstein. True, Chadbourne put Rothstein through a strenuous grilling, but nothing ever came of that grilling. And only a few weeks after the hearings the pair were linked by Mayor Hylan.

Hylan, fighting for renomination, declared, ". . . as advisers in Tammany Hall . . . [are] . . . a B.M.T. lawyer, who is striving to get an increased fare, Tom Chadbourne, and Arnold Rothstein, the big gambler. Hylan . . . stands in the way of an increased fare. . . . Hylan stands in the way of the wide-open town Rothstein and the Tammany designee for Mayor [James J. Walker] will give you if they are successful on Primary Day."

It is late to set up a cry of "Fake," yet all the evidence seems to point to questioning the complete honesty of all the investigations. The ground rules that had obtained for so many years, during the Mazet and Lexow investigations, during the hue and cry after Rosenthal was killed, appear to have been rigidly observed in the bucketshop investigation.

There is no doubt, however, that the various bonding and surety companies would have liked a more thorough investigation, one which might have helped them to recover stolen or looted securities. They never did give up in their efforts to trace such securities to Rothstein. Not, at any rate, until after his death, and then only tangentially.

In May, 1929, Gene McGee, Fallon's former law partner, was tried in General Sessions Court, Manhattan, on charges of receiving stolen property, in this case bonds valued at $137,000, stolen in 1927 from a messenger working for the firm of Taylor, Bates and Company, of 100 Broadway.

These bonds had been recovered shortly after they were stolen and returned to their rightful owners. Now McGee was charged with having effected their return, though knowing they were stolen.

Gene McGee was a pitiful figure when he appeared in the courtroom to defend himself. Fallon was dead. The great days of the Forty-second Street Bar Association had passed even before Fallon's death. And in the intervening years McGee had been barred from the practice of law.

Now he had to fight to stay out of jail.

He defended himself, maintaining that he had acted in good faith. He testified that he had been approached by an attorney for the security house and asked if he would help in locating the bonds. He said he had gone to Rothstein to ask his help.

Judge Nott asked, "Why did you go to Rothstein?"

"Because he knew all the people in the underworld," McGee replied.

McGee said Rothstein had been most reluctant to help. "He told me," McGee testified, "that if the District Attorney found out he had anything to do with any stolen bonds he'd be back in court again. He said he'd already had enough trouble with bonds."

McGee then said he had pleaded with Rothstein, for old time's sake, to help him. "I told him that, if I could help recover the bonds, it would be of assistance to me in my plea to be reinstated as an attorney. I had already been disbarred."

McGee said that, on the basis of this appeal, Rothstein offered to help him through a third party—Phil Kastel. Rothstein arranged a meeting between the two, but Kastel told McGee he could not help him.

"He said," McGee testified, "that he was not in any trouble and did not want to get involved in any. He said, 'If I have anything to do with bonds, next thing you know, people will be saying I stole them.'"

After the Kastel rebuff, McGee testified, he returned to Rothstein and Rothstein agreed to help on condition that his name not be mentioned. A few days later, McGee continued, Rothstein telephoned him and said, "I can get those bonds back, but it will cost $13,000." McGee got the money from the attorney who had approached him, brought it to Rothstein, who gave him the bonds, still in their original container.

"Did you ask Rothstein from whom he secured the bonds?" Judge Nott asked.

"No, your Honor, I didn't ask him. He volunteered that he got them from somebody who was about to send them west to dispose of them."

The "somebody" remained unidentified.

There is one sidelight to this story. Before McGee was approached, the attorney went to Fannie Brice and asked her if Nicky Arnstein would use his good offices in recovering the bonds. Miss Brice, who testified at McGee's trial, said, "I told him Nicky wasn't available and I asked him why didn't he go to Gene McGee."

This was the old trinity, Rothstein, Arnstein and Kastel. Whenever there was a big bond theft their names were mentioned in every conjecture.

McGee was acquitted of the charges brought against him, but he was never readmitted to the bar. However, through the years, until his death, he was part of the legal brain trust of the mobsters and racketeers who had found a far more profitable field than either bond robberies or bucket shops.

Like Arnold Rothstein and Phil Kastel and many thousands of others, McGee became involved in breaking the prohibition law.

Chapter **16** *The Secret Self*

he ten years between 1912 and 1922 saw Arnold Rothstein transformed from a slim, white-skinned, deep-eyed young gambler, lost in anonymity, to a wealthy, notorious figure.

At the end of that decade the man who had chosen to live for money had more than enough for all the rest of his life. And a greater appetite for money. He knew his belief that money was power was true. Did he not have far more power than he had ever believed possible?

Arnold Rothstein, who had once run errands for Tim Sullivan, had become at least the peer of Sullivan's successors. He was welcome in the Scarlet Room in Delmonico's.

Arnold Rothstein, who had once worried about the cop on the beat, now controlled the destiny of that cop and thousands of others.

How had all this affected him?

Bulwer-Lytton wrote: "There are two lives to each of us, the life of action and the life of our minds and hearts. History reveals men's deeds and their outward characters, but not themselves. There is a secret self, that has its own life, unpenetrated and unguessed."

How true was this of Rothstein? Was not his public life his entire life? Could this man, who lived in secrecy, have a secret self?

Much more happened to Arnold Rothstein than he caused to happen. Opportunism was a reflex action. He was always ready for that

213

"tide in the affairs of men which, taken at the flood, leads on to fortune." It all resolved itself into the one word—money.

He could smell it, anywhere, any time.

Money had a morality all its own. It was omnipotent and could therefore make its own rules. It could buy anything, including men. His own experience proved it and so the belief required no proof beyond that.

Rothstein became really rich in that—his—great decade. "Until the end of the war," Carolyn Rothstein said, "he had money, but it was not too much for him to be able to count it. Afterward, there was so much he could not keep track of it. Of course the amount varied, from day to day, from race to race.

"When we married, it was his ambition to have $100,000. Then he raised the limit, first to a quarter of a million, then to a half million, and, finally, to a million. When he had his million, he took off the limit. All he wanted was more."

He was neither spendthrift nor miser with money. He liked to live well, but not as a grandee. As he grew richer he wanted larger, more expensive, quarters. This was because he thought this would make Carolyn happier. If he made her more happy, she might love him more. As to the rest of the world—he did not have to prove to it that he was rich. He knew it and that was enough.

He dressed well and quietly. Carolyn bought his accessories for him, many of them on her European trips.

He worried about his health. He feared sickness. He was told that ripe figs were healthy. From that day on, he carried a bag of figs in a coat pocket. He prescribed figs for anyone who remarked he did not feel well.

He was vain of his personal appearance. The one gibe of Fallon's that he could not forgive was "Who ever heard of a mouse with false lowers?" Actually, it was Rothstein's upper teeth that were false. These had been soft and chalky from childhood. He lost them, one by one. Finally, the dentist told him those few that remained had to come out, that Rothstein would have to wear an upper plate.

Rothstein appeared at the dentist's office early one morning, bringing his books and ledgers with him. Both dentist and Rothstein worked all day. Rothstein conducted his business from the dentist's chair, over the dentist's telephone.

Rothstein bled and pained and gambled. At the end of the day the blood-flecked ledgers showed a profit of $11,600. And Rothstein had his upper plate.

He was ashamed of his body, of the bodies of others. He and Carolyn always occupied separate bedrooms, always had separate dressing rooms and baths. He removed the last of his clothes in the dark, unable to bear the light on even his own nakedness.

He and Carolyn were married friends, not married lovers. They spent little time together. During those years when Rothstein had his racing stable she would go with him to the race track a number of times during the week. Otherwise she saw him only during that brief period between his arising and his leaving for "business."

There was no mention of Bobbie Winthrop between them. She existed, but she was no part of the life that they shared.

Always he was anxious to please Carolyn. Was there anything she wanted, anything he could buy for her? She loved the theater and he got tickets for the shows she wished to see. Usually, she went with a woman companion. When she was accompanied by a man, it was frequently Jack Rothstein.

Sundays were different from other days. There was no racing and, for a long time, no baseball. On arising, Rothstein would sit down in his study, work on his ledgers. He would open the Sunday paper to the sports section, turn quickly to the results of the Saturday races.

He would show interest in what Carolyn read. He depended upon her to tell him what news there was in the papers. That way he kept up with things outside his sphere that were happening in the world. Like psychology. He did not think much of psychology.

"All right," he said, "so there's something inside one man's head that makes him smart and makes another man dumb. But they were born with it and you can't change it. It's like one man who's crooked and another one who isn't. They were born that way, and there's nothing anyone can do about it."

In the early years of their marriage, the Rothsteins talked about children. After a time, they knew they were not going to have any. The knowledge had no effect upon him. He never expressed a desire for a child. Surprisingly, he liked children. Once he brought a child to the house.

Each morning, when Rothstein returned home, he would find notes and messages for him on a small table in the foyer. If he had any message for Carolyn, he would leave it there. One morning she found a note asking her to look in the library.

Going into the room, she found a freckle-faced, red-haired boy, about ten, asleep on a couch. His face, his hands, and his clothes were filthy.

When the boy awoke, he introduced himself. "I'm Red. I'm hungry." He told Carolyn that Rothstein had brought him home and told him to sleep in the library.

Carolyn fed Red. When he had eaten, he wanted to know when Rothstein would be getting up. When she told him, he said that gave him time for some errands. He would return after completing them.

Later Rothstein came downstairs, asked for Red. He told Carolyn he had discovered the boy singing and dancing for pennies outside a restaurant just before dawn.

"I gave him a dollar," Rothstein said, "and he began to cry. It made me feel silly. I took him into the restaurant and fed him. You'd be surprised how much a little kid like him can eat."

"I wouldn't. I fed him breakfast."

The boy had told Rothstein a pitiful story. His mother had worked as a cleaning woman in office buildings, but had broken down from overwork and could not make enough to support Red and his brother, who was "sick wit' de T.B." It devolved on Red to make some money, which he did by his singing and dancing. He said he lived in Harlem and often walked back and forth from home to the mid-town section to save the subway fare.

"I just felt sorry for him," Rothstein said. "When he told me he often stayed out all night, I brought him here."

"What are you going to do with him?"

"Help him out," Rothstein said. "I told him I'd match what he made if he went to school."

Shortly afterward, Red returned, as dirty as he had left.

Over his protests, Red was forced to submit to a bath and then Carolyn took him shopping. When they returned, Carolyn insisted that Red again bathe before he put on his new clothes. He asked logically, "How dirty can I get in a couple of hours?"

"It depends upon how dirty you started out. You can use another bath."

The boy was torn between cupidity and habit. Cupidity won. He again bathed and then dressed in his new clothes. He looked strange when he emerged from the bathroom.

Carolyn started to take his old clothes, which he was carrying, from him. "We'll burn those up," she said.

"You can't. Dem's my workin' clo'se."

"But Mr. Rothstein said you weren't going to work any more. He'll give you money and you can go to school."

The boy shrugged. "How do I know he won't change his mind?"

Carolyn had no answer. Red kept the clothes, but he never wore them on his visits to the Rothstein home.

He became a daily visitor. Each Saturday he collected his "pay." He was shrewd, curious, always asking questions.

"I became quite fond of him," Carolyn said. "He would sit with me and tell me things he shouldn't have known, and to which I should not have listened, about well-known Broadway people. He had learned a great deal on the streets. He had a worldly wisdom greater than mine and a vocabulary that called for constant editing."

This had been going on for some two months when Rothstein received a letter from Red's mother. She wrote that she would be glad to permit Rothstein to adopt her son, but added, "If you don't want to, I'll settle for a house or an apartment."

The letter irritated Rothstein. He sent one of his employees to the address given by Red's mother and told him to find out all he could about the family. The result was disillusioning.

Red's mother, it developed, was well known to the police. The "sick brother" was a prisoner in Sing Sing, serving time for an armed robbery. There was a "father," who appeared at the family flat occasionally, beat up the mother, took what money she had, and disappeared.

When Red appeared at the Rothstein home the next day Rothstein gave him $100. "You earned this," he said. "Now get out and don't let me ever see you again."

Rothstein's pride was badly hurt. He had been played for a sucker by a kid in short pants. A kid who had probably snickered up his sleeve each time Rothstein had given him money.

That was the last time the Rothsteins saw the boy, but not the last time they had anything to do with him. Some two months later a call came for Rothstein. Red had been picked up as a juvenile delinquent and was being held by the authorities. He wanted out.

Carolyn called a lawyer, asked him to help Red. Later she was told that Red had been released. Red, himself, never called to thank her or Rothstein.

"I missed Red for a long time," Carolyn said. "He was company. I don't think Arnold missed him at all. He had acted on impulse, not from emotion."

Only his family appeared able to penetrate to Rothstein's emotions. The cotton market collapsed in 1922 and, when it did, Abraham Rothstein found himself in deep financial trouble. Many of his competitors chose bankruptcy as the easiest way out, but not Abraham. "I owe the money," he said, "I will repay it, every penny." He began to sell and mortgage everything he owned.

Jack Rothstein called Arnold. "Papa's stripping himself and it won't do any good. He can't raise enough money."

"Why doesn't he ask me? I'll give it to him."

"You know he wouldn't ask you."

Arnold Rothstein did know. One did not ask anything of the dead, and he was dead to his father. He was alive to all the rest of the world—important, powerful, rich to all the rest of the world—but to his father and his father's world he was dead. "How much does Papa need?"

"A lot. More than $200,000."

"Tell him to go to the main office of the Bank of United States tomorrow and ask for a loan."

"He's been there. They refused him."

"I'll see to it that they change their minds."

"If Papa knows it's your money, he won't take it."

"He won't know unless you tell him."

The next morning Rothstein was at the Bank of United States when it opened. He went to the office of the president and took a thick manila envelope from his inside pocket. "There are $300,000 in Liberty Bonds here. My father will be asking you for a loan this morning. This is the collateral for the loan."

The bank president opened the envelope, counted the bonds. "We'll be happy to make the loan."

Rothstein understood this. He liked making loans on just such collateral. He rose. "My father is not to know about the bonds, understand?"

"Whatever you say."

Abraham Rothstein got the money from the bank. With it he paid off every one of his creditors, had enough to weather this financial storm. Within three years he paid back the loan and the bank returned the last of the collateral to Arnold Rothstein.

It was not until Arnold's death that Jack told this story to Abraham Rothstein. The old man lowered his eyes, his lips moved. *"Yisgadal, ve visgadash. . . ."*

Jack was the favorite brother. Still there was one time they were estranged. Jack went into the brokerage business, called his firm, "Rothstone and Company."

"Are you ashamed of me?" Arnold demanded.

"You called your racing stable the 'Redstone Stable,' didn't you?"

"That was different. Everyone knew I owned it."

"Well, everyone knows you're my brother. I tell them so."

"But you call yourself 'Rothstone.' "

It was three months before Arnold spoke to his brother again.

And there was one other time. One other time when there was an insight into Arnold Rothstein's "mind and heart." These seemed so small a part of him, so much less than they were with other men.

In the winter of 1923 pneumonia struck hard. Esther Rothstein was one of the victims of the epidemic. Arnold was called and told his mother was dying. He rushed to her side. It was on a Friday afternoon.

The family was gathered about her. Abraham was there, and Jack and Edgar and Edith. And Arnold. The doctor told them, "It is in the hands of God."

A little before sundown, Abraham picked up his fringed prayer shawl and his prayer book. He spoke to Jack and Edgar. "It is time to go to the synagogue."

Arnold said to his father, "I'll go with you."

"You cannot," Abraham said softly. "Have you forgotten? You are dead." There was no cruelty in his voice, no wish to hurt. Only the fact was cruel.

After a time Arnold left the house, had his chauffeur drive him to Reuben's restaurant, then his headquarters. He went back to his table without speaking a word. There was something about him that forbade words. Only Sid Stajer ignored it.

Stajer was quite young, a pasty-faced boy who stooged for Rothstein and those about him. A young punk. "What's the matter, Mr. Rothstein?" he asked.

Rothstein lifted his head, started to stare Stajer down. Then he changed his mind. "I'd like to go to the synagogue and pray for my mother," he said, "but I can't." His lips twisted into a bitter smile. "Besides, I've forgotten the prayers."

"I know them," Stajer said. "I'll go to the synagogue and pray for her in your place." He got up and ran from the restaurant.

Maybe that was why Rothstein liked Sid Stajer. No one could figure any other reason. Stajer was a drug addict and a dope peddler. He was arrested for counterfeiting Internal Revenue stamps and for bank robbery. He was a liar, a thief, a petty crook. But Rothstein liked him, protected him, and, when he died, Rothstein left an inheritance to Sid Stajer.

"There is," wrote Bulwer Lytton, "a secret self that has its own life, unpenetrated and unguessed."

Shortly after Rothstein's death Carolyn received a short note from San Francisco. It read "I'm awfully sorry" and was signed "Will Davis."

She finally recalled Davis, a tall, emaciated man with a sallow complexion and thick eyebrows that met above the bridge of his nose.

The first time she had seen him was one dawn when she was awakened by noises in the kitchen. Throwing on a robe, she went downstairs and found Rothstein and a stranger drinking milk and eating cookies.

Rothstein greeted her and said, "Carolyn, this is _____" He looked toward the stranger.

"Will Davis." The man spoke only a little above a whisper. His eyes were on the linoleum that covered the kitchen floor.

"Will Davis," Rothstein said. "He wants to borrow $1,000. I've got his collateral." Rothstein took a revolver from his pocket and placed it on the kitchen table.

Carolyn looked from the gun to Davis. He raised his eyes, guessed that she might be a friend. "I was desperate," he said, his voice a husky monotone.

"Tell her why you wanted the money," Rothstein said.

"To play the races. I know I can beat them. My figures prove it."

"No one can beat the races," Rothstein said. "Not with figures."

"I can." Davis spoke doggedly.

Rothstein opened the gun. It was not loaded. Rothstein laughed. "That's like your figures."

"Please, Mr. Rothstein," Davis pleaded, "give me a chance. I'm not a holdup man. I'm a school teacher. At least, I used to be. I've got a wife and kid in California. It's like I told you. I saved up a stake to come here and bet the horses. Someone picked my pocket."

"So you decided to get a fresh bankroll from me."

Davis averted his eyes again. "I was desperate. I didn't think. All I wanted was a loan. I would have paid you back."

Carolyn said, "My God, Arnold, can't you see he's telling you the truth."

Davis thanked her with his eyes.

Rothstein said, "I'll give you a chance, Davis." He took out his roll, peeled some bills off it. "You give me your figures for ten days. If they're good, then I'll back your play. Meanwhile—" he pushed the bills over to Davis—"meanwhile, here's eating money."

"I'll prove they're good," Davis said. "Wait and see."

Each day Davis brought his selections to the Rothstein house. Some days he picked but one horse and never more than three. His winning percentage ran extraordinarily high.

At the end of the ten days Rothstein said, "I'll take a chance. It could be you've just been lucky. I won't lend you any money, but I'll make you a partner. I'll bet your picks and give you a percentage of the profit at the end of the meeting."

"I've got to have some money for my wife and kid."

"Give me their address. I'll send them fifty a week as long as your figures stand up."

Davis gave Rothstein the address and each week, thereafter, Rothstein sent the $50.

Davis now became part of Rothstein's entourage. He went to the track with him each day.

"Davis," Carolyn said, "was a fanatic about his figures. He would work all night on them and have only a couple of hours' sleep before going to the track. He would be sitting in the box and suddenly say, 'Don't bet this race. The wind has changed.' He would go downstairs between races to look at the track. Sometimes, before the first race, he would tell Arnold, 'The track was furrowed this morning. That throws my figures out.' "

Fanatic or not, he had a remarkable streak of winners. At the end of the New York season, Rothstein was ahead $160,000 on bets made on Davis' choices. He owed Davis $24,000, fifteen per cent. But Rothstein did not settle with Davis. Instead he insisted that Davis accompany him to Maryland, for the tail end of the season there.

Davis was reluctant. "I'd like to go west and see my wife and kid."

"And leave all that money behind? Do you realize how much money I've made for you?" This was typical of Rothstein. He had won on advice from Davis, but he acted as if he were doing Davis a favor.

"I know, Mr. Rothstein. Could I have some of it?" he asked tentatively.

"After the Maryland season." So far, all that Davis had received was a weekly $50 for himself and that other $50 which went to his family. Rothstein was going to hang on to the balance as long as he could. One way or another, he was getting interest on it.

They went to Maryland. Davis' luck—or his figures—held up. When that season ended, Rothstein was ahead a total of $250,000 on the figures.

Davis said, "If you'll just give me $5,000, I'll call it even. I want to go home."

For once, Rothstein did not take advantage of another man's hard luck. "I made a deal," he said. He took out his little black book. "I owe you $34,000. I'll give it to you tomorrow."

He paid Davis off the next day in his office. He gave him $30,000 in Liberty Bonds—those ubiquitous bonds—and the difference in cash. "Put those away," he said, nodding at the bonds. "They're as good as gold." Then he did an unusual thing. He counted off another $5,000 and gave it to Davis. "For your kid," he said.

Davis promised to return the following spring, but he did not. Rothstein tried to find him, even had a friend in California go to the address where he had sent the weekly money. Word came back to Rothstein that the Davis family had moved, no one knew where. That made Rothstein uneasy.

"There's something fishy about it," he told Carolyn. "Did he play me for a dub?" A "dub" was his own synonym for "sucker."

"Maybe he has all the money he wants?"

Rothstein's brow lifted. "Nobody ever has that much." Worry darkened his eyes. "Do you think he was a detective or a government man?"

"Isn't that silly?"

"Then why doesn't he come back? Or at least write?"

"I don't know."

Rothstein remained uneasy about Davis for a long time. He never heard from him again. Only Carolyn did.

Rothstein did not want friends. Companions, yes. But friends, no.

He had hangers-on. Abe Attell and Curly Bennett. They were his bodyguards also. There would be others to perform that function, including thin, handsome, cold-eyed, Jack Diamond and pudgy, bushy-haired Fats Walsh.

There were his lawyers. He always had lawyers about him.

And respectable, upright acquaintances from Broadway, like Edgar Selwyn and George White, the theatrical producers. Once he attempted to attain an intimacy with Irving Berlin, even going so far as to offer to finance a new music publishing company for Berlin. But Berlin brushed him off. "I don't need you for a partner and I don't need your money."

Few men could have been so cavalier with Rothstein, but Berlin had no skeletons in his closet.

Yes, there were people he knew, but he didn't have friends.

"He didn't want them, really," Carolyn said. "They were a luxury." She added an afterthought. "Like a wife."

Then why did she stay with him all those years?

"I suppose I loved him. When two people live together over the years, they become part of each other. I guess Arnold was much more a part of me than I was of him."

And, still, there were moments.

A night—it was during the period of the Fuller-McGee investigation—when he came home, taut as the high wire in a circus. He awakened her and asked her to come to the living room and talk to him. They sat in silence for a time and then he said, "There's something inside keeps driving me and I don't know what it is. There's something I want and I don't know what that is either. That's a terrible feeling, because if you don't know what you want, how do you know when you get it?"

"Has something gone wrong?" she asked.

He shook his head. "No, it just came over me tonight. I won a big hand on a bluff. There was a time that would have made me high as a 'junkie.' It used to mean something; it doesn't any more. And then I began to wonder what did mean anything to me. What did I want? I couldn't get the answer. I just want something. Maybe—"

he laughed, a high, brittle laugh—"maybe to be king of the world."

"Would that make you happy?"

"I don't know. I don't know."

And then there was the night Rothstein suggested they drive down to Atlantic City. Carolyn was happy to go any place where one day would be different from all the other days.

On the way they were caught in a dense fog near Hammonton. The chauffeur slowed the car to a crawl.

Rothstein looked out the window. Looked into the misty blankness. "Maybe this is the way it ought to be all the time. Just us alone in the world." He waved a hand at the fog. "There's nothing out there. There's just the two of us here. I'm glad you're here. I wouldn't want to be alone. I used to be alone at night when I was little. All the lights were out and the door was closed.

"At first I used to be afraid. I thought it was like being dead. And then I got used to it. The whole world was inside my room. And it was my world. Nobody else had any part of it. It belonged to me, like the world belongs to me now. We could drive over a cliff and not know it. We could run right into the ocean and not know it. But that can't happen to my world. I won't let it."

A short time later the fog lifted. He sat back and stared at lights burning in the distance. It wasn't his world any more.

Chapter **17** *A New Nation*

Arnold Rothstein was not prepared for prohibition. He had no concept of the effect it would have on his life and activities—or his bankroll. In this respect he was no different from the rest of the population of the United States.

The Volstead Act, named for the otherwise undistinguished congressman from Minnesota who introduced it, became effective at 12:01 A.M., January 17, 1920. It put teeth into the 18th Amendment, which had become part of the Constitution exactly six months earlier. The act made it a crime to manufacture, transport or sell beverages containing more than one-half of one per cent alcohol by volume.

For some months before the law became effective the New York branch of the Anti-Saloon League had been conducting a public relations campaign whose theme was that, with prohibition, a "new nation" would be born. Of all the prophecies made about prohibition, this one was the most completely fulfilled. However, the "new nation" that was born on that bleak January morning bore little relationship to that envisioned by the jubilant Prohibitionists.

The League was a poor soothsayer, but there was none more accurate. Certainly the criminal world had no idea of the impact—the changes—that prohibition would have on its structure and operation.

Most persons, among them Arnold Rothstein, felt that the law would be effective, that it would be observed and enforced. The United States was a law-abiding country. Its people might grumble,

226

but they would not revolt because of a law a small minority apparently opposed and a great majority seemingly favored.

From his personal viewpoint Rothstein thought the law a good one. He did not drink. He did not like men who drank too much. Besides, a great many of his customers spent money on whisky, and now they might spend some of that money with him. (This was a feeling shared by other businessmen.)

The advent of Prohibition brought him no boon. He had arranged a poker game at a rented flat on West Fifty-fifth Street. Gamblers, however, were scarce. Try as he and his steerers did, they could not flush a quorum for the game. Tom Farley and Nat Evans remained alone in the flat.

Rothstein walked the length of Broadway in his search. He stopped at Reisenweber's, where a funeral ball for John Barleycorn was being held. The same burlesque mourning was in evidence at other places. The waiters at Maxim's were dressed as pallbearers, down to the white gloves.

At the Golden Glades, a coffin was wheeled about the room as the clock struck twelve. The "corpse" was a jeroboam of champagne, donated by Harry Kessler, famed champagne salesman. At Murray's Roman Gardens there was a mock funeral for "King Alcohol." The entertainment at the Café des Beaux Arts ended with the orchestra playing Chopin's Funeral March.

At the Café de Paris, which had once been Rector's, there was a variation from this pattern. The café was the scene of a Cinderella Ball, with a cover charge of $10 per person.

One of the largest crowds gathered at the Hotel Vanderbilt. It had been drawn by an advertisement which promised that "one hundred cases of the finest champagne ever held in one cellar" would be opened at midnight and dispensed free.

Rothstein ended his search for gamblers at Jack's, his old headquarters. A bibulous party was in progress in the private, upstairs room. Wilson Mizner presided, but he was not in his usual sardonic form. He and his companions—newspapermen, gamblers, idlers—were not interested in witticisms. They were too busy trying to drink up enough liquor to last them the rest of their lives.

Rothstein left Jack's and went to the flat. He told Farley to return the gambling paraphernalia to the containers in which it had been transported. There would be no game. He talked with Evans and then went home, earlier by many hours than was his custom. And there he took a drink. Milk.

Prohibition was one of those coming events which had long cast its shadow before it. Kansas had passed the first state-wide prohibition law in 1880. In 1882 Iowa followed Kansas. By 1914 nine states had adopted absolute prohibition. Eighteen others passed such laws by 1917. And six more joined these twenty-seven before 1920. Some form of local option was already law, or in the process of becoming law, in most of the remaining fifteen states.

The first demand for a law against liquor was apparently made in 1826 by Lyman Beecher. He sought "legislative interference to protect the health and morals of the nation."

There was not, even in those times, complete unanimity as to the value of such legislation. One of the leading temperance advocates of the day, Dr. Dioclesian Lewis, warned against this tactic. He favored education and persuasion. His thesis was that prohibition was a moral, not a legislative, matter. He even wrote a book, *Prohibition a Failure*, in which he stated that legal action would violate personal liberty, "that great, pivotal fact of human life."

The result was his excommunication from the prohibition movement.

The driving force behind enactment of the 18th Amendment was the Anti-Saloon League. Founded as a state organization in Ohio in 1874, it became national in 1895.

By 1909 it had established its own publishing house. By 1912 it was turning out forty tons of material—newspapers, books, pamphlets, magazines—each month.

All this, of course, was legitimate enough. Even the expenditure of vast sums of money was legitimate in its inception. Wayne B. Wheeler, general counsel for the League, admitted in 1926 that the League had spent more than $35,000,000 up to that time, first in its campaign for prohibition and then in efforts to keep the law enforced.

What Wheeler did not admit—but what everyone had come to know—was that the League had become the most powerful pressure group in American politics. It operated the toughest, best-financed lobby in the national capital and in most of the state capitals.

The League was interested in but one issue, and it was an issue that transcended party lines. If a candidate for office favored national prohibition, he got the support of the League. It did not matter what else the candidate stood for.

In a basic sense the Prohibitionists made up a third party. The League provided campaign funds and campaign workers for the candidates it backed. It published literature for them.

The Prohibitionists campaigned in the name of morality, but they had no real sense of morality. André Siegfried, the Frenchman who made a study of the American scene in the twenties, reported in his *America Comes of Age:*

"It is openly admitted that Congress voted under direct and formidable pressure from the Anti-Saloon League. . . . Its agents had carried on an ambitious and vigorous campaign . . . and had even gone so far as blackmail. In some cases, with the aid of detectives, they had unearthed the private life of the local Congressman, noting his debts, his moral weaknesses and any strains on his reputation. Then they were in a position to order him to vote as he was told, or be exposed."

The Prohibition Amendment was born of a mixture of high-mindedness and low principles. It was effected on the theory that the end justified the means. That was its innate weakness. It was what doomed it to failure. The blackmailer exacted his tribute but made himself liable to jail.

It would be more than a decade before the Wickersham Committee would report to President Hoover:

". . . the prohibition law . . . [is] . . . not regarded in the same light as other laws; the prevailing attitude is one of defiance, resentment, or merely indifference. . . ."

The "defiance," the "resentment" and the "indifference" began simultaneously with the enforcement of the prohibition law. Within twenty-four hours of its becoming effective arrests were being made by the scores throughout the country. Millions of otherwise law-abiding men and women entered a conspiracy to thwart, to outwit and to break the law.

And they became willing accomplices of the thousands of criminals who slowly became aware that there was big profit in prohibition.

Whatever good prohibition might have done was interred with its bones on December 5, 1933, when it was repealed. The evils have continued to live. Of these the greatest was that it provided tens of millions of dollars to finance all types of crime.

The criminals did not immediately sense this potential. They could not believe that much of the nation would aid and abet them. It was beyond their imaginations to conceive that some of them would become folk heroes, machine-gunning Robin Hoods, in a new American legend.

Nor did they realize that prohibition would change the whole structure of the underworld.

In New York this change took many forms. One of these was racial. The Irish, who had for so long been the leaders, were to be replaced by the Italians. "Peg Leg" Lonergan, "Dandy Johnny" Dolan, "Bum" Mahoney, "Duck" Rearden, "Mush" Riley, "One Lung" Curran, "Wild Jimmy" Haggerty, and even "Ownie the Killer" Madden were replaced by the "Lucky" Lucianos, the "Scarface Al" Capones, the "Terrible Johnny" Torrios, and, ultimately, by Frank Costello, whose nickname was "The Boss."

And the organization of crime—its gangs—would undergo the same change. The "Whyos," the "Hudson Dusters," the "Plug Uglys" and the "Gashouse Boys" would yield to the "Mafia," to the "Syndicate."

The big change would be in the matter of organization. Where hoodlums once controlled a few square blocks, the new gangs would control cities and states. Where anarchy had ruled there would be a chain of command.

The profits of prohibition would be responsible for all this. The power of the criminal would increase geometrically as his bankroll grew arithmetically. Prohibition gave crime the Midas touch. It made Maecenases of hoodlums.

Prohibition was an acid that quickly spilled on the law and started eating it away. Corruption, which had been local and limited, became national and unlimited. No law-enforcement agency—local, state or federal—would remain uncorrupted.

Police, district attorneys and judges would be bought. Customs agents and the Internal Revenue Service agents would go on the payrolls of the crooks.

Newspapers and newspapermen would be bribed.

Honest merchants and workmen would lose their honesty.

Murder would go unpunished. Lesser crimes would be ignored.

The man who first grasped so many of these potentialities was Arnold Rothstein. He saw, sooner than most, that a new Golconda had been unearthed. Its development called for two important possessions. Capital and protection. In those early days he was still the one principal source of both. Especially in New York City.

Recalling the millions that passed through his hands during prohibition, he might well have forgotten his first profit from the law. That was a ten-dollar fee for providing bond for a cab driver, Harry Koppel. Koppel was arrested on January 18, 1920, and charged with transporting a case of liquor in his taxi.

The first of Rothstein's intimates to be arrested for violating the 18th Amendment was Sid Stajer. On May 16, 1920, Stajer was charged with selling ingredients to make home brew. He was running one of the many newly opened shops which sold copper coils, malt and hops. A chain of such shops had appeared overnight. The lease for Stajer's place, like the leases of many such, was in the name of the Redstone Material and Supply Company.

Arnold Rothstein headed this corporation, which had stated in its papers of incorporation that it would deal in "construction material." Someone with a sense of humor had prepared the papers.

Rothstein was always in search of the big dollar, but he never lost the opportunity to make the small one. Like the Chicago meat packers, he sought to sell everything but the squeal.

Rothstein was one of the first rumrunners. He made the smuggling of uncut diamonds and narcotics a side enterprise.

He operated one of the largest bail bond businesses in New York. Each man for whom he provided bail had to give Rothstein his insurance business.

Rothstein had "pieces" of many night clubs and cabarets. This was a bonus he took for financing them, at his usual rate of interest. His "partners" found that they had to purchase or rent such equipment as silver and linens from firms that Rothstein owned. They also had to place all their insurance with Rothstein's firm.

Rothstein financed many retail outlets for bootleggers. His realty firms negotiated rentals and leases.

He bankrolled many bootleggers and provided them with trucks and drivers to transport their illegal cargo. This was a division of his activities which he turned over to Jack ("Legs") Diamond, his quondam bodyguard, and his brother, Eddie Diamond. In some instances, when the bootleggers had their own trucks and drivers, they were hi-jacked by the first organized gang, led by the two Diamonds.

Rothstein's main function was organization. He provided money and manpower and protection. He arranged corruption—for a price. And, if things went wrong, Rothstein was ready to provide bail and attorneys. He put crime on a corporate basis when the proceeds of crime became large enough to warrant it.

In the fall of 1920 he was approached with a proposition by Irving Wexler, better known as "Waxey" Gordon. Gordon was a dope peddler, a pickpocket and a sneak thief. He had worked for Rothstein in the garment center, protecting either strikers or strikebreakers, depending on which group had turned to Rothstein for help.

Gordon was accompanied by Max ("Big Maxey") Greenberg, of Detroit. Greenberg had become a bootlegger almost with the passage of the prohibition law. He had been bringing in whisky from

Canada and it had been quite profitable. Now he wanted to expand. He needed, he said, $175,000.

Knowing Gordon, Greenberg had come to him to help raise the money. In 1920 Gordon was hardly in a position to help. (Later Gordon would own a number of hotels in Manhattan, a line of sea-going ships, shares of numerous night clubs, a brewery, a distillery and a castle, complete with moat, in New Jersey.) However, Gordon could take Greenberg to Arnold Rothstein.

The first meeting was held on a bench in Central Park. Greenberg told his needs to Rothstein and offered to pay the usual rate of interest for a loan. He explained that a great deal of money was tied up in such equipment as trucks and warehouses. And he added that costs kept going up because the Canadians, aware of the law of supply and demand, kept raising wholesale prices.

Rothstein listened to Greenberg's story and said he would give him an answer the next day.

At the next meeting, this time in Rothstein's office on Fifty-seventh Street, Rothstein came up with a counterproposition. Instead of buying the whisky in Canada, why not buy it in England and bring it over? Greenberg said this was a fine idea, but how could it be done with just $175,000. Such a proposition would call for much more money.

Rothstein agreed. He was ready to put up the money. And he would declare Greenberg in to the extent of the $175,000. He would lend this to him and take the trucks and real estate Greenberg owned in Detroit as collateral. Of course Greenberg would pay the usual high interest fees. And, as a matter of protection for Rothstein, Greenberg would also take out as much life insurance as Rothstein could place on his life.

This hardly approximated the proposition Greenberg had originally made, but he accepted it.

Gordon also asked to be included in the deal and he was given a small "piece." It was from this piece that Gordon built his bootleg empire.

When arrangements were concluded, Greenberg had given Rothstein a chattel mortgage on his equipment and real estate. He owed Rothstein $175,000. But he did not get one penny in cash. In addition, he was obligated to take out life insurance in wholesale lots.

Rothstein's next step was to find an English agent to act for him. This was not too difficult, since a number of bucket-shop operators had fled to Europe to avoid prosecution. One of these was Harry Mather, a former associate of Phil Kastel, who was under indictment in the United States on two charges, operating a bucket shop and fraud.

Mather had been useful to Rothstein earlier in some dealings with Swiss bankers and Dutch diamond merchants. He proved equally useful in arranging for the purchase of whisky and its transportation to the United States.

Mather had no trouble purchasing 20,000 cases of Scotch whisky. On his own, Mather also included some hundreds of cases of ale. Next came the problem of transportation. Mather found a Norwegian ship that was under a libel in England. He arranged to pay off bills outstanding against the ship and have the libel lifted so it could sail.

All this took time. While Mather was making his arrangements in Europe, Rothstein was facilitating the landing and retailing of the whisky in the United States. His first step was to purchase a half dozen specially built speedboats, each capable of carrying from seven hundred to one thousand cases of whisky. Rothstein found a boat builder in Bayonne, New Jersey, who got these boats for him.

The next step was to facilitate transportation once the liquor was landed. At this time Rothstein had exceptional connections on Long Island. He had made these when he first opened a gambling house on the island and he had maintained them. There was no trouble getting assurance that Rothstein's whisky trucks would travel the highways unmolested.

That left just one danger—the time between unloading from the Norwegian ship and loading on the waiting trucks. The open water in this area was being patrolled by the Coast Guard, whose headquarters was on Montauk Point. It took a little time, but Rothstein was able to establish most friendly relations with the Coast Guard-men.

When all this was completed, Rothstein notified Mather that he could order the Norwegian ship to set sail. He also told Mather that there would be a shipment from Holland that should be placed aboard. This shipment was of uncut diamonds.

The voyage across the Atlantic was hardly uneventful. The ale froze and the bottles popped. The ship was undermanned and the crew threatened, a number of times, to turn the ship about and head back to England. However, the boat finally reached the agreed-upon rendezvous point.

There it was met by the speedboats and by a delegation from the Coast Guard station, who helped unload the boat and even transported some of the cargo to shore. Once landed, the trucks were waiting, along with a motorcycle escort which convoyed the whisky to Long Island City, where Rothstein had rented a warehouse.

This was the first of eleven transatlantic crossings the ship made. Late in 1921, when the ship was on the high seas on its eleventh voyage, Rothstein was tipped off that a new commander had been stationed at the Montauk Point Coast Guard headquarters and that his ship was marked to be "taken."

Rothstein made radio contact with the ship and the captain was ordered to change course and head for Cuba. When the ship landed there, an agent for Charles A. Stoneham picked up the cargo. Stoneham at that time was operating the Havana race track and casino.

Rothstein told his partners that he was no longer interested in running rum. The last cargo had brought no profit, being sold to Stoneham at cost.

A final accounting was made, with Rothstein collecting all sums due him, plus interest. It had been a most profitable enterprise and, if Rothstein profited more than the others, he had taken the greatest risk.

What he did not tell Gordon or Greenberg was that he had been the actual purchaser of the final cargo. Now, on his own, Rothstein arranged through Stoneham to have the liquor brought into the United States by small boats from Cuba.

Rothstein was now finished with the importation of whisky. He had a number of good reasons for giving up this business. Rumrunning tied up large sums of money over a long period of time. It involved risks that could not be avoided. The chance of loss grew continually. And if a shipload of liquor were "taken" by the authorities, the cost could be as much as a half million dollars.

There was one most important reason he did not reveal. It was a reason he could not reveal to anyone.

Prohibition was a game he could not "bull." It was too big for him, or any one man, to control. Since he could not control it he wanted no part of it.

This was the first time since his rise to power that Rothstein had found himself in this position. It was to become a recurrent pattern in the next few years.

He could pioneer in breaking the prohibition law, developing new techniques. He could find ways to grow wealthy from prohibition that did not occur to others. But there was no way for him to patent these methods, copyright a new technique. Others could move in and profit by his brains, his contacts and his influence.

When he ended his partnership with Gordon and Greenberg, it hardly inconvenienced them at all. They stayed in business. And Rothstein even continued to finance them at times. But he was no longer essential to them. It was as easy for Gordon to make Mather his European agent as it had been for Rothstein.

Collaterally, Rothstein continued to use Gordon's rum boats for smuggling diamonds and dope. By 1922 so many diamonds had been imported that the market for them became flooded. However, there was never any surplus of dope. After Rothstein's death, Gordon sought to continue that operation. He had to give it up when a message was delivered that others of Rothstein's heirs claimed that inheritance.

If rumrunning was the first of Rothstein's innovations, probably the most important was the development of the modern "mob."

Rothstein created the modern type of gang out of necessity. A need arose for such an organization and Rothstein was quick to meet that need. He saw in it an opportunity to make money, big money. And he never passed up such an opportunity.

Luck was with him at the start. He had the right man at hand to head the operation. This was Legs Diamond.

Chapter **18** *An Amazing Pertinency*

The history of organized gangs in New York starts with the "Five Pointers," who came into being about 1840. Then came the post-Civil War gangs, led by "Butcher Boy" Poole and John Morrissey, among others.

These gangs were tied together by neighborhood pride, by racial ties or by political affiliation. It was essentially this type of gang that was led, up to the time of prohibition, by such as Monk Eastman and Paul Kelly. Their greatest value was to politicians, who owned them and used them on Election Day.

These gangsters, to use an expression of later vintage, even the Eastmans and Kellys, were "punks." They took orders and lived off what they could scavenge. They were rabble, for sale to the highest bidder, and the price was never high.

All these gangs were anarchic. They preyed on each other as much as they did on outsiders. With the coming of prohibition, a new type of gang came into being. It had discipline and order. It possessed a chain of command. And, most important, it was financially independent.

Arnold Rothstein fostered the first such gang. Like so many innovations for which he was responsible, it was not the result of planning. These gangs—Rothstein's gang—came into being because there was a need for them. They came into being because they worked.

Rothstein had known gangs and gangsters all his life. He had known Monk Eastman and had used Eastman's services. From the time of his apprenticeship at the Hesper Club he had seen the political importance of the gangs. It became obvious to him, soon after prohibition went into effect, that this new law called for a different type of gang and gangster.

It needed hoodlums who could take orders, hoods who could take big chances. It demanded a close-knit organization. And it called for a leader who could keep his men under control, have them available when the need arose, and subject to discipline at all times.

Rothstein chose a frail, white-faced, handsome, sadistic former package thief as the first gang leader in the new era. This was Legs Diamond, who had been born John T. Nolan. He had earned his nickname by his speed in running away from the law in his petty larceny days.

Diamond had one special attribute. He was totally without sentiment. Where other gangsters wept when they heard "Mother Machree," his eyes remained dry. He did not believe in sending flowers to funerals, even those of his friends. If a hoodlum was good to his mother, Diamond felt this was a sign of basic weakness.

He went to work for Rothstein in 1919. Like Waxey Gordon, he got his first job in a labor dispute. He helped "settle" a strike by using brass knuckles, acid and the butt of his gun. His cold-blooded attitude made him valuable to Rothstein. He became Rothstein's bodyguard. And he kept a watchful eye on Rothstein's various floating games.

He was not averse to some independent work on his own. Stanley Walker, in *The Nightclub Era*, wrote:

"It became the thing at Police Headquarters, when a gambler was found murdered with all his pockets empty, to ask, " 'Did Legs take him home?' "

When Rothstein became involved in rumrunning he found a fresh use for Diamond. He told him to round up a small group of dependable men to protect the whisky once it reached land. The first members of the Diamond gang were Legs' brother, Eddie, and Gene Moran, later to become an outstanding jewel thief.

These three rode in the trucks, guns ready, from Montauk Point to Long Island City. Just as in the old days of the West, when the stagecoaches traveled through hostile or dangerous territory, they "rode shotgun."

They were so proficient that Rothstein even rented the trio out to other rumrunners. This was part of the "protection" which Rothstein provided. And it came high.

Late in 1921 Diamond brought a proposition to Rothstein. He wanted to operate on his own, but as an outlaw. There were literally thousands of rumrunners and bootleggers operating all over the New York area. Many of them were amateurs, moving into a field they saw was quite profitable. Diamond figured on making these his prey. He saw, with basic cunning, that these amateurs would have no redress if their trucks were hijacked.

Diamond wanted financing. He needed money for trucks, for drops, and even for occasional protection. More than anything else, however, he needed a "fence," someone to take the contraband off his hands. He asked Rothstein to provide the financing and buy the loot.

The proposition was to Rothstein's liking. It offered a chance for big profit at relatively small risk. He would be able to buy cut-rate whisky from Diamond. And by late 1921 Rothstein was already interested in a considerable number of places where whisky was sold at both wholesale and retail.

Rothstein lent Diamond the money, arranged to give him his services. That meant protection, bonds and lawyers.

In the beginning Diamond stuck to his original idea of preying on amateurs and lone wolves. Sid Feder and Joachim Joesten wrote in *The Luciano Story:* "Along about this time . . . [1921] . . . the Diamond brothers—Jack and Eddie—appeared on the West Side with a nondescript mob that practically advertised its willingness to handle any line. It is historic as the first of the really modern gangs. Its specialties were bootlegging, fur and silk robberies, and hijacking, plus a sideline of narcotics when the price was right."

With Rothstein behind him, and his own disregard for any kind of rules, Diamond gained immediate importance.

The quick and easy money Diamond made attracted recruits for his gang. True, he was still ostensibly working for Rothstein, but it was common knowledge that he was doing considerable free-lance work on his own. Extremely profitable free-lance work. No wonder he was able to get such volunteers as Charles Lucania, who became Lucky Luciano, and Arthur Flegenheimer who evolved into Dutch Schultz.

The gang's jobs for Rothstein included guarding Rothstein's various enterprises, working for whatever side hired Rothstein in labor disputes, and keeping Rothstein supplied with various types of contraband at bargain basement prices.

Diamond was satisfied with the arrangement for some time. And so was Rothstein. One reason was the mutual profit involved. As good an instance of this as any involved that notorious gentleman, Robert Arthur Tourbillon, known as Ratsy to some, as Dapper Dan Collins to many more.

Collins was a blackmailer, a shakedown artist, a confidence man and the "great lover" of the underworld. He served time in Atlanta for violation of the Mann Act and did assorted stretches in assorted jails for assorted crimes. Over the years Rothstein bankrolled him in a number of endeavors and Collins worked for Rothstein, in the United States and in Europe, in a number of liquor and dope deals.

Collins possessed that most necessary qualification for success in confidence games—a magnificent "front." He was tall, handsome and had a head of blond hair that women envied and could not attain with a peroxide bottle. Whereas most con men practiced their wiles on males, Collins used his on women.

An attorney who represented him said, "Collins could meet a woman at nine o'clock in the evening, and be holding her hand in ten minutes. By nine in the morning, he'd be holding her bankbook."

He told so many stories concerning his antecedents and background that even the authorities never did learn where he came from. He was probably of French descent, for he spoke that language fluently and without a trace of accent.

His personality was engaging. So engaging that he was able to take in many who knew him well, including Bill Fallon and Arnold

Rothstein. Fallon, when asked why he associated with Collins, replied, according to Gene Fowler:

"Because he is a philosopher as well as the Chesterfield of crime."

Some of that philosophy was uttered in discussing Rothstein. Fowler quotes Collins as saying, "Everyone hates Rothstein because he makes them pay back what they borrow" and "He gets everyone sore if they borrow his money; that's so he'll be the first person they'll pay back when they get flush."

In 1921, shortly after Collins was released from a term in Atlanta, he appealed to Rothstein for funds to finance a rumrunning deal. He was not in Rothstein's good graces at the time because of an overdue marker for $11,000 in Rothstein's little black book. Only Collins, already in debt to Rothstein, would dare ask for further funds.

Collins told Rothstein that he had a boat at his disposal which was faster than any possessed by the Coast Guard. He had a friend in the Bahamas who had arranged the purchase of 1,200 cases of Scotch whisky at $75 a case, less than one-fourth of what such whisky was retailing for in New York.

What he lacked—and what he wanted Rothstein to provide—was the $90,000 to pay for the Scotch.

Rothstein did not at once leap at the idea. There were few men to whom he would advance $90,000 without security. Collins was not one of them. Besides, as he implied to Collins, he had great doubts about Collins' ability to tell the truth at any time about anything.

If Collins would give him all pertinent information, Rothstein would investigate and see if the proposition was as appealing as Collins made it sound.

Collins grudgingly told Rothstein where the boat was anchored. "By the way," he said, "you'll find that people there know me as Cromwell, Charles A. Cromwell."

Rothstein's emissary went to Philadelphia and checked. He found the boat, as described, and was informed that it was in the process of being purchased by a "Mr. Cromwell," a member of the wealthy and social family of that name. "Related to the Stotesburys," he was told.

So far so good.

Rothstein's next step was to find buyers for the whisky. This was not very difficult. What was difficult, however, was getting a deposit on an undelivered cargo. Here Waxey Gordon was helpful. He put up $30,000, a ten per cent deposit at the rate of $250 a case, a very good price.

Now Rothstein's investment was limited to $60,000 of his own money. That is, if he accepted the price originally quoted by Collins. He had no intention of doing this.

Next, Rothstein held another conference with Collins. He said he was prepared to go into the deal. However, while he trusted Collins implicitly, he felt it would be too much of a risk for Collins to carry $90,000 in cash with him. Anything could happen on the high seas, including mutiny or piracy. And there was always the danger of a stickup on dry land, even before Collins set sail.

To cut down the danger of any such eventuality, Rothstein said, he would send one of his own men to the Bahamas immediately. The man would make the purchase and have the whisky ready for storing on Collins' boat when it arrived.

Collins caviled. He accused Rothstein of lack of faith. He said Rothstein was making him look like a tin-horn. It did him no good. Finally he told Rothstein the name of the man in the Bahamas. As a sop to Collins, Rothstein advanced him $1,000, saying, "This is a loan and it makes you $12,000 in the hole."

Rothstein chose Sid Stajer to go to the Bahamas. He gave Stajer precise instructions. "Check that price. Collins wouldn't know how to tell the truth even if he wanted to. Offer $50 a case and see what happens."

Stajer, on his arrival in the Bahamas, found the liquor wholesaler, told him he was acting for Collins, and offered $50 a case for the Scotch.

"Not a chance," the man said. "I told Collins I wouldn't take less than $60 and that was a favor to him. [It turned out he had been in Atlanta with Collins.] If you don't want the load, there's a dozen others who'll take it."

"It's a deal," Stajer said, and counted off $72,000. This represented an actual cash outlay by Rothstein of $43,000. He had already received $30,000 and advanced Collins $1,000.

A few days later Collins steamed into the Bahamas. He not only loaded the 1,200 cases on board, but an additional 150 cases, purchased with money he had "promoted" from various sources. There was nothing in his agreement with Rothstein to prevent this.

The return trip to the United States was uneventful. No Coast Guard ships or other revenue boats were sighted. Late one night the yacht pulled into a private dock in New Jersey, the skipper explaining to the dockmaster that he was having engine trouble and wanted permission to make some minor repairs. Some hours later a fleet of trucks pulled up and removed the 1,200 cases of whisky which belonged to Rothstein and Collins. They left Collins' own 150 cases on board.

There was some discussion about the excess liquor, but Collins explained to Jack Diamond, who was with the truckers, that these were a separate deal. Then Collins, Diamond and the liquor rode into New York City and the warehouse.

Shortly before dawn a second truck pulled up at the dock. The driver got out, boarded the tied-up ship, and said he had been sent to pick up the 150 cases. He got two of the crew members to help him load this whisky on his truck and then drove away. The driver was Eddie Diamond!

As far as Collins was concerned, this venture into free enterprise and rugged individualism turned out to be a total loss.

A day later Collins and Rothstein sat down to divide the profits. The whisky, Rothstein told Collins, looking him in the eye, had cost $90,000. Collins offered no rebuttal. Sale price was $300,000, leaving a profit of $210,000 to be equally divided. From Collins' share, Rothstein then deducted the $12,000—the amount of the old marker plus the $1,000 loan. That left Collins with $93,000 due him. And that was what Rothstein paid him.

Rothstein's profit on the deal came to $139,000, plus the $12,000 recovered from Collins, previously a dubious asset, plus half the selling price of the 150 cases of liquor which the Diamonds had hijacked from Collins.

The entire deal was marked by cynicism. Collins had started out to get the edge on Rothstein and had failed. Rothstein had succeeded in outmaneuvering Collins. There were no hard feelings on either side. This was the way both did business. If this time Collins was the "pigeon," next time it might be Rothstein.

The Diamonds, in addition to their other payment, shared some $18,750, good pay for a couple of hours' work.

It was large "touches" such as this one which caused Diamond to turn outlaw. As petty thief, as holdup man, he had managed to garner just enough money to pay for flashy clothes and flashier women. As gang leader he had more money than he had ever believed existed. His wants—always basic—could be sated.

As gang leader he was able to compensate for his slight stature, for his sickness, for his lack of physical courage. The sawed-off shotgun truly was an equalizer for him. It made him as good as, if not better than, the biggest and the strongest. The person whom it was hardest to convince was himself. He had to prove himself, for himself, time after time.

As the underworld became more organized, Diamond was faced with a choice. He could take orders, become subservient again. There would be slight financial loss, perhaps none. But the bubble that was his ego would be deflated. And that he could not accept.

He was able to keep going for a short time because the new underworld had other problems. And because Rothstein was still his protector. In the first couple of years, Frankie Yale and Frankie Marlow, the rising Frank Costello, the already arrived "Big Bill" Dwyer, and Waxey Gordon did not want to take a stand against Rothstein and his power.

However, by 1924 the business of breaking the prohibition law had shaken down. Individual operators and small-timers were being eliminated. Many of them went out of business because the price of protection, plus the depredations of the Diamond gang, made it unprofitable to continue to operate. Others were simply told to get out of the business and they took the hint.

And by this time Rothstein found that his affairs were intermingled with those of others. He was no longer operating on his own. He had money in dozens of night clubs, those combinations of restaurant, bar and café that had sprung up in New York. These took the place of the famous restaurants of an earlier era. Jack's and Shanley's, Reisenweber's and Churchill's, Joel's and Bustanoby's, all were forced out of business. If they couldn't—or wouldn't—serve liquor they couldn't get customers. People in New York were no longer interested in dining. They wanted to drink.

There came into being such places as the Silver Slipper, the Rendezvous, the El Fay Club, the Ambassadeurs and the Cotton Club. All of them sold liquor. All of them were operated by the new dynasty of the underworld.

As in the late nineteenth century, these were robber barons, but more literally so than their predecessors. They sought—and gained —monopoly. They used any means to stifle competition. The simplest and most effective was death.

Rothstein knew all of them. Luciano had pushed dope for him. Louis ("Lepke") Buchalter and his partner, Jacob ("Gurrah") Shapiro, had first been thugs in labor wars, working for him. Larry Fay had borrowed the money for his first taxicab fleet from Rothstein and Rothstein carried the insurance on Fay's silver "El Fay" cabs.

Frank Costello's biographers report: "As early as 1921, it was common knowledge in New York that Arnold Rothstein . . . was associated with Costello in various forms of business. . . . [Costello] got his first instruction in the art of operating gambling rackets from the master financier of the underworld."

Costello's partner in those days, and for many years thereafter, was Dandy Phil Kastel. In the early days of that partnership, when the pair had a virtual monopoly on all the punchboards that sprang up about New York, Rothstein was the money source for them.

Herbert Asbury, again in *The Great Illusion*, wrote that ". . . [Costello] has made no secret of his association with and friendship for Arnold Rothstein."

Dutch Schultz served an apprenticeship with the Diamonds, drove a truck for Rothstein.

Even William V. ("Big Bill") Dwyer, who had no liking for Rothstein and, beginning in 1922, would have no business with him,

owed his start to Rothstein. Dwyer had Costello as an early associate and, through Costello, borrowed money from Rothstein. Their
break came because of Diamond.

By 1923 Dwyer had become the King of Rum Row. He was the
biggest importer of whisky into the United States. Taking over
where Rothstein had left off, he instituted a wholesale corruption
of the Coast Guard that extended all along the Atlantic coast. A
good part of all the whisky that Diamond hijacked belonged to
Dwyer.

Dwyer served notice that he did not care who was behind Diamond. He was going to put the hijackers out of business.

Rothstein by this time had wearied of Diamond. The hoodlum,
grown cocky, was as likely to steal from his employer as from a
stranger. His lust to hurt—to kill or maim—shocked Rothstein. Not
that Rothstein was sensitive, but he did not believe in waste of any
kind and Diamond's sadism was waste.

Informed that Dwyer had declared open season on Diamond,
Rothstein gave his blessing to Dwyer.

In October, 1924, as Diamond was driving his sleek limousine
along Fifth Avenue, another car drew up alongside and the occu-
pants of that car let loose a barrage of shotgun slugs. Diamond
somehow escaped a serious wound, though he was peppered with
pellets. He stepped on the gas and drove to a hospital, where he
received treatment.

Questioned by the police, Diamond said he had no idea who
might have shot at him. "I don't have an enemy in the world," he
said.

From that time on, Diamond was "no price" on Broadway. Not
even those who bet on the longest of long shots wanted any part of
him. If someone had offered to bet that Diamond would outlive
Rothstein, he would have been trampled in the rush of takers. Yet
Diamond did survive Rothstein by almost three years.

After this first attack on him, Diamond's gang disintegrated. No
one on Broadway stayed with a loser and Diamond looked like a
sure loser.

But, even though the Diamond gang broke up, the new type of

gang remained. Rothstein had created it and it outlived him. He had taught the underworld that it could create private armies that operated for the underworld's benefit, not that of politicians. True, the politicians got value from these gangs, but it was no longer their right. They had to pay an increasingly heavy price.

With the dissolution of his partnership with Gordon and Greenberg, and the end of his protection of the Diamond gang, Rothstein stepped out of actual bootlegging and rumrunning. He gave up the warehouse in Long Island City, Waxey Gordon taking it over. Gordon also took over a warehouse on West Thirty-eighth Street.

However, Rothstein's entanglement in beating the prohibition law increased, rather than decreased, over the years.

New York State passed its own enforcement act in 1921. This was the Mullen-Gage Law, whose provisions were far harsher than those of the Volstead Act. The new law turned enforcement into a state function. And it created a legal chaos such as no state had ever before faced.

Arrests were made on a roundup basis. Less than a month after the law became effective, court calendars were so clogged that it became impossible to set trial dates within a three-year period. Bailiffs and their deputies were sent into court corridors in an effort to fill jury panels. The police force in New York City could make little effort to enforce other laws.

The city chemist reported that more liquor was turned over to his department for analysis in a single month than the department could check in a year.

The Grand Jury became so involved in liquor cases that it had time for little else. In the two years that the Mullen-Gage Law remained on the books, just a little less than seven thousand indictments for violations of that law were handed up. Out of this total just twenty persons were convicted!

A situation like this was made to order for Rothstein.

His strength, as did the strength of such politicians as Tom Foley, Jimmy Hines and other district leaders, rested with their connections in the District Attorney's office and with the minor judiciary, especially the Magistrates' Courts of New York. District leaders virtually had the power of appointment to these offices, though nominally such appointments were in the hands of district attorneys and the mayor.

Fixes are made at the bottom of the chain of legal procedure. By the time a case goes to a higher court, the odds on fixing have become astronomical. However, when a case is in its beginning, that is the time deals can be made.

This explains why on the police records of such as Costello, Luciano, Yale, Marlow and others there are so many charges marked "dismissed." The fix was made at the preliminary hearings. Assistant district attorneys reported that they had "insufficient evidence" or witnesses just didn't appear or police officers suddenly found that they had overstepped themselves.

Evidence as to how widespread this practice was lies in the official figures. Of the 6,902 liquor law cases called up, 6,074 were dismissed at their inception. This does not mean that there was a "fix" in every case. It simply means that seven out of every eight cases never went past the Magistrate's Court. The record also shows that another 400 cases were never brought to trial.

What this meant to Rothstein was shown in the record of his bonding business. Between 1921 and 1924 Rothstein's office provided bonds amounting to over $14,000,000 in liquor cases of various kinds!

However, Rothstein functioned in many different ways in helping to make a travesty of the prohibition law. A good example was in the manner in which he thwarted the padlock law.

In 1921 the government began to use the padlock as a means of closing places where they had found violations of prohibition. This was highly effective for some time. Not so much because it put individual places out of business but because it prevented their being used for any purpose.

Landlords, able to exact high rentals for night clubs, cabarets and speakeasies, soon learned that they stood to lose long-term revenue if a padlock went on their property. Some landlords met this problem by boosting rents sky high. Others, however, decided they would rent only to law-abiding, if lower-paying, tenants.

However, there was one big loophole in the padlock procedure. It required that the law prove its case. If the owners of the raided premises, or the persons arrested on the premises, were acquitted or the cases against them dismissed, then they had a just grievance. And they could seek an injunction against further raids on the premises.

It was Gene McGee, Fallon's law partner, who called this to Rothstein's attention. He pointed out how near perfect this loophole was. The original injunction would be normally forthcoming. Such an injunction was equivalent to being licensed to operate as a speakeasy or night club.

The only way for the law to get the injunction vacated would be for the authorities to be able to prove that the premises were being used illegally. However, so long as the injunction was in force, the authorities were forbidden to raid the premises to get such evidence.

Rothstein sought out premises that had been raided, but where no convictions had resulted. He leased these. Then he had his attorneys go into court, in the name of a quickly formed corporation, and ask for an injunction against further raids. Rarely did he fail to get the injunction. Then Rothstein would turn around and sublease the premises to someone who wanted to run a speakeasy or night club, or, as happened in some instances, a gambling game or horseroom.

By 1924 Rothstein was receiving as much as $50,000 as a bonus for subleasing such a property.

Rothstein's cupidity made him go one step further in procuring injunctions. After all, before there could be an injunction there had to be a raid. So Rothstein began to arrange with his friends in the police department for such raids. One such instance, one of the few that received any publicity, involved the Park City Club.

This club, located at 107 West Forty-eighth Street, was raided early in 1925. The raiders, a group of plainclothes men, found nothing illegal on the premises. Some three days later a bond was filed and the club applied to Supreme Court Justice Aaron Levy for an injunction restraining the police from any further action against the club.

The case was assigned by Justice Levy to Referee Joseph Kahn, who held an open hearing. Joseph Shalleck represented the petitioners. He was one of Rothstein's many attorneys, a brilliant young lawyer who had begun his career in the office of Fallon and McGee and was known, even then, as a protégé of Jimmy Hines. Assistant Corporation Counsel Russell L. Tarbox argued against granting the injunction.

Tarbox made an immediate point that the bond which had been filed had been negotiated by Rothstein and issued by the National Surety Company, with whom Rothstein had many dealings. Shalleck asked that all mention of the bond and Rothstein be stricken from the record, on the ground that neither of these was pertinent to the case at hand. Referee Kahn remarked dryly, "Mr. Rothstein appears to have an amazing pertinency in many of these injunction proceedings."

How pertinent it was in this case was revealed by the testimony of Policeman Arthur Stearne, one of the raiding officers.

Stearne swore that the orders for the raid came "from upstairs." It developed that this meant they came from a source outside the department. The orders were given to Stearne's commanding officer, who had, some time earlier, ordered that the Park City Club be placed under observation.

Referee Kahn asked, "Was there any evidence that the premises were being used for any illegal purposes?"

"As far as I knew, no."

Stearne then pointed out that the raid was ordered for some time in the morning, hardly a time to catch any lawbreakers. "Some of us talked this over," Stearne testified, "and we decided the raid would be used for an injunction." Because of that suspicion, he added, he and some of the other raiders agreed they would try to gain entrance to the premises without identifying themselves. In that way, if they found nothing, it would not have been a raid, but merely a visit.

"In other words," Tarbox interposed, "you did not wish to lay the foundation for just such an action as this?"

"That is correct."

Stearne then went on to relate what happened. "We reached the place. The door was open. A couple of men were sitting around reading newspapers. There was no sign of any violation. We were all ready to leave when one of the men in the room asked, 'Is this a raid?' Before I had a chance to answer, another officer said, 'Yes, this is a raid. You're under arrest and we're going to search this place.' I knew right away we had been right thinking there was something smelly about the whole thing."

The search, of course, yielded nothing. The men were arrested and booked, bailed out by bonds obtained through Rothstein, then freed on action of the District Attorney's office.

"You think then," Tarbox asked Stearne, "that this raid had been prearranged?"

"I certainly do."

"For the purpose of seeking an injunction against further interference?"

"That's just what I think."

"Has anything happened to you since the raid?"

"I was put back in uniform. I am now assigned to Staten Island."

"Did this happen to any of the other officers who accompanied you?"

"Only to those of us who planned to cover up in case we didn't find any evidence. It did not happen to the officer who said that this was a raid."

Tarbox then asked, "Have you any idea who might have been behind all these happenings?"

Shalleck quickly objected, but even as he was objecting, Stearne said, "Everybody figured that Arnold Rothstein had something to do with it."

Once again the referee had a dry comment. "What everybody figures too often is something nobody knows. Strike the last question and answer from the record."

Despite Stearne's testimony, the referee recommended that the injunction be granted. He had no other course under the law. Judge Levy accepted the recommendation and the Park City Club was now virtually immune from the law.

It became the site of one of the biggest gambling games in New York. The man who ostensibly ran it was Jimmy Meehan. He was operating on a bankroll supplied by Rothstein.

The Park City case was in the courts during the 1925 mayoralty campaign in New York. Hylan had been informed that he would not be backed by Tammany, which was throwing its support to Jimmy Walker. In a press conference, he was asked to comment and he said, "Too many policemen are friends of Rothstein. Too many public officials are also his friends. That explains why places with which he is reported to be connected seem able to operate without molestation."

Whether this comment was factual or not, it was a stupid remark for Hylan to make. He had been mayor for eight years. Richard Enright had been police commissioner all these eight years, Hylan's appointee. If Rothstein had too many friends among the police and among the public officials, the fault must have been, at least in part, Hylan and Enright's.

What Hylan could have truthfully said was that Rothstein's connections and influence transcended his. This, however, would have been an admission that Hylan had been an ineffective mayor and his appointees equally ineffectual. So, he too chose to make an "everybody figures" statement. It was, of course, the best he could do. Not he, not Enright, not even the Hearst papers, still engaged in their battle against Rothstein and against Tammany Hall, were able to get any evidence to back up what they "figured."

Yet even at this period, when his influence appeared greatest, Arnold Rothstein was moving over on his underworld throne to make room for others who, if they were not to be his superiors, were certain to be his peers.

They were a motley crew and, where Rothstein had used finesse to attain his place, they used brute force. Where Rothstein had used cunning, they used a sawed-off shotgun. In only one respect were they like Arnold Rothstein. They, too, knew the power of the bankroll.

Chapter **19** *Who's for Italy?*

In 1932 Jimmy Walker, a disillusioned, heartbroken man, preparing to resign as mayor of New York, stood at the grave of Charles F. Murphy, looked down at the flower-covered plot, and said, "There lies all that is left of the brains of Tammany Hall."

Murphy had died in 1924. His successor as leader of Tammany was George W. Olvany. He held the title for five years, but never the power that had been Murphy's. The fault was as much Olvany's as anyone's. He had not wanted the position. From the day he assumed it he looked wistfully ahead to the day he could abdicate.

Power rarely goes long unclaimed. If Olvany did not want it, there were others in Tammany who did. These fought not for Olvany's title but for the might that went with the title. In the course of their struggle they came close to destroying Tammany.

John F. Hylan, vainly struggling in 1925 to retain his office against the challenge of a young, cocky Jimmy Walker, sensed the change in the Hall. He singled out Arnold Rothstein as the cause, called him "the gambler boss of Tammany," "the king of the underworld," and "the hidden power behind Tammany."

The bumbling, fumbling Hylan was wrong, as he so often was. But by some chance he had put his finger on a change taking place in the organization and on the man who, more than any other, was causing that change.

Rothstein was neither "king" nor "boss." If anything, he was a prime minister; the underworld, then as now, operated in a manner similar to the European parliamentary system. And, as is the case in many such instances, Rothstein led a coalition rather than a united party.

Rothstein had great power, but this was circumscribed. He was the link connecting the two men who sought, from the day Olvany became leader, to assume Olvany's power. These men, engaged in the real battle for control of Tammany, were James J. Hines and Albert C. Marinelli. Rothstein was necessary to both of them—and he was necessary to Olvany.

But, even more, Rothstein was necessary to the groups backing Hines and Marinelli. These were the now-rich, now-important gangsters. The underworld had grown, fertilized by gains from prohibition. It already had fortunes at its command. And it was in the process of increasing those fortunes. The gangster had become a force in American society and sought constantly to make himself an increasing force.

Once Rothstein's strength had rested in his bankroll. That was now thicker than ever, but it was no longer the thickest in the underworld. Even a Waxey Gordon had more money. A Big Bill Dwyer could have bought both Rothstein and Gordon in 1925.

Rothstein's strength lay in his being Arnold Rothstein—and nothing more. He was unique in his world. He was the lone solvent for politics and crime, for Hines and Marinelli. He was a bridge between the still-green past and the just ripening future.

The structure of the new criminal world was already visible. System and cartelization had made their appearance. Crime now transcended local limits, state lines and even international boundaries. Prohibition had caused this.

Crime could go into the open market place and buy whatever it wanted. It had its eye on Tammany Hall.

Murphy's death was the signal for the first offer.

When Murphy died, the politicians still controlled the criminals. The favors came from the Hall. Murphy, no fool, had seen the power of the criminals increasing and had moved to keep that power subject to his.

Olvany, succeeding him, stepped into a job for which he was not fitted. He had no stomach for a knockdown, dragout fight. He was essentially a compromiser. He lacked the steel of his predecessors.

During the five years that Olvany reigned, but did not rule, the relative positions of crime and politics altered, so that they balanced. And after Olvany's time, when John F. Curry became the head of Tammany Hall, that balance shifted. The criminals became the bosses; the politicians, the favor seekers.

The depression capped this change. During the depression the gangsters had money and no one else did. It enabled them to solidify their position.

This is how it came about. And Rothstein's part in it.

The changing American society of the twenties was influenced by many factors. Prohibition. A rise in wages and living standards. The revolt against authority, both public and private. The booming economy. The change in the ethnic structure of the country, especially in the cities.

In New York this last was marked by the rise of the Italians. Italian immigration to the United States came late, almost a half century after the great wave of Irish immigration. A trickle in 1880, it was a torrent by 1910.

Some Italians early entered politics in New York. One of the first was Anthony Rinaldo, who, like many other nineteenth-century Italian immigrants and first-generation Americans of Italian descent, joined the Republican party. These Italians were fired by dreams of liberty and, if they could not join the party of Garibaldi and Cavour in the United States, they could join that of the Great Emancipator.

Rinaldo was named as the Republican candidate for Congress in an East Side district. His opponent was a Tammany hack, a veteran congressman, Timothy Campbell.

During the campaign, Campbell had one set speech which he delivered whenever he made a public appearance. It was short.

"There is two issues. A national issue and a local issue. First, the national issue.

"There is two bills before the country—the Mills Bill and the

McKinley Bill. The Mills Bill is for free trade with everything free. The McKinley Bill is for protection, with nothing free. Do you want everything free or do you want to pay for everything?

"Having thus disposed of the national issue, I will now devote myself to the local issue, which is the Dago, Rinaldo. He is from Italy. I am from Ireland. Are you in favor of Italy or Ireland?

"Having thus disposed of the local issue, and thanking you for your attention, I will now retire."

Campbell won a smashing victory. The time had not yet arrived when an Italian could compete politically with an Irishman in New York City.

(Returned to his seat, Campbell made his mark in American history. He asked a favor of President Cleveland and was informed that the action he requested was unconstitutional. Indignantly Campbell snorted, "Mr. President, what in hell is the Constitution between friends?")

After Rinaldo's time, other Italians entered local politics. As time passed, the Italians veered to the Democratic party. The Democrats were better organizers. They did the favors. They could provide the jobs. And they usually had the power in New York City.

Murphy had early sensed the importance of the Italian vote in New York. The census figures were enough for him. In 1920 these showed that there were almost a half million persons of Italian birth in New York City, as opposed, for instance, to 160,000 who had been born in Ireland.

Murphy knew a third force had been added to the Irish and the Jews.

Murphy had begun to parcel out political patronage to the Italians as early as 1910. At first this patronage consisted of menial jobs, laboring jobs. At best they were in the Department of Sanitation. By 1920, however, Murphy was distributing more important patronage to the Italians. Even judgeships.

There was no complete unanimity in Tammany over this growing recognition of the Italians. Tammany from the end of the Civil War had been controlled by the Irish, for the Irish, with some *lagniappe* after the turn of the century to the Jews. Basically, however, it was an Irish fief, its coat of arms a shillelah rampant on a field of shamrocks.

And its leaders were Tweed, Croker, Kelly, Sullivan, Foley and Murphy. An obvious heir apparent, whose background was the same racially, who came from the same saloon-infested school, was James J. Hines.

Until 1921 it appeared that Hines, ex-blacksmith, ex-saloonkeeper, would succeed Murphy as leader when Murphy's reign ended. He was intelligent, a good mixer, a man who could get the vote out and get out as much as he needed. He had a small army behind him, an army of hoodlums, gangsters and thugs. But in 1921 Hines engaged Murphy in open warfare.

It grew out of a business deal. Hines had brought together Murphy and Louis N. Hartog, a manufacturer of glucose, during the war. In return for certain favors which Murphy could do for Hartog, Hartog would make Murphy his business partner. The deal had resulted in much bitterness and Murphy felt that Hines was to blame. As a result, he cut off much of Hines's patronage.

And Hines, in 1921, had sought to unseat Murphy's own district leader. The result was a bitter primary fight, in the course of which Hines's friend, ally and some-time attorney, Joseph Shalleck, was beaten, blackjacked and shot in the chest. After that battle Hines and Murphy were bitter enemies.

However, they had to do some business with each other. As the medium through whom they would deal they chose Arnold Rothstein. He remained friendly with both, to the advantage of all three.

When Murphy died, Hines was the obvious choice for leader. However, many of the district leaders felt that this would be a sign of lack of respect for the so-recently dead. Instead they chose Olvany, who had Hines's support.

But the first cracks in the Tammany monolith appeared when this choice was made. There was a demand for greater recognition of the Italians in Tammany Hall. This demand came, principally, from a thick-chested, tight-spoken, grim young man named Albert C. Marinelli.

Marinelli was shrewd, hard and ambitious. He entered politics while still in his teens and worked up to become an election district captain under Tom Foley. He and Arnold Rothstein early became acquainted. They found it easy to work together, both in politics and in business.

Marinelli was appointed a port warden in 1921. His duties included policing and patrolling parts of the waterfront, protecting them against use by bootleggers and rumrunners.

In the term that Marinelli served as port warden there was not a single seizure of contraband on the docks under his supervision. Nor, for that matter, was there any great number of arrests for such things as pilferage, robbery and smuggling.

It might have been that he enforced the law so rigidly that law-breakers avoided his docks. It might also have been that his friends did not want to embarrass him by doing business on his docks. Among those friends were Joe ("The Boss") Masseria, Lucky Luciano, Frankie Yale, Frankie Marlow and Albert Anastasia. Frank Costello was another intimate.

It might have been sheer coincidence, or just good luck, but during this same period Marinelli became wealthy. He established a trucking business in Little Italy, on the corner of Kenmare and Mulberry Streets, which prospered from its inception. It was primarily a rental business and among Marinelli's customers were the Borough of Manhattan, the City of New York, the Diamond brothers, Frankie Yale and Big Bill Dwyer.

Marinelli's friend Arnold Rothstein insured the business for Marinelli, wrote liability and property damage policies for him, and even a $40,000 policy on Marinelli's life.

Marinelli, who was later to become county clerk of New York, met a rebuff when he sought recognition from Olvany. He blamed Hines for this. To fight back, Marinelli decided to run for district leader against the incumbent, Harry C. Perry.

Hines backed Perry to the limit, with cash, votes and fists. Perry won.

Marinelli appeared to accept his defeat without rancor. He pledged his support to Perry and to Olvany. He worked diligently in the next election.

Olvany rewarded him with a type of bar-sinister recognition. Though Marinelli was not a district leader, he was consulted on patronage, much against the advice of Hines. Hines maintained that Marinelli was too ambitious to be trusted. And he pointed to the political support that Marinelli was getting.

This was coming from two anti-Hines district leaders, Daniel ("Battery Dan") Finn, whose family had long controlled the lower West Side, and Edward Ahearn, leader of the lower East Side.

He did not point out a far more important source of backing which Marinelli had accepted—even encouraged. This was the type of backing which would cause Thomas E. Dewey to describe Marinelli, some years later, as "the political ally of thieves, pickpockets, thugs, dope peddlers and big-shot racketeers."

The gangs made up Marinelli's shock troops, as they made up the shock troops of Hines. Behind Marinelli—perhaps a little ahead of him already—were the Italian gangsters, led by Joe Masseria. Allied with Hines were the old-line gangsters such as Ownie Madden, Big Bill Dwyer, Vannie Higgins and Larry Fay.

Later Hines would become the partner and supporter of Dutch Schultz. That time was still some years ahead.

A picture of the relationship at that time was given before a United States Senate committee, headed by Senator Copeland of New York, by two witnesses.

The first witness was George Z. Medalie, who had been Rothstein's attorney, later United States Attorney for the Southern District of New York and the political godfather of Thomas E. Dewey. Medalie said bluntly, "Gangs are part of the machine for political control and not until politics is divorced from municipal affairs will we get rid of gangsters."

The second witness was Frederic Kernochan, Chief Justice of the New York Court of Special Sessions. He testified:

"Gangs exist because they have some usefulness connected with district leaders. . . . Their special work is performed on primary days and election days and that is how they get their protection from district leaders. They could not exist a minute—no, I won't make it that strong—but they would be given a tremendous blow if, somehow, the protection of district leaders could be taken from them."

Medalie and Kernochan were testifying to the best of their knowledge and awareness. They gave the district leaders credit for more power than they possessed at the time. And the gangsters credit for less.

The new type of gang, put together so cavalierly by Rothstein for Diamond, had grown, expanded, just about taken over. A gang, for instance, like the one that early supported Marinelli, the gang headed by Joe Masseria.

Masseria was leader of the Mafia, which a few years later would become the Unione Siciliano. The Mafia was imported into the United States from Sicily about 1900. It was a secret society of cutthroats like the "Thuggees" of India. It came complete with blood brotherhood, secret codes, and of paramount importance, an enforcement branch, which took care of enemies, traitors and balking victims.

The first leader of the American Mafia was Ignazio Saietta, known as "Lupo" and "Lupo the Wolf," the latter a redundancy, in that "Lupo" was Italian for "wolf."

Saietta was a blackmailer, a sadist who preferred torturing some of his victims to collecting from them. He operated in the United States as he had in Sicily. His victims were his fellow Sicilians. Under Saietta, the Mafia was not part of the American underworld, but a branch of a foreign terror organization.

However, some of his followers were more Americanized. Among these were Joe Masseria, Ciro Terranova and Frankie Yale. Later these were to be joined by Johnny Torrio, Lucky Luciano, Frankie Marlow and Al Capone, among other recruits. Whether it was his own idea or that of his followers, Saietta decided to branch out into American-type crime. Here he made his mistake, for he chose to go into the counterfeiting business.

Federal authorities might later prove to be lax, inept and corrupt in enforcing the prohibition law, but they were highly efficient, always, in enforcing the laws against counterfeiting. Lupo was arrested in 1920, tried, convicted and given a thirty-year sentence.

Now began a battle to see who would succeed Saietta. Masseria found he had competition from Salvatore Mauro. Mauro was killed on Chrystie Street. Immediately his partner, Umberto Valenti, took over. Like Masseria, he sought support from the rising young toughs. He put together a small army headed by Silvano Tagliagambo.

Masseria's strong-arm men were headed by Luciano. And they made their headquarters in Marinelli's trucking office. In the end Masseria won his fight. To win it he got some help from an outside source, the Diamond gang, to which Luciano was then temporarily attached. And the Diamond gang, of course, was then being financed by Rothstein.

The new organization really organized. Ciro Terranova was given control of the Bronx and Westchester and the artichoke racket was made his special province. Frankie Yale was liege lord of Brooklyn, and overseer of the produce markets. Masseria was top man, with headquarters in Manhattan. His right-hand man was Luciano.

The new leadership—and prohibition—changed the whole complexion of the Mafia. It continued to collect tribute from the Sicilians in the United States, but it branched out into bootlegging, rumrunning, beer running, gambling and any other illicit activities that might yield a profit. But, like most gangs of the period, its main source of revenue was illegal alcoholic beverages.

This group, like any other gang, needed protection in its operations. It needed lawyers, bail bonds. It needed friends in positions of influence. It needed to make itself felt in New York politics.

That was the reason for the alliance with Marinelli. It was the reason the group maintained such close ties with Rothstein.

Hines was completely aware of what was going on downtown. He had his own gangster army. He knew that Marinelli was seeking to replace him as the dominant power in Tammany Hall. He made no secret of his knowledge, but he was unable at this time to get enough leaders behind him to destroy Marinelli politically.

Nor did Hines's gangster allies want to start a war. They saw something that Fourteenth Street did not see. They saw that Marinelli was giving the gangs and the gang leaders an importance they had never before had. Marinelli might be the political leader, but his leadership depended upon the whims of Masseria and his followers. The other gangs were not averse to reaching that same position. They would rather take over Hines and Tammany than wage war against their fellows below Forty-second Street.

This suited Marinelli and Masseria. They were hungry, scratching, kicking, gouging newcomers, not interested in any ground rules laid down by tradition. Time, they felt, was on their side.

So there was no war, but a truce. One side did not want war and the other side was not sure if it was ready. There might be a skirmish—like Marinelli's original effort to become district leader. But there would be no pitched battle.

Someone had to supervise the truce. Someone trusted by both sides. He had to be apart from both, yet a common denominator. Like the primary exercise in logic. No part of "A" is in "B." Part "A" is in "C." Part "B" is in "C."

"C" was obvious. "C" was Rothstein.

He was tied to both groups, friendly with both. Marinelli had a trucking business and Rothstein handled his insurance. Jimmy Hines and Larry Fay owned the New York Milk Chain Association, a group that blandly practiced extortion and called itself a "co-operative," and the Association rented office space from Rothstein.

Frank Costello needed $40,000 to purchase a brewery and borrowed it from Rothstein, giving him a note. The note was still in Rothstein's possession when he died. His executors collected the debt. And Jimmy Hines, always an inveterate gambler, found himself owing $34,000 to the bookmaker, Kid Rags, and got Rothstein to pay the debt for him, giving Rothstein an I.O.U. that he never collected.

Both groups owned night clubs and cabarets and Rothstein was their partner. Rothstein and Yale, Rothstein and Marlow. Rothstein and Madden, Rothstein and Fay.

Hoodlums, gunmen, pickpockets, bookmakers—joined to both sides—were arrested, found themselves in trouble. Rothstein posted their bail, arranged for attorneys to handle their cases.

Both sides needed a fence—and Rothstein was ready to buy.

Rothstein, the lucky middleman.

He was always available for favors. Did Joe Masseria want a pistol permit, Rothstein could arrange for one to be granted by State Supreme Court Justice Selah B. Strong. A permit that was stamped UNLIMITED, so that Masseria could carry a gun anywhere in New York State.

Rothstein, the common solvent. The man who could go to Olvany, Hines, Marinelli.

More, he was still a teacher, an improviser, for the underworld. He was showing how crooked profits could be turned into legitimate channels. He was deeply involved in real estate. His bonding business was one of the largest in New York. His insurance firm led all the others in writing insurance for the company he represented in 1924 and 1925.

He was a pioneer and these newly rich, newly important hoodlums and gangsters followed in his footsteps.

He was not truly aware of his importance, of his uniqueness. He was still blinded—would remain blinded—to anything but money. These others did not have to envy him that. They had money too.

Just as a dozen years earlier Rothstein had been the right man in the right place when Murphy sought a successor to Becker, so now he fitted precisely when this revolution was taking place in the underworld.

He could fill this special job circumstances created for him. And he could also go about his own business, still growing, still developing.

Especially he could keep his hold on industrial racketeering. Others watched as he profited from this field. But it really was no great concern of theirs at the time.

The gangsters were still primarily involved in the liquor business and their eyes had only now turned to their opportunities in politics.

However, there were some who already were getting their training in the garment center. Such as Louis ("Lepke") Buchalter, Jacob ("Gurrah") Shapiro, Albert Anastasia, and Tommy ("Three-finger" Brown) Luchese. Some of them were already making plans.

Chapter **20** *The Workingman's Friend*

abor racketeering in the construction industries goes back many centuries. The builders of the Pyramids were laborers enslaved by an Egyptian labor boss who had a connection with the Ptolemies. The ruling Inca of Peru, Pizarro reported, farmed out labor contracts to local caciques.

It is no wonder, then, that it should have made its first appearance in the United States in these same building and construction trades.

The actual labor boss—union leader, strong-arm man, crook, and political power—came into being at the end of the nineteenth century. His appearance was almost simultaneous in three places—Chicago, San Francisco, New York. In each instance it was in the construction field.

"Iron Sam" Parks began his career in Chicago, went from there to New York. His friend Martin B. ("Skinny") Madden succeeded him and was, in turn, succeeded by Michael J. ("Umbrella Mike") Boyle and Timothy ("Big Tim," of course!) Murphy. The man who controlled the labor field in San Francisco was Patrick Henry ("Pin Head") McCarthy.

The labor crooks attached themselves to the dominant political party. In New York it was Tammany and the Democrats. In Chicago it was the Republicans. And in San Francisco it was also the Republicans.

The Parkses, Maddens, Murphys, Boyles and McCarthys came

into existence, and gained their power, because of collusion between them and crooked employers and equally crooked politicians.

The American Federation of Labor was made up of craft unions, unions of skilled workers. Much of its organizing efforts went into the construction field. As a result, hundreds of new union locals came into being throughout the country. The AFL gave great autonomy to its locals. This was costly from its beginning to the present.

As the AFL membership grew, so, too, did its political power. Samuel Gompers, head of the Federation, enunciated a political creed for labor. It would "reward its friends and punish its enemies." Politicians, who had for long been on the side of management, now had to take into consideration the votes of labor. In most instances it was the Democrats who decided in favor of the unions.

The loose structure of the AFL made it possible for local labor strongmen to emerge from the ranks and take on great power. These men could make their own rules, call their own strikes, and impose the terms of settlement. These strongmen became the first labor crooks, the first labor racketeers.

For almost a score of years the crooked labor boss would be the heart of labor racketeering. Then a change would take place. And Arnold Rothstein, who had worked with the old-line labor racketeers, would introduce the new ones and the racketeering form in which they would operate.

He would invade new labor fields. He would introduce stand-by gangster armies. He would serve as protector of unions. And exact tribute from them. And he would lay the foundation for his successors, who would profit far more than he, terrorize as he had not, and become a part of the union framework.

But his beginning in this field would be by working with the first labor bosses, who were the first labor crooks.

Sam Parks was the father of labor racketeering in New York. He had been a workingman, a lumberjack, a coal heaver, a railroad brakeman, a roustabout and a construction worker. Working as a housesmith in Chicago, he had joined the union, become its walking delegate. The walking delegate had much power.

He was the liaison between union and employer. He served as union organizer and work overseer. The first walking delegates had to be tough. They were always in danger from paid strikebreakers and goons, from discontented union members.

Sam Parks was tough. He was well over six feet, big-fisted and foul-mouthed. He had fought a thousand battles and claimed never to have been defeated in a rough-and-tumble fight. Certainly he fought from poverty to wealth.

His was a case history of labor racketeering about 1900. A walking delegate, he so favorably impressed the mammoth construction firm of George A. Fuller Company, that the firm made him its "labor counsel." As labor counsel, he dealt with Sam Parks, walking delegate, changing hats as he bargained with himself. Other Chicago firms followed the lead of the Fuller company and Parks prospered in his dual capacity.

It was the Fuller company that was responsible for Parks leaving Chicago for New York. The firm decided to enter the New York construction field and wanted to protect itself against trouble from both competing firms and local union leaders.

Parks was offered a raise in salary as labor counsel if he would move himself and his operations to New York. The raise would cover any temporary loss of Chicago graft.

This was agreeable to Parks. In Chicago he was splitting his take with Skinny Madden. New York had no real labor boss and promised far greater profits.

Arrived in New York, Parks set his sights on control of the House-smiths, Bridgemen and Structural Iron Workers' Union. He attended a meeting of the union and appointed himself its new walking delegate. He offered to fight anyone who challenged his right to the job. There were no takers.

The union had 4,000 members. In a short time they were 4,000 groveling subjects of Iron Sam who had become "King Sam."

Parks was astute. From the start he realized that his basic job was to satisfy, not antagonize, the rank and file of the union. So, in the process of lining his own pockets, he also got higher wages and better working conditions for the union members. But he always settled for terms with which the construction companies had little quarrel.

Parks associated himself with two groups in New York. One was the Board of Building Trades, composed of heads of unions in the building and construction fields. The other was Tammany.

The construction field has always been in need of friends holding public office. No other type of business is so vulnerable to political harassment. Local bodies grant licenses and issue permits. Building inspectors, fire inspectors, all kinds of inspectors, delay construction, even halt it. There are dozens of city and county ordinances that can cause delays—and delays always cost money.

And, in Parks's time, there was constant need for workers to have physical protection from antiunion goons or dissident union members. It was a lot cheaper to get this protection from the uniformed police, whom the city paid, than to hire private guards.

The obvious place to go—the obvious ally—was Tammany. And there Parks went. He did not get all the promises he wanted. After all, there were long-standing political alliances between local construction interests and Tammany. Parks saw an opportunity to advance both himself and his own cause.

At this period Murphy was seeking to consolidate his position. And Big Bill Devery was challenging him. Parks allied himself with the Devery challenge.

His first overt move was to lend some of his strong-arm men to Devery in the mayoralty election. He also contributed to Devery's campaign chest.

Parks immediately found himself in trouble.

The Hecla Iron Works, holding a number of municipal building contracts, complained to the District Attorney that Parks had extorted money from Hecla and its owners. Parks was arrested, arraigned and his bail was fixed at $5,000.

What then followed was told by Harold Seidman in his book, *The Labor Czars.*

"His $5,000 bail," Seidman wrote, "was quickly supplied by Bill Devery, New York's former police chief. 'This whole roll,' said Devery flashing the money to the gaping multitudes gathered at the prison, 'is for my friend Parks. It is all money earned by honest labor, and will go to get an honest man who is under arrest out. There is nothing crooked about Parks. He is the workingman's friend and so am I.'"

This case was somehow settled. However, Parks's troubles were only beginning. He was again indicted for extortion, this time on the basis of charges preferred by the Hamburg-American Line, so dependent on Tammany for dock facilities and other privileges. Once again, Devery supplied bail.

This case went to trial and Parks was found guilty and sentenced to Sing Sing. His attorney obtained a certificate of reasonable doubt and Parks was returned to New York City. Bail was, once more, supplied by Devery.

Parks was grateful to Devery, but he was also a realist. Tammany had defeated Devery badly. Big Bill's political power was at an end.

Parks held a meeting with Assemblyman Dick Butler, a Tammany "regular," and asked for peace.

Murphy was amenable. He was more interested in friends than in enemies. He realized that the labor vote was growing ever more important and that the labor bosses were in a position to help Tammany in many ways. And even provide sinecure jobs for deserving Tammany Democrats. However, he made it a condition that Parks tone down his more blatant extortions and be more careful of those whom he chose as victims.

Parks agreed, but he soon violated the agreement. Called on the carpet, he was arrogant and boastful. As quoted by Ray Stannard Baker in *McClure's* magazine, Parks's answer was, "Don't talk to me about the boss. I'm the boss."

He learned that he was not.

He was again indicted, this time for trying to shake down a company which was building a theater for Big Tim Sullivan and his partner, John Considine.

Parks sent an emissary to Butler with the message that he wanted bail posted immediately. Butler turned the message down. Now Parks turned to his old friend Devery. He let Devery know that he was prepared to join him in another fight on Tammany. This time, he assured Devery, they would win.

Devery's answer was a formal statement, quoted by Seidman: "I will not stand for a man who carries water on both shoulders. Mr. Murphy and his friends are not friends of the laboring man. When Mr. Parks commences to flirt with Mr. Murphy and Company, I have no further use for him."

Parks remained in jail until he went on trial. It took a jury just fifteen minutes to convict him. Parks was given a sentence of two years and three months. He was serving this sentence in Sing Sing when he died.

It was some time before a successor to Parks appeared. But when he did he caused one prominent builder to say, "Today Sam Parks would be a saint. He was a hundred-dollar grafter. I wish he were here today."

The man who evoked this nostalgia for Parks was Robert P. Brindell.

Like Parks, he was a native Canadian. Like him, he had known poverty as a youth, had worked as a laborer. It was on the docks of Canada and the United States that Brindell served his apprenticeship. He was in New York, just another dock-walloper, when Parks rose to power.

He began his career as a minor functionary in the Dock and Pier Carpenters' Union. By 1907 he headed that union. In the next six years he began to make his influence felt in other unions. Among those who supported him in this drive were Tim Sullivan, Tom Foley and Charles Murphy.

Brindell early became a member of the Florrie Sullivan Association, though it is a question whether he was ever a United States citizen. His union members were active in primary and general elections.

Brindell, shrewder—or better advised—than Parks, sought to centralize all the building unions in New York and put them under his control. His first step was to affiliate his union with the national Brotherhood of Carpenters and Joiners, headed by William L. Hutcheson. With this as an entering wedge, Brindell was able to get other conservative union leaders to join him in forming the Building Trades Council.

This group, under an AFL charter from the national organization took unto itself the power to call strikes and negotiate wage and working conditions for all workers in the building industry. Brindell had himself elected to a life term as president of this body and then arranged that all delegates should be his appointees and none could be rank-and-file members. These delegates, further, were to be the business agents of the various unions.

Had Benito Mussolini ever sought a model on which to build his fascist state, he could not have chosen a better one than this charter and constitution of the Building Trades Council.

Almost at once this organization became known as the "Tammany Hall Annex." Its attorneys were John J. O'Connor, assemblyman from Murphy's own district, and Francis X. Sullivan, Tammany commissioner of public works. William P. Kenneally, one of the sachems of Tammany Hall and later its leader, was a vice-president of the Council. Tom Farley, who was to serve as sheriff of Manhattan and go down in history as "Tin-Box" Farley when he told the Seabury Committee that he found all his wealth in a tin box, was a business agent for the Cement and Concrete Workers.

Brindell also had some outside activities. He was a partner in an agency selling Simplex automobiles. The other partner was Arnold Rothstein. He got a kickback from life insurance sold to members of his and other unions. The insurance was placed by Rothstein. At one time Rothstein wrote almost $700,000 worth of insurance in one day, all on the lives of persons working for, or doing business with, Brindell.

There was still another field from which Rothstein prospered. When any new project was begun, contractors and builders had to supply performance bonds. These always met requirements when they were provided by Rothstein's firm.

The performance bonds, of course, had to be provided by the

employers. However, organization of the employers was as streamlined and centralized as organization of the unions. Where the unions had their council, the employers had their "employers' association."

The fifteen largest construction firms were members of this association. The members had a monopoly on building and installing every product needed in construction work—except labor. No sand, marble, tile, stone, plumbing or electrical supplies could be used in construction unless supplied by a member of the Association.

A shrewd attorney, John Hettrick, had conceived of the Association, and, when it was formed, managed its affairs. He supervised all bids from members, setting any arbitrary figure he wished. Since he represented a monopoly group, he believed in charging all—and, as eventually happened, more than—the traffic would bear.

Two men, Hettrick for the employers and Brindell for the unions, had complete control of construction in New York. The Association would hire only workers under Brindell's discipline. The unions would boycott any construction work not performed by the Association.

Brindell policed the agreement. He collected tribute from the members of his union or they could not work. If any employer dared hire a worker who had not paid off, the Association would cause the worker to be fired and would discipline the employer.

Employers outside the Association could not hire union men. If they hired nonunion men, Brindell would use hoodlums to wreck both the job and the workers. He could always get a supply of hoods through his good friend Arnold Rothstein.

It was their own greed which finally caught up with both Brindell and Hettrick. The latter, drawing up bids, approving specifications, raised prices so high that he priced all New York City construction out of the market. Both private and public building came to a standstill.

New York City authorities refused to take any action but, once again, a State Senate committee acted. The Lockwood Committee, with Samuel Untermyer as its counsel, came to New York and held a series of hearings. There was no lack of witnesses.

The facts concerning both the workers' Council and the Employers' Association became public knowledge. The District Attorney was forced to act. Brindell was indicted on three counts of extortion. When he was arraigned, bail was set at $10,000, and Rothstein posted the bail for him.

Then Hettrick was indicted as a fellow conspirator. Again Rothstein was on hand to act as bondsman.   -

There was, as always, a political issue involved. Brindell, the big man of labor, was tied to the Tammany machine. He was able to provide votes and money whenever these were needed. The Republican legislature was hoping to cut off the flow of both.

Tammany fought back. Assemblyman O'Connor rose on the floor of the Assembly and called on God to witness that "this entire investigation is part of a deep-seated propaganda to discredit organized labor." His fellows on the Democratic side of the chamber cheered the speech. Other Tammany stalwarts made the same charge.

But the evidence, assembled by Untermyer and handed, iron-riveted, to the District Attorney, was overwhelming. Brindell was convicted and given a five-to-ten-year sentence. Hettrick and a half dozen others also were sent to jail.

The costs of construction fell. Once again there was new building.

That was the only real result of the investigation and the trials. It did not affect the relationship between crooked labor leaders, crooked employers and politicians. Men like Joseph P. Ryan and Joseph Fay would replace Brindell. They would be replaced by others when they were caught. Men like Johnny Dio and Vincent Squillante and their like.

And Rothstein would go on. Brindell was in jail, but there were other union leaders who required his services. Other employers, like his old friend Sam Rosoff, who would call upon him for help in dealing with unions.

His influence, in many labor fields, far transcended the geographical limits of New York.

Arch Selwyn, the theatrical producer, told the *New York Times* how far that influence extended.

"When we and Sam Harris," he said, "were building our theaters in Chicago, we got into a jam. They pulled a strike on us and tried to hold us up for a sum of money we did not have. We were absolutely in the hole.

"It was some of Big Tim's [Murphy's] stuff.

"Murphy gave Al Woods the works. Woods wouldn't come across so they put a bomb in his theatre. I told Arnold what we were up against. He was very fond of Sam Harris. He called Tim up on long distance and told him: 'Listen, Tim, these fellows haven't any such dough as that. They're friends of mine, and what you're doing to them, you're doing to me. You leave it to me and I'll treat you right. You can trust me. But call your dogs off and see that the boys get a square deal.'

"We had no more trouble after that."

Selwyn added that the original demand had been for $50,000, but that Murphy had been placated with just $10,000 after Rothstein's call. "He [Rothstein] had influence in every big city in the country. And he loved it."

One place where that influence was potent was just across the Hudson River, in New Jersey. Boss Frank Hague had close relations with Tammany Hall and when he was fighting for control of the Democratic organization in 1916 and 1917 he got help from the Hall. Rothstein sent a large group of floaters and toughs across the river to give what assistance might be needed.

Hague showed his gratitude by giving Rothstein a bookmaking monopoly in Hudson County. Rothstein first opened a big book in Weehawken and later moved it to what was then Union Hill and is now Union City.

More important, Hague brought Rothstein together with Theodore Brandle, then business agent for the Iron Workers' Union and later as powerful in New Jersey as Brindell had been in New York.

Brandle became labor boss, businessman, politician and even banker. Brandle also had a bonding business. It bonded all companies which did work for public agencies. It became the second largest such firm in New Jersey. Its New York representative was Arnold Rothstein.

One hand fed the other.

Crooked as all this was, vicious and larcenous, it still came under the head of "honest graft." It was not gangsterism. Not the gangsterism which Arnold Rothstein introduced into the garment trades. It would be some time before the methods used in that field would be imposed in other union fields.

The garment industry—call it cloaks and suits, needle trades, or all of these—had its beginnings in New York City, and New York has remained its major headquarters for some seventy-five years.

Like many industries and businesses, it started in New York because there was an ample supply of cheap labor. The workers came from Europe to Castle Garden, to the slums, and then to the sweatshops. The last two steps frequently took place on the same day.

The first disorders in the garment industry occurred in 1897, when some radicals incited a few of the workers to ask for an increase in pay. One employer met this demand by calling on young Monk Eastman, who led a group of toughs into an attic workroom on Allen Street and beat up two men supposed to be the union ringleaders.

This was just a day's work to the unimaginative, hard-fisted Eastman. He did not sense he had been offered a continuing source of revenue. His work done, his pay collected, Eastman returned to robbery, slugging and general assault and battery.

In 1909 the first large-scale strike of garment workers took place. By that time, according to a report made by the Federal Immigration Commission, a marked change had taken place in the garment workers. There were as many Italian workers as there were Jews, and women had become the majority.

There was hardly a family in the lower East Side ghetto or in Little Italy, to the north and west, which did not have at least one member working in a sweatshop, taking home cloth to be sewn, or working as presser or fitter.

Hours were long, sometimes as much as eighteen hours a day. Pay was low, sometimes as little as fifty cents a day. Tens of thousands of the workers were contracting, or had already contracted, tuberculosis. This was an occupational hazard, stolidly accepted.

From the same homes that the workers came the gangsters came. There was not a gangster who did not know about these working conditions firsthand. They could see a mother, a sister, a father, a brother, working at the garment trade.

Gangsters are surprisingly literal. Most of them are highly emotional. (Recall the deathbed mumblings of Dutch Schultz: "Mamma. Mamma. Mamma." "Put a roof on the doll.") In 1909 most of the gangsters had been reared in homes where the honest, hard-working members damned the "bosses" and the "padrones" even as they worked to make these rich. No wonder the hoodlums had their sympathies on the side of the workers.

To a great extent this influenced their action in the 1909 strike. Their mothers and sisters were being beaten and kicked by "guards" whom the employers hired. It was as important a factor to the gangsters as the few dollars they earned during the strike.

The unions, splintered into factional groups on the basis of racial, religious and political differences, could not have survived without the aid of the gangsters, many of whom were volunteers. The unions had little money in their treasuries and had not yet attained any political importance.

The union leaders knew they had to win or die. They believed their cause was just. Like so many other fanatics, they also rationalized that the end justified the means. So they brought in gangsters to fight their battles for them.

Among the first to be hired were Big Jack Zelig, so close to Charles Becker, Joseph ("Joe the Greaser") Rosensweig, and Pincus ("Pinchy") Paul. Zelig and Rosensweig worked together. Paul was a member of another gang.

When the strike was concluded the unions had gained a precarious foothold. And the gangsters a firmer one. Zelig stayed on as an organizer for two unions. He held this job when he was killed.

Rosensweig wanted a job as organizer for the Furriers' Union. Unfortunately Paul already held that job. First, Rosensweig tried persuasion to get Paul to resign. Two beatings did not persuade Paul. So Rosensweig decided he had to take sterner measures. He called in one of his followers, Benny Snyder, and told Snyder to kill Paul.

Snyder followed orders too literally. He went right out and murdered Paul in front of a half dozen witnesses.

District Attorney Charles A. Perkins, an anti-Tammany office-holder, had little trouble getting a full confession from Snyder. Snyder swore that he had been paid five dollars by Rosensweig to commit the murder. He even had the five greasy dollar bills in his pocket when he confessed.

The cooperative Snyder received a twenty-year term for second-degree murder. Rosensweig was able to plead guilty to manslaughter and get off with ten years. Perkins preferred this to putting Snyder on the stand as his only witness.

All three of the original gang leaders who had found soft pickings in the garment industry were now out of circulation. A vacuum existed. The unions still needed physical protection; "finks" and "goons," some of them with deputies' badges, still harassed union members and owners of union shops. Benjamin ("Dopey Benny") Fein soon filled the vacuum.

There was little "dopey" about Benny except his name, and this derived not from any lack of intelligence but from the vacuous, slightly sleepy expression he wore because of adenoids.

Excepting his open mouth, Benny's was a good-looking face. He had brown, curly hair, large, limpid, brown eyes, a straight nose, and a strong mouth and chin.

This was a period of disorganization among the gangs. Eastman was in jail. Paul Kelly had moved to Harlem, where he was organizing the ragpickers. Zelig, one of the few strong leaders, was dead. A reform administration was arresting and convicting gangsters who had long been immune from law.

Fein was intelligent enough to sense that this was no time for an ambitious gangster but a good time for a clever one. He sought to act as peacemaker among the different gangs, such as those led by "Porkie" Flaherty, Abie Fisher, "Little" Rhody and Billy Lustig. He pointed out that there was enough loot for all, provided they acted together.

Sweet reason temporarily prevailed and a general agreement was reached. Benny staked out the garment center as his own preserve.

Within a short period Fein was employed by twelve locals, drawing a weekly salary from each. That salary ranged from $25 to $50. In addition, as he later confessed, whenever trouble arose and he had to hire outside "help," he received a bonus of $100, and $10 daily for each helper. He paid the helpers $7.50 a day and pocketed the difference.

Benny also received protection. The unions agreed to engage lawyers for him, provide bail when that was necessary, and counsel should such help be needed.

The unions had gone to a third party for this protection and these services. They had gone to Arnold Rothstein.

There was a deep irony in the reason they had asked Rothstein's help.

Many of the union leaders were Jewish. One of the earliest workers' organizations in New York was the United Hebrew Trades Union. This organization, like most of the early unions, was not founded by fire-eating labor leaders but by idealists, theoreticians and social philosophers.

They knew their Karl Marx. Many of them were followers of such Utopians as Fourier and Robert Owen. Some were Platonic Socialists and others were soapbox anarchists. But they knew very little about the practical side of unionism.

They needed a middleman to act for them. They picked Arnold Rothstein—and here was the irony—not because he was involved in politics, not because he was Jewish, but because he was the son of Abraham Rothstein.

They had learned they could trust the father. So they placed their trust in the son.

This was just another business proposition to Rothstein. He had something to sell and here were people who wanted to buy it. They were willing to pay a good price both to him and to those to whom he would go in their behalf. He would take the cash and let the votes go—where they would do the most good.

He agreed to use his influence with Tammany Hall. He agreed to provide bail bonds, lawyers. That was his business.

He could not promise too much. New York City, as the result of the Becker scandal, had once more elected a reform mayor, John Purroy Mitchel. Perkins, the District Attorney, was a Republican. Both were antilabor.

Mitchel and his police commissioner, Arthur Woods, were carrying on a campaign against the unions. Arrests were being made by the score. Finally, even Dopey Benny was arrested. He was held on four counts of felonious assault.

Fein sent out a hurry call for bail and a lawyer. The call was relayed to Rothstein. He advised against bailing out Fein. The advice was not unpleasant to the union leaders. Fein had become a most expensive employee. In addition, he had insinuated himself and some of his followers into various union offices. Legitimate union leaders had feared his revenge if they moved against him.

But now they had Rothstein on their side. Rothstein and his own group of hoodlums.

Rothstein had his own reasons for offering the advice. In the first place, Fein was not dependent upon him. In the second, he felt Fein could be sacrificed.

The union leaders followed Rothstein's advice. Fein stayed in jail. It took some time, but finally Fein realized he was being made a sacrificial offering to placate the authorities. He moved to save himself. He sent a message to District Attorney Perkins offering to make a full confession in return for a light sentence.

Perkins agreed. He saw an opportunity to connect his political enemies, Tammany, with protected lawlessness. Charles Whitman was sitting in the governor's chair in Albany as the result of just such an exposé.

Fein proceeded to make a full confession. He told about his activities, his pay scale, the numerous assaults and acts of terror he had committed. But he could not put a finger on any big politicians or on Tammany. The closest he could come to this was to inform Perkins that arrangements had been made by the unions for Arnold Rothstein to provide bail and counsel for him and his followers.

Rothstein was summoned to Perkins' office. He appeared, accompanied by his current attorney, Isaiah Lebow. He admitted posting bail in numerous instances. That was his business. He admitted nothing else.

The meeting ended almost immediately. Perkins had to admit, when Lebow pressed him, that he was not against the right of accused persons to bail.

However, armed with Fein's confession and Grand Jury testimony, Perkins got indictments against eleven gangsters and twenty-three union officials. Rothstein posted bail for all of them.

Trial of the union officials was delayed on one pretext or another until the end of Perkins' term in office. He was succeeded by Edward Swann, a Tammany choice.

In 1917 Swann appeared in court and asked for dismissal of the indictments on the ground that there was not sufficient evidence to warrant prosecution. Judge Delehanty granted Swann's request, almost a matter of form.

There were immediate cries of "fix" and "undue influence." L. S. Breckenridge, who, as assistant district attorney under Perkins, had prepared the cases, charged that the wholesale dismissal was the result of "a disreputable Tammany plot and the dismissal . . . was a part of a pre-election promise which gained for Judge Swann the support of the East Side labor leaders and a well-known gambler when he ran for District Attorney."

Judge Delehanty, on the basis of affidavits from Breckenridge and others, accused Swann of presenting a false recommendation to him and demanded that the Governor remove Swann from office.

Whitman held a series of hearings and concluded that, while the evidence was not sufficient to warrant Swann's removal, it was enough to cause Swann to be censured.

That slap on the wrist concluded the legal maneuverings.

Rothstein had proved his value to the unions. He had provided them with the protection for which they had asked. For Rothstein, the unions now offered an ever-expanding source of revenue. The larger they grew the more they needed him.

Rothstein had placed his own crew of gangsters inside the unions, opened the way for them to grow ever stronger within the industry. The first leader of this group was Jacob ("Little Augie") Orgen. Little Augie, one of Benny Fein's lieutenants, proved his worth in the garment disorders of 1919 and 1920.

He was clever rather than brave. He was a schemer. He disliked physical combat, but when forced into it fought with the desperation of the born coward. He wanted to rise above himself, to become a "sport." To that end he dressed in flashy clothes and even wore fawn-colored spats.

Those spats must have been a constant challenge to the gang of hoodlums who worked under him. They were as hard, mean, cruel and ambitious a group as had ever been gathered. Receiving their $7.50 a day from Little Augie were the Diamond brothers, Lucky Luciano, Waxey Gordon, Lepke Buchalter and Gurrah Shapiro.

Little Augie held control until 1923. Then he became involved in a battle with a gangster called Kid Dropper, who sought to muscle in on the Wet Wash Workers' Union. Dropper was killed by a follower of Little Augie's, Louis Kushner.

The police could not connect Little Augie with the murder, but they placed him under such close surveillance that his usefulness in the garment industry ended. His place was taken by Lepke Buchalter.

Little Augie, in 1925, became a bootlegger and prospered. He was a partner of Jack Diamond in 1927, when he was killed. He and Diamond were talking together on Norfolk Street, on the East Side, when four men drove up and opened fire on them. Diamond was not touched. It has remained moot whether the killers were after Orgen or Diamond. It did not make any difference to Orgen. He was dead and, if that was a mistake, it was not a rectifiable one.

Lepke Buchalter, the man who took Little Augie's place as leader of the gangsters in the garment industry, was a complex character. When he took first rank he was scarcely more than twenty, a presentable, soft-spoken individual with soft, collie eyes and a dimple in one cheek. He already had a police record, the first notation going back to 1915.

Lepke came from a good family, his antecedents much like Rothstein's. His people were honest, in comfortable financial condition, pious and educated. Of their children they had trouble only with one, Louis. And he was the most intelligent and, seemingly, the best behaved.

By his mid-teens, he had become an outlaw. He was tough with his fists, but he did not like to use them. Of medium height and weight, he was no match for real bruisers. But he did not have to be. His brain more than made up for lack of brawn. The young hoodlums with whom he hung out early made him their leader. They might out-fight him, but they couldn't outthink him.

Lepke had a talent for organization. He made friends easily. But he was an unrelenting enemy. He could be double-crossed only once. That was why, in later years, he could play so large a part in putting together the Syndicate.

Lepke had imagination. He was a dreamer with a touch of megalomania, a disease so common to gang leaders.

When Rothstein gave him his opportunity in the garment rackets, Lepke grasped it. He saw possibilities in it—for wealth and power —that Rothstein could not envision. He bided his time, made his plans. Ultimately the time came when he could put those plans in operation.

Lepke's partner, Jacob (Gurrah) Shapiro, was different. He was big, hulking, loud-mouthed. His education was limited, his imagination even more restricted, and his appetites completely animal. But he was a terror in a fight, had complete loyalty to Lepke, his senior partner, and the physical ability to keep recalcitrants in line.

A good index to the differences in the men stemmed from the source of their nicknames. "Lepke" derived from "Leb," Buchalter's Jewish name, and was an affectionate diminutive, bestowed by his mother. "Gurrah," on the other hand, evolved from Shapiro's difficulties with the English language. When annoyed, he would shout, "Gurrah'd a here." Translated, this meant "Get out of here" and was usually accompanied by a blow or kick.

For some time the only importance they had in the gang world came from their jobs with Rothstein. They had no other connections, had not yet earned any type of reputation. They ranked, for instance, far below Luciano, who was already known as a lieutenant of Joe Masseria.

It was while working for Rothstein that Lepke and Luciano became friends, a friendship that was to play so important a part in later years when they were among the heads of the national crime cartel.

Lepke's great chance came during the vicious, damaging, bitter strike that erupted in the garment center in 1926. Only then did he emerge as a man of importance.

The 1926 strike went far beyond the classic struggle between worker and management. Unions fought unions. Factions within the same union fought each other. Employers found themselves on opposite sides of the battle.

In some locals right wing fought left wing. In others two left-wing factions fought each other. One union might join an employer to fight a second local. And an employer might give aid to a local that the shop on the floor below was trying to destroy.

Such a situation was made to order for Rothstein. Everyone needed his services and he had no loyalties, except to his pocket-book.

Writing of this strike, Harold Seidman, in *The Labor Czars,* said:

"Arnold Rothstein maintained a flourishing business . . . supplying gangsters to the furriers' and garment workers' unions. In addition, he 'fixed' the police so that they would not club the strikers. For his services, he received fees running into the hundreds of thousands of dollars."

And Joel Seidman, in *The Needle Trades,* part of the series of books on "Labor in the Twentieth Century," wrote:

"In the . . . 1926 strike . . . the General Strike Committee expended some $3,500,000. . . . While negotiations were in progress with manufacturers, it became known that . . . the notorious gambler, Arnold Rothstein, had been sitting as mediator."

The furriers were deeply involved in this great strike, primarily a battle of ideologies between different sectors of the union. During their strike the late Matthew Woll, vice-president of the American Federation of Labor, wrote a letter of protest to Mayor Walker. In it he declared:

"It is a common rumor, if not an understanding throughout the fur district, that 'police protection' has been assured the Communist leaders and sympathizers. [The left-wing faction was led by Ben Gold, destined a quarter of a century later to be found guilty of violating the Smith Act.] It is said that nearly ten days before the beginning of the present reign of terror, one Arnold Rothstein, said to be a famous or infamous gambler, had been the means of fixing the police in behalf of the Communists."

This charge was met by a barrage of denials. Walker announced that Rothstein had no influence with his administration or with the police. Rothstein said his only connection was to post bail for persons arrested. Gold issued a statement pointing out that far more of his followers had been arrested and clubbed than members of the opposition. And Morris Malkin, one of Gold's associates, said he had documentary proof that Rothstein not only was not on the left-wing side of the argument but that he was in the pay of the other side.

In 1933 Malkin was a witness before a Congressional committee investigating labor troubles. By this time Rothstein was five years dead and Malkin had turned on his former beliefs, recanted his Communism. He now recanted on another level. He swore that it was true that the Communist faction had purchased Rothstein's support.

"We felt," he said, "we could not win without outside help to keep the police and the politicians from interfering with us. We knew the man to see was Arnold Rothstein. We went to him and paid him and we had no trouble with the police during the strike."

The committee counsel then asked if Rothstein was a Communist.

"He didn't know or care about the politics of a strike. He named a price for his help and we paid it."

Malkin was next asked, "Did he ever work against your—I mean the Communist—side?"

"Yes. Whenever they got to him first, or if they paid him more."

Rothstein profited greatly from the 1926 strike—in cash. But he lost greatly too. Even as he seemed strongest he was growing weaker.

The strike hurt many locals, decimated their memberships, bankrupted their treasuries. The gangsters, however, had to be kept on the payrolls. Lepke sensed his opportunity. Instead of taking pay from the unions, he simply took over the unions. They became his property.

Lepke the dreamer was on his way to making his dream come true. He and his cohorts gathered more and more garment unions into their hands. And they moved into other union fields. Soon Lepke's domain included painters' unions, motion-picture operators' unions, dockworkers' locals and teamsters' locals.

After 1926 Lepke worked not for Rothstein but with him.

Lepke needed Rothstein for his political importance. Neither Lepke nor any other gangster had yet made direct contact with Tammany. Rothstein was still the link.

But the unions—and the employers—soon learned that the man who dominated their industry, who would dominate it for years, was Lepke. He and Gurrah were "The Boys." And the Boys milked the garment industry as long as they lived. It was their heirs—Anastasia, Plumeri, Levine and Luchese—who would take over after them.

All, however, would owe a debt to Rothstein. He had opened the vein, showed them how to exploit it. Showed them how to double-deal and cheat.

For Arnold Rothstein, protector of the unions, the workingman's friend, had also sold them out.

The facts came to light when the Seabury investigation filed its report. Buried in it was this, about the 1926 strike:

"Manufacturers had sought or welcomed the aid of underworld characters like Arnold Rothstein . . . in an effort to avoid unionization."

Anything for a buck.

Even narcotics.

Chapter **21** *The Juice of the Poppy*

Wah Kee, a slender Chinese with a stringy goatee, arrived in New York from San Francisco in 1868 and opened a shop at 13 Pell Street. He sold Oriental curios, bean sprouts, other vegetables used in Chinese cooking, candied ginger and sweets. In a flat over his shop he sold opium pellets and provided pipes for smoking them.

This was the beginning of commercialized use of narcotics in New York City.

Soon others opened "opium dens." The places attracted the attention of the police, not because of the use of narcotics but because they became gathering places for thieves, footpads and gangsters. The opium dens were regarded as in a class with saloons and, for many years, were no more illegal.

When Arnold Rothstein was growing up he occasionally visited these dens. Joseph Lilly, in a series of articles in the New York *Telegram,* reported that Rothstein had been an occasional opium smoker. He might have been; a great many of his contemporaries were. But if he smoked opium as a youth he had long since foregone the pleasure by the time of his death.

By that time his interest was in the smuggling and sale of drugs, not in their personal use. There was big money in dope and Rothstein was always interested in big money, never more so than in the last few years of his life.

To Arnold Rothstein the dope traffic had no moral connotations. It was a question of trying to "beat the government," just as in the importation and sale of liquor. And hardly as bad, for there was a constitutional amendment against the importation and sale of liquor and only a hazy law, more hazily enforced, against traffic in narcotics.

When Rothstein was growing up, the use of narcotics was widespread. It was encouraged by some of the best—and richest—people. Harry J. Anslinger, United States Commissioner of Narcotics, has stated that one out of every four hundred Americans was a narcotic addict in 1900!

George E. Pettey wrote, in *The Narcotic Drug Diseases and Allied Ailments,* that "At the turn of the century, patent medicines containing opiates in some form were sold in every drugstore in the country. They were offered for relief of headaches, general aches, various pains, the 'misery' and that 'tired feeling.' School children could go to a local soda fountain and buy a medicated drink containing cocaine."

When heroin came into use in 1898, the medical profession hailed it as a great advance in healing and enthusiastically endorsed it for virtually every use. One advertisement, in *Ainslee's* magazine, called it "the greatest boon to mankind since the discovery of morphine in 1803," and offered it for sale to the general public in various forms.

It was not until some years later that its addictive properties became known. And then another type of advertisement appeared in the magazines.

In 1910 the St. James Society of New York advertised it would "send any one addicted to Morphine, or other drug habits, a trial treatment sufficient for ten days, *free of charge,* of the most remarkable remedy for this purpose ever discovered . . . dissimilar in every respect from any other known treatment. Our remedy . . . leaves the patient with health entirely recovered, and free from all desires formerly possessing them."

But there was still no law against importation, manufacture or sale of narcotics.

By that time narcotics had been in use some seven thousand years. It was the Sumerians, who occupied the lower part of Mesopotamia, now called Iraq, who discovered the euphoric properties of the poppy. They extracted its juice and gave the resultant nectar the name "gil," which meant "joyous" or "rejoicing." Narcotics are still called by this name in the Middle East.

Not until the tenth century A.D. did the poppy, with its joys, its illusions and its noxiousness reach the Far East. Arabian traders then introduced it into China. Barbosa, the Portuguese explorer, reported in 1511 that he saw much of the "opium which Moors and Indians eat."

At about that time Western Europe became acquainted with opium and its doctors wrote, in words that were forerunners of the advertisements of four centuries later, that the drug was useful in treating "poison, deafness, asthma, colic, coughing, jaundice, fever, leprosy, female troubles and melancholy."

Opium became a trade weapon and later an instrument of diplomacy. A war was fought because of it, the "Opium War" between England and China, fought to prevent China's banning the importation of opium. The British East India Company was bringing it to China from India by the shipload and it represented the difference between a favorable and an unfavorable balance of trade for the British.

That war resulted in British victory and, ultimately, in the "Open Door" policy.

The Yankee traders of Boston were not without guilt in this instance. Russell and Company and Augustine Heard and Company, both of Boston, were fighting side by side with the East India Company, and profiting, though hardly as greatly.

Narcotics were in use by physicians and surgeons in the United States from the beginning of the Republic. Each new discovery was adopted and accepted by the practitioners of medicine. A flourishing trade developed in proprietary medicines which contained narcotic drugs of all kinds. There was big money in peddling narcotics and it was part of big business.

Mark Sullivan, in Volume II of *Our Times,* wrote:

"Along with the rest went the adulteration of drugs; the . . . use without restrictions, in patent medicines, of opium, morphine, cocaine, laudanum, and alcohol; the preposterously false and cruelly misleading curative qualities claimed. These patent medicines were sold in every drugstore . . . in the land. . . . It was an immense traffic. In 1900, the total volume of business was $59,611,355. The patent medicine manufacturers comprised, at that time, the largest single [national] user of advertising space in newspapers."

It was the magazines, not the newspapers, which took up the fight against promiscuous sale of narcotics. Edward W. Bok instituted the campaign in 1904 in the *Ladies' Home Journal*. Shortly afterward Samuel Hopkins Adams wrote the first of a series of articles to appear in *Collier's Weekly*.

Adams revealed the formulas of the "opium-containing soothing syrups, which stunt or kill helpless infants; the consumption cures, perhaps the most devilish of all, in that they destroy hope where hope is struggling against bitter odds for existence; the headache powders which enslave so insidiously the victim is ignorant of his own fate; the catarrh powders which breed cocaine slaves."

But there was no widespread condemnation of narcotics, of their manufacturers or sellers. The newspapers remained discreetly silent. And the drug manufacturers, employing the biggest lobby then in existence, were able to prevent any legislation which materially affected them.

When the Pure Food and Drug Law was enacted in 1906, it touched the narcotics problem only lightly. The restraints which it imposed were picayune. An act to control the narcotics traffic was finally passed in 1916, the Harrison Act, but it was primarily a revenue measure and the questions of morality and health were almost ignored in its drafting.

None of this is an apology for Rothstein's entrance into the illegal traffic in narcotics. It is intended to show that his attitude toward drugs was the attitude of a businessman. He regarded himself as in competition with the drug manufacturers. He could beat them to the market by finding an "edge" for himself in the form of drugs on which no taxes were paid. He would have a further edge in that the legal obstructions to sales, imposed on the drug manufacturers, would not affect him.

There was no big, general market for illicit drugs until 1921. By that time the Harrison Act had been carried to the Supreme Court, where it was held constitutional. Teeth had been inserted in it which prevented physicians' writing unlimited prescriptions for drugs. That meant legitimate drug outlets were drying up.

But the demand was not. There were thousands of addicts—made addicts by soothing syrup, by cough medicines, by paregoric, as well as by dope pushers—who wanted something to alleviate their craving.

Most of these were poor. Many of them were Italians and Levantines. Some were Orientals.

The first illicit drug traffic began among these groups. Charles Lucania, who was to become Lucky Luciano, started his criminal career by becoming a runner for a dope peddler. Luciano was still in short pants; his lids did not yet droop from a razor's cut.

When, a number of years later, Luciano joined the Legs Diamond mob and became acquainted with Rothstein, he suggested to Rothstein that there was money, big money, in dope. It was as a result of this suggestion that Rothstein entered the traffic when he started to import whisky.

Waxey Gordon, too, saw the potentialities in dope before Rothstein did. However, in those early days he did not have the capital to finance the racket on any large scale.

Gordon, even more than Luciano, was responsible for Rothstein's making a continually larger investment in dope.

By 1925 Rothstein was up to his nostrils in the traffic. He had hundreds of thousands of dollars tied up in drugs throughout the world. He would extend, rather than lessen, this investment in the next few years.

However, it was not Luciano's glowing words about the money to be made in dope or Waxey Gordon's evidence that this was so that pushed Rothstein into the dope business. It was his own vanity.

For many years Rothstein had been the most important man in the underworld. His had, for long, been the fattest bankroll. Now he saw others rising to challenge him. Big Bill Dwyer, grown rich in rumrunning. Frank Costello, who had come to Rothstein for loans only a short time before and was now preparing to take over Dwyer's empire. Phil Kastel, who had been bankrolled so often in petty larceny con games and in bucket shops, but who now bankrolled others.

True, none of these had yet challenged Rothstein in his most important field. None had moved into his place as the "man to see," "the man uptown." They had political connections, but these connections still went through him. In this field he was still top man.

But he had always believed that a man was only as important as his bankroll. The law of relativity applied to that as much as it did to the world of science. And he knew his bankroll was growing relatively smaller all the time, even if it grew greater absolutely.

He had, of course, a number of lucrative enterprises. But, while these yielded a large and steady income, they were not the gold mine that prohibition was proving to others. And some of his more rewarding activities had been either curtailed or liquidated.

The bucket shops were gone, wrecked by publicity and more stringent laws.

The stolen bond racket had fizzled out.

He had retired from rumrunning.

He no longer operated gambling houses.

His one big source of income was bookmaking and, even here, he was beginning to feel the squeeze of competition.

No wonder the dope traffic intrigued him. Here was a chance to make big, big money. It was virtually an untapped field and one that he could develop and profit from.

The traffic was unorganized. There was little competition on the level where he would enter it. What competition there was came from small-lot smuggling, from unethical doctors.

Rothstein saw an opportunity to put the dope traffic on an international basis, to regulate supply and demand. He would deal in lots too big for anyone else to enter the market against him. And the risks involved did not seem too great. Not in view of the potential profit.

A kilogram of heroin (2.2 pounds) could be purchased in 1923 for $2,000. When finally sold it could bring in more than $300,000!

One kilo could be used to make some 15,500 pure one-grain capsules, but no addict ever would get a pure heroin capsule. By the time it reached him the narcotic would have been cut so that the capsule for which he paid $10 or $15 contained only five per cent pure heroin. The rest would be lactose, quinine, anything that was white and powder soft.

Dope-running called for a large and effective organization. The source of supply was a long way from New York. Rothstein realized he would need "buyers" overseas to obtain supplies for him. And purchasers in the United States to take those supplies off his hands. He was interested solely in the wholesaling, not the retailing, of narcotics.

He found there was a ready market for drugs. Luciano and Gordon wanted as much as they could get. The Torrio-Capone organization in Chicago was in the market. So was "King" Solomon in Boston. And "Nig" Rosen in Philadelphia. Customers were waiting avidly in Kansas City, in St. Louis, and in Atlantic City, New Jersey.

Rothstein began his operations on a modest scale. Harry Mather did the first buying. Later he was joined in Europe by Dapper Dan Collins. And in 1926 Jacob ("Yasha") Katzenberg added the purchase of drugs to his activities as a buyer of liquor. (Ten years later Katzenberg would be described at a meeting of the League of Nations Committee to Control Narcotics as "an international menace, involved for years in the operation of a narcotic ring.")

Nat Ferber, so instrumental in revealing the bucket-shop ring, wrote that his investigations revealed that "Rothstein established himself as the financial clearing house for the foreign dope traffic. . . . He was the only man in the United States who could, and did, establish a credit standing with the foreign interests sending drugs into this country."

Ferber reported that his investigations showed many transactions between the bucketeers and foreign bankers. Evidence in the case of Dillon and Company, owned by Phil Kastel, showed more than $300,000 of such transactions.

But Rothstein's connection with the dope traffic does not rest on such tenuous threads. There is far more solid evidence.

Until 1925 Rothstein limited his drug purchases to European sources. Late that year he turned to Asiatic sources and sent Sid Stajer, a narcotics addict himself, to Asia. Stajer visited China, Formosa and Hong Kong. He was able to make "buys" in all three places.

The next year Rothstein sent George Uffner to Asia. Uffner was to continue to act as a buyer long after Rothstein was killed. He would work for Buchalter, for Luciano and for others who needed supplies. He would become a favorite of such as Frank Costello and Frank Erickson.

Building his dope racket, Rothstein enlarged his "legitimate" interests. There was an old, well-established importing house in New York City called "Vantine's." It had long been engaged in importing from China and the Orient. Rothstein bought the business.

Customs officials had long known Vantine's, known it as a legitimate enterprise. When shipments arrived for Vantine's they were given only a cursory inspection. Beginning in 1925, that type of inspection made it possible for pounds of pure dope to be smuggled into the country. Vantine's was a perfect front.

Rothstein had other such fronts. He operated a number of art galleries and antique shops.

Rothstein was not content with his illegal profits from these businesses. As long as they were his he wanted to make them self-supporting. He was fearful of the other fellow's game and sought to protect himself in his buying and selling of art objects and pictures. To that end, he employed an art expert, Jons McGurk.

McGurk was a specialist in Renaissance art and Rothstein insisted that McGurk show him how to tell the genuine from the fake. For months on end, McGurk spent Sunday afternoons at the Rothstein home, teaching the gambler how to judge pictures.

Rothstein was an apt pupil, but not a conceited one. He never made a purchase or put a picture on sale without McGurk's advice. After all, if a Morgan could employ a Duveen, a Rothstein could employ a McGurk.

Because he was smuggling narcotics, Rothstein became a connoisseur of *objets d'art*, old paintings and Oriental rugs.

Rothstein saw in dope the opportunity to make unlimited profits. He pressed his luck, parlaying his profits. Instead of cashing in, he put his profits back into the business. At the time of his death he had at least $2,000,000—and possibly double that amount—tied up in drugs that were scattered all over the world.

As overlord of the racket, Rothstein had to care for even the meanest of his subjects. That was why, in the last years of his life, so much of his bail bond business involved dope pushers, dope peddlers and dope addicts.

Jack Diamond and Max Gross were arrested on drug charges in 1926, released on bail. The bail bonds were issued by the Detroit Fidelity and Surety Company and were guaranteed by Rothstein.

Charles Webber and William Vachuda, arrested on July 14, 1926, charged with Harrison Act violations, were freed "twenty minutes after their arrest," according to Assistant United States Attorney Blake, on bond posted by the same company and, again, guaranteed by Rothstein. Short time, indeed, for bonds of $25,000 each.

Irving Sobel, an employee of Rothstein, Inc., an investment firm headed by Arnold Rothstein, was arrested in June, 1926, on charges of wholesale peddling of heroin. Rothstein posted bail for him. He got this bond back two months later when Sobel pleaded guilty to the charge.

Jack Solomon, arrested in 1927 on a narcotics charge, was freed on bail posted by Rothstein.

In 1928 Sid Stajer was arrested on charges of violating the Federal Narcotics Act. Rothstein posted his bail and Stajer was free on this bail when Rothstein was killed.

Those last years—from 1926 to 1928—more and more of Rothstein's time was taken up by attention to his dope empire. Yet not until after his death did this facet of his life and career get any public attention.

It was a routine request, made by United States Attorney Charles H. Tuttle, which resulted in exposure of Rothstein's activities.

A few days after Rothstein died Tuttle asked for, and received,

permission to examine some of Rothstein's records. Tuttle specifically requested papers dealing with the Rothmere Corporation, one
of many Rothstein enterprises. He did not reveal the reason for his
interest.

This was made public on December 8, four days more than a
month after Rothstein died. On that date federal agents raided a
hotel on West Forty-second Street in New York. In a room for which
a "J. Klein" had registered, they discovered a cache of dope on
which they placed a value of $2,000,000.

That same night other federal agents boarded the Twentieth
Century Limited at Buffalo and removed Joseph Unger from his
berth. Searching him, they found baggage checks for two trunks.
When these trunks were opened, they were found filled with dope,
wrapped in red and green ribbons like Christmas packages. At retail prices this dope would have brought between two and three
million dollars.

In Chicago, on the night of December 8, a third group of federal
agents raided the North Sheridan Hotel. They arrested Mrs. June
Boyd and confiscated drugs which they also valued "in the millions."

Figures released by federal agents are nearly always inflated, and
these were. However, the drugs which they seized had a value of at
least a half million dollars and possibly twice as much.

After the seizures Tuttle announced that the drugs were part of
Rothstein's "estate."

Tuttle then added that his office and the office of the Federal
Bureau of Narcotics had been investigating Rothstein's connection
with the dope traffic for more than a year. "It became obvious to us
in 1927," he said, "that the dope traffic in the United States was
being directed from one source. More and more, our information
convinced us that Arnold Rothstein was that source."

Tuttle revealed that the seizures and arrests had resulted from
his examination of the Rothmere Corporation records. "Among those
papers," he said, "we found the evidence which led us to Unger and
to the seizure of the drugs. These same records also revealed to us

the headquarters of the Rothstein organization in a number of foreign countries, among them France, Belgium and Holland.

"We are requesting the State Department to arrange for assistance in breaking up these foreign outlets of the Rothstein ring.

"Other papers in the Rothmere records revealed Rothstein's close connections with drug peddlers and distributors, for whom he provided bail and lawyers after their arrest by local or Federal authorities."

Tuttle then went on: "As a result of our efforts here, in Buffalo and in Chicago, enough dope has been taken to create crime enough to fill Sing Sing and to create mental disorders sufficient to fill all our state hospitals for the mentally defective."

Hardly had this series of raids been completed when federal agents made another seizure, this one at the French Line pier in New York. A dozen packing cases, marked "scrubbing brushes," were found to be filled with dope. The official valuation set on this shipment was $4,000,000. Again it was stated that the information leading to the seizure had come from "the Rothstein papers."

Tuttle, in a fresh statement, said, "This seizure is the second development in the plans which this office, in conjunction with the narcotics bureau, has made to destroy the traffic in illegal drugs in this city at the source.

"This seizure is a very large fraction of the drug supply of the biggest drug ring in the United States, and the papers we have seized, and the evidence we have in our possession indicate that Arnold Rothstein had to do with arranging the financing of this ring."

There followed some more arrests and some raids. Among those arrested were Samuel ("Crying Sammy") Lowe, with a long record for violations of the narcotic laws, and Mrs. Esther Meyers, identified as a friend of Unger.

The December Federal Grand Jury called a number of witnesses, among them Stajer, Abraham Stein, Lowe and Unger. Assistant United States Attorney Blake questioned Mrs. Rothstein, asking her for "any information she could provide on any of Mr. Rothstein's transactions that might interest the government."

Afterward Blake said his questioning had convinced him "Mrs. Rothstein had no knowledge of any acts in which we might be interested. We are grateful for her co-operation."

Unger was arraigned on December 21. Before the arraignment Tuttle said he expected that evidence would be forthcoming at Unger's trial that would "definitely show the relationship of Arnold Rothstein to the international drug traffic."

Unger, however, pleaded guilty at his arraignment. That meant there would be no trial and no evidence.

Tuttle and Blake, however, continued their search of the Rothstein papers. On January 2, 1929, Blake announced: "Startling evidence, involving important figures in New York public and political life, and disclosing more fully Arnold Rothstein's overlordship of the narcotics rings of the United States, will be presented to the new Federal Grand Jury next week.

"We will have both witnesses and documents to take before the Grand Jury to show how sinister were Arnold Rothstein's operations in the drug traffic. The evidence we expect to produce is more startling than anything so far disclosed."

Neither Blake nor Tuttle would say anything further. Neither would they identify any of the "important figures." However, they did point out that they had done all their investigating without any co-operation with local authorities. "We felt, under the circumstances, that this was best."

The January Grand Jury heard the testimony. Nothing new developed.

Months passed and still there was no "startling disclosure." After a time the whole investigation appeared to have been pigeonholed.

Even after his death the power of Rothstein was strong enough to stifle yet another attempt to reveal his secrets. Tuttle undoubtedly was sincere. And his efforts were equally sincere. But he could not get witnesses to talk. And when he sought fresh access to Rothstein's papers many of the papers could not be found.

He had told the truth when he said that Rothstein was the financier of the drug traffic in the United States. He had, temporarily, disrupted the operations of the drug ring when he made his raids and arrests. But that was all. In a few short months that traffic had been resumed, was continuing on the foundation, and with the organization, which Rothstein had created.

Luciano and Lepke were the new overlords. They made Katzenberg their principal "buyer" in Europe. After repeal, Katzenberg was sent to Asia. "Curly" Holtz, a thug who had operated in the garment district, first as a lieutenant of Little Augie and later as a strong-arm man for Lepke, replaced Unger as roving contact with various sources of supply.

Rothstein had pioneered, developed a new, great source of illicit revenue. He had taken a disorganized, hit-or-miss operation and turned it into a businesslike machine. His heirs took up where he had left off. They collected the millions that Rothstein had hoped for and for which he had so carefully planned.

Of all Rothstein's enterprises, this had been most carefully developed. He had given it time, effort and all his intelligence. Yet, it was the most costly business that ever occupied his time, his interest and his money.

He never made a dollar from it. That is, a cash dollar. He had great paper profits, but these were not worth the paper on which he figured them. In addition, he had made actual cash investment in the drug traffic that ran into the millions. Why not? He was like a gambler who knew that he had a pot cinched.

But a bullet ended the game before he had a chance to turn over his hole card.

There was no way for him to collect. Death had closed the books.

Just as it had closed them on so many other ventures in which he was involved in these, his last, days.

Chapter **22** *With Me, It's Brains*

It was Damon Runyon who dubbed Rothstein "The Brain." Of all the titles ever given him—or names that he was called—this was the only one he liked.

He held his own intelligence in high esteem and that of most others in low. This was a subject he would even discuss publicly.

"The majority of the human race," he told Zoe Beckley of the Brooklyn *Eagle,* "are dubs and dumbbells. They have rotten judgment and no brains and when you have learned to do things and how to size up people and dope out methods for yourself, they jump to the conclusion that you are crooked."

On the same theme he told Edwin C. Hill, of the New York *Sun,* "With me, it's brains—that's all. I can tell any man how to make money and how to make it straight. It takes brains, personality and opinions. I'll back my judgment any time."

In answer to a further question from Hill, Rothstein said, "You want to know how I make my money? There are two million fools born for every intelligent man. That ought to answer you."

He relished being a public figure and a man of mystery at the same time. Everyone knew who he was; he thought no one knew what he was. He realized that the concept of the "Boss Gambler," the "Man who fixed the Series," was general. He was satisfied to have it that way. It concealed so many other things he was.

His life, even now when he was wealthy, important, a man in his forties, still began at sundown and finished its daily course at dawn. Age showed lightly on him. His face had grown a little more pale,

300

the once-fair complexion now chalky. He had gained a little soft, flabby weight. Just enough to show, but no more.

He remained a creature of the night.

His breakfast was served in the late afternoon. There were notes, messages, on the tray. The phone, cut off in his room, had been ringing since early morning. Carolyn or Thomas Farley, now butler in the Rothstein home, had answered it, taken the messages.

Fats Walsh, stolid and patient, would meet him at the door when Rothstein left for the office. Fats Walsh, last of his bodyguards.

The office occupied a half floor of the Fifty-seventh Street building. There were many names and legends on the frosted glass windows. "Rothmere Investment Co." "Rothmere Sand and Gravel Co." "Nassau Heights Engineering Co." "Pan-Continental Film Distributing Co." "Redstone Material and Supply Co." "Texas Chief Oil Co." "Insurance." "Bonds." But nowhere the name "Arnold Rothstein."

There were more messages at the office. Freda Rosenberg, once Fallon's secretary, now his, would have them ready for him. Miss Rosenberg was used to working hours that began when those of most secretaries were ending. She was discreet. She was, even by Rothstein's standards, "smart."

Rothstein would ignore these messages temporarily, unless Miss Rosenberg had placed something urgent at the top. He had to look at the ledger sheets, see what the "action" had been that day. The long columns of figures would list the bets made by bookmakers all over the country, on races run all over the country. There was a separate ledger sheet for baseball bets. And a third for prize-fight wagers.

Then, a mental balance sheet drawn up, Rothstein would go to the small room at the rear of the big office, which served as his private office. He would lock himself in, lift the receiver from the private phone whose number had been removed from its glassine cover. No one but Rothstein ever revealed this number. And then only to a private few.

It was on this phone that Rothstein transacted business with Luciano, with Marlow, with Yale, with Marinelli, with Hines, with Judge Vitale or Judge McQuade.

There were always "contracts," that euphemism for "fix" or "favor," that politicians used then and still use. A call to a judge to arrange for bail. A call to a lawyer, informing him of a client who needed his services. A call to his good friend, Ciro Terranova, for whom he provided a suite of rooms in his Fairfield Hotel. Perhaps a call to Teddy Brandle.

It might be any time after ten in the evening that he finished in the office. Then he would go to "headquarters." Once that had been Jack's. Later it was Reuben's, on the West Side. Now, and for all the rest of his life, it would be Lindy's at Broadway and Fiftieth Street.

One table was reserved for him. It bore no reservation sign, but, no matter how crowded the restaurant, it remained vacant after nine each evening. It had to be vacant when Rothstein appeared.

Entering the restaurant, he would find more messages. Leo Lindy would hand these to him or, sometimes, the night cashier. Rothstein would take these messages, walk to his table. Walsh would drop back, sometimes taking a place near the door, sometimes sitting at a table close by.

Rothstein would run through the messages. He had his little black book before him and, each time he made an entry in it, he would wet his pencil stub. The messages read, their contents noted, he would shred them and place the shreds in an ashtray. Then he would light the scraps of paper and sit staring at the papers turning to ash until they were destroyed.

Next he would go to the phone, place the little black book before him, and give numbers to the operator. Sometimes he made just a few calls. Sometimes he made a dozen. The calls completed, he returned to his table.

This was the sign that he was ready to talk with those who had been waiting for him, some of them for hours. Every night was petition night at Lindy's.

One by one these would go to Rothstein's table, sit down close to him, lean even closer, and whisper to him. No one ever spoke above a whisper to Rothstein. To each of these Rothstein said, "Tell me the story."

Sometimes, when the whispered colloquy reached its end, Rothstein would just shake his head. The petitioner would shuffle away, his eyes averted from all the others who were watching him. More frequently, for this was his business, Rothstein would peel some bills from his roll, let them fall to the table, where the petitioner would dart out his hand and gather them up. Rothstein's lips would move, easy for those watching to read. They knew what Rothstein was saying. "God help you if you don't." It was his warning that he expected to be paid on the dot, interest included.

Most of the petitioners were "characters," that Broadway term for individuals with no visible means of support who, somehow, continue to exist, to go on from day to day. They were like prospectors in the mother lode country, certain that with just one more grubstake they would find a gold mine.

Sometimes they did. Like Walter ("Good Time Charley") Freidman, who was a small-time gambler, one-time cab driver, errand boy for Rothstein. He became comanager of a heavyweight champion of the world, Primo Carnera, and lived high off the hog for a time.

Or Murray Garson, small-time con man, now down on his luck. A score of years later Garson would have as his partner in a bigtime con game the chairman of the House Military Affairs Committee and the pair would steal some millions of dollars from a nation at war. And go to jail for the swindle.

There were others, important in show business, who came to Rothstein. Like Selwyn, who had had trouble with "Big Tim" McCarthy. Or Gus Van, of the famed vaudeville team of Van and Schenk. Van needed money to pay off his bookmakers and had to borrow $7,800 from Rothstein for that purpose.

Anne Nichols came to Rothstein in 1922. A few weeks earlier her play, *Abie's Irish Rose,* had opened on Broadway and been flailed by the critics. Just the same, it was doing some business. If she could borrow enough money to keep it open for a little while she was sure it would turn into a hit.

"How much?" Rothstein asked.

"I know $25,000 will be enough. I'll give you a half-interest in the show for that."

"I'm not in show business," Rothstein said. "I'll lend you the money if you have collateral." Did she own any real estate? Or stocks or bonds? How about jewelry?

She listed her assets.

Rothstein counted them off. "I'll take your personal note for the money," he said. "Of course you'll have to post collateral. Interest is ten per cent."

She hesitated.

"You're sure the show's going to be a hit. What are you risking?"

Almost everything she owned, of course, but she did not say that. "I'll give you the note," she said.

There were other conditions, Rothstein whispered. She would have to give him all the insurance she carried and take out a life insurance policy to cover the loan. "I have to be protected," he said.

They were harsh terms, but the best thing that ever happened to Miss Nichols. The show ran five years, broke every long-run record in New York. A half interest in the show would have yielded Rothstein a million dollars. He wanted the sure thing, not the gamble, and so all he received for his loan was a profit of about $3,000.

Miss Nichols, however, felt Rothstein had taken advantage of her need. On the day that she paid off her debt she canceled every policy Rothstein had written for her.

George White did a lot of business with Rothstein at the table in Lindy's. The money that White made on his successful productions of the *Scandals* quite often was insufficient to pay off his unsuccessful parlays at Belmont Park.

Hoodlums stopped for a moment's talk. Larry Fay. Frankie Marlow. Marlow was quite a sportsman. He had a stable of race horses and a stable of prize fighters. Rothstein was very interested in prize fighters. It was profitable to him.

In 1925 Mickey Walker and Dave Shade fought in Madison Square Garden for the welterweight championship of the world.

All the spectators in the Garden, with three exceptions, were certain that Shade had won the championship.

The three who disagreed were the referee and two judges.

The *Morning Telegraph*, spokesman for the sporting world, headed its story of the fight WALKER WINS ON RANK DECISION. Just beneath this head was one sentence in boldface type: "It was reported at ringside last night that Arnold Rothstein won $60,000 on the fight."

Rothstein said that the boldface sentence was all wrong. He had won $80,000, and not $60,000 as the paper had reported. He said he did not know if Marlow had a "piece" of Walker.

A year later Rothstein was involved in another big-money deal involving a prize fighter. It started with a conversation he had in Lindy's with his old friend, Billy Gibson, now managing Gene Tunney, matched to meet Jack Dempsey in Philadelphia for the heavyweight championship of the world.

Gibson told Rothstein he had heard "rumbles" that Tunney could not win. Powerful underworld interests were going to see to that. "If we get a fair shake," Gibson said, "we win." A fighter was always "we" to a manager except when he was catching punches.

"Do you know who?" Rothstein asked.

Gibson shook his head. "I just got the word."

"I'll take care of it," Rothstein promised.

The next day Rothstein called Maxie ("Boo Boo") Hoff, top man of Philadelphia's underworld and bootlegging set. In 1921 Rothstein had delivered Hoff's first big load of whisky to him. "Gibson's my pal," Rothstein told Hoff. "I want you to protect him."

"Tell him to see me."

Gibson went to Philadelphia and had a conference with Hoff. He returned from it, told Rothstein, "Boo Boo says it's all right. Can he make good?"

"Yes," Rothstein said. A little later he called Hoff.

"I sent the word out," Hoff said. "This is my territory and what I say goes. I'm betting Tunney." (He pronounced it "Tooney.")

Odds on the fight were 4 to 1 that Dempsey would win. Knowing that Hoff and his influences were riding with Tunney's left jab and right cross, Rothstein spread $150,000 around the country on Tunney.

Tunney did not need any help to beat Dempsey in Philadelphia. He won because he gave Dempsey a clear, and obvious, beating. Of course, a year later there was the "long count" in Chicago. Hoff was at ringside there with his friend Al Capone. It might have had something to do with that long count.

Hoff implied that it did when he sued Gibson for a share in Tunney's earnings. It was in the trial of that suit that Rothstein's part in bringing Hoff and Gibson together was revealed. Hoff said that the price for his "help" was a "piece" of Tunney. Everyone agreed Tunney had no knowledge of these machinations.

After all, as Gibson told the court, a fighter's job was to fight. His manager had to do the thinking, the planning and the maneuvering.

Yes, all kinds of people made their way to Rothstein's table. A cop who wondered if Rothstein would help him get a promotion to detective. A garment manufacturer who was a friend of Abraham Rothstein—so many of them were—who needed help in a union dispute. A bookmaker who wondered if Rothstein would help get him an "okay" to operate in New Jersey.

These were casual visitors, changing from night to night. But there were others, regulars, who sat with Rothstein as night blended into day. Lawyers like Maurice Cantor and Freddy Kaplan. Sid Stajer and Abe Stein, taking some time off from their activities in handling dope. George Uffner, when he was in town. Mike Best and Remy Dorr, two bookmaker friends whom Rothstein bankrolled. Jimmy Hines, to say a word or two about politics or gambling. Gene McGee, with whom Rothstein remained friendly and to whom he paid a legal retainer up to the time of Rothstein's death.

For a time young Draper Daugherty, son of Harry Daugherty of Teapot Dome and Harding scandal fame, used to sit with the regulars. He had a job in Rothstein's insurance firm and liked to be seen with Rothstein. He had to quit that job when it became public knowledge. His father feared that it would hurt his reputation.

And toward the end the most regular of all at the Rothstein table was Bill Wellman, last of Rothstein's protégés and probably the most legitimate.

Bill Wellman was tall and blond and self-assured. He was a great salesman. As a boy, hardly out of his teens, he had sold himself to Barney Oldfield, the racing driver, and become his manager. Then he had become manager of the old Madison Square Garden. It was while with the Garden that Wellman met Rothstein.

In 1926 he interested Rothstein in a grandiose real estate promotion. It would be a housing development, Juniper Park, at Maspeth, Long Island. He knew the place and insisted that Rothstein look at it.

Rothstein took one of his few trips across the Queensboro Bridge and looked at one hundred twenty acres of what had once been farm land.

Then Wellman made his pitch. The city was expanding, moving eastward. Soon Queens would be a flourishing residential area. It would be the site of thousands of low-priced and middle-priced homes. Here was Rothstein's chance to get in on the ground floor of something that could make millions. His prime selling point was, "Negroes don't have a decent place to live. This can be the first decent Negro section in the country."

Rothstein was impressed by this. It was not that he was a humanitarian, but that he owned some Harlem real estate and it yielded a big return.

He bought the land for $400,000. And put Wellman in charge of developing it. As the plan was outlined, Rothstein would build the houses through one company, finance the mortgages through another, and insure them through a third. In addition, every person buying a house would have to take out a life insurance policy equal to the amount of his mortgage!

The plan was foolproof on paper.

It turned out to have a number of drawbacks. Developing and building cost a great deal of money. Beginning late in 1926, Rothstein had to lay out an average of $5,000 weekly in cash. This money went to contractors, builders and suppliers. It paid for radiators and stoves and electrical equipment.

At the end there were some two hundred houses on the development.

Wellman worked at Juniper Park each day, came into New York each night, went to Lindy's, where he sat with Rothstein till early morning. His enthusiasm was as high at the end as it had been at the beginning. And, by the end, Rothstein had put more than a million dollars in cash into Juniper Park.

There was another real estate development in which Wellman participated. This was the Cedar Point Golf Club in Woodmere, Long Island. This cost Rothstein some $400,000 in cash.

When the club was opened, Rothstein took part in the ceremonies. He was prevailed upon to play with the club professional. Three holes were enough for him. "Golf is too slow for me," he said. "Besides, there's no way to gamble on it."

Rothstein's major real estate holdings, however, were in Manhattan. He owned houses on West Fifty-sixth and West Fifty-seventh Streets. He had property on West Fifty-ninth Street. He had large holdings on Forty-seventh Street, on East Sixty-eighth Street, on East Nineteenth Street. He owned the Fairfield Hotel on West Seventy-second Street through the Hooper Realty Corporation, ostensibly controlled by Carolyn Rothstein. And there were the two big tenements in Harlem.

For a time he was a partner in the Longchamps chain of restaurants. His sister Edith had married Henry Lustig, then a wholesale dealer in fruits and produce. Lustig talked Rothstein into backing him in a restaurant, the first of the Longchamps chain.

The partnership was relatively successful but it came to an abrupt ending. Lustig had continued in his original business and Lindy's restaurant was one of his customers. Rothstein was in Lindy's one morning when a Lustig truck made a delivery. Rothstein asked Lindy for a copy of his bill.

The next day Rothstein went to the Longchamps restaurant and asked the bookkeeper to quote him the prices that Lustig was charging Longchamps for fruit and vegetables. Comparing the two sets of figures, he discovered that Lustig was charging his own business more than he was charging Lindy.

Rothstein delivered an ultimatum to Lustig. "Buy me out or I'll close up the place." Lustig raised the money to buy Rothstein out and the two parted, never again to speak to each other.

It was some years after Rothstein's death that Lustig was sent to jail for cheating the government of taxes due from the, then, most successful chain of restaurants in New York.

The first Longchamps restaurant was in a building Rothstein owned. That was part of his technique in finding tenants for his property.

When he became a partner in Wallach's, the clothing chain (a partnership ended before Rothstein's death), he had Wallach move into one of his buildings. Rothstein spent $40,000 fitting up an elaborate establishment, according to Carolyn Rothstein in her book, *Now I'll Tell*. Rothstein gave Sid Stajer a part of his interest in the business.

Stajer, telling Mrs. Rothstein of this, said admiringly, "Then Arnold went out into Broadway and made every punk on the street buy himself a new outfit at two hundred and fifty bucks a throw."

Other activities took up time. Vantine's and the art gallery were primarily cover-ups for his narcotics activities, but he tried to make them profitable. Whenever he heard someone was furnishing a home, he sought to get the business for his own firm. Norman Katkov, in *The Fabulous Fanny*, tells how Fannie Brice was made to buy thousands of dollars' worth of furnishings and bric-a-brac for a new apartment.

Rothstein sought to interest his friend Sam Rosoff in buying some paintings for his home. He told him a fine painting was not only a thing of aesthetic value, it was also a good investment. He suggested that Rosoff attend an art auction with him.

Rosoff was far more interested in shooting crap, but it was early in the evening and there were still a few hours before any sort of gambling would start. Rosoff agreed to accompany Rothstein to the auction.

A portrait of a young girl was put up for sale. The auctioneer announced that it was a painting by Sir Joshua Reynolds, certified as such by the Sotheby Gallery in London, and estimated by that gallery as being worth 5,000 guineas. This the auctioneer translated roughly into $25,000.

Rosoff asked Rothstein if this was on the level and was assured it was. Rosoff scoffed, saying no picture was worth more than five dollars to him.

Then the bidding began and, as the bids climbed, Rosoff grew more and more excited. His chins trembled and his head swiveled from side to side as the bidding went to $17,500. Then, unable to contain himself any longer, Rosoff bid $18,000.

There was a sudden cessation of voices. The auctioneer looked about. "Going. Going. Gone to the gentleman with Mr. Rothstein for $18,000."

Rothstein said, "You've got a bargain, Sam."

Still caught up in the excitement, Rosoff went to the cashier, wrote out a check for $18,000, and insisted that the picture be wrapped so he could take it with him.

Outside the auction gallery the pair separated. They met again some hours later in Rothstein's office on West Fifty-seventh Street. Rosoff was still carrying the picture, but his enthusiasm had waned in the intervening period. He offered it to Rothstein for $15,000. "People," he said sadly, "think I'm nuts buying a picture."

Rothstein assured him that buying a masterpiece was no sign of insanity. As a matter of fact, he owned some pictures himself. So did J. P. Morgan and Andrew Mellon. No one had ever believed any of this trio insane. However, he added, he was not in the market at the moment for any further artistic masterpieces.

Rosoff offered to sell the picture for $12,000 and then for $10,000. "You said yourself it's worth a lot more. So did that gallery in England."

"Tell you what I'll do," Rothstein said. "I'll cut you high card. The picture against $10,000."

"It's a bet," Rosoff said.

Rothstein pulled a fresh deck of cards from his desk, broke it, shuffled the cards. Rosoff took them from him, gave them another shuffle and placed them on Rothstein's desk. "Cut," he said.

Rothstein cut a six.

"That's easy to beat," Rosoff said. He lifted some cards, turned them over to reveal a three.

The picture was sent to Rothstein's home and Carolyn hung it in the living room. Shortly thereafter Rothstein sent home another picture, a Gainsborough titled "Miss Gwathney," a companion piece to the artist's "Age of Innocence." This picture had come into Rothstein's possession as had so many other valuables. It had been collateral for a loan made by an art dealer who loved art, but loved gambling more.

The loan had gone unredeemed and now Rothstein had taken title to the collateral, which also included a painting Rothstein did not consider fit for public display. This, he said, was "a dirty picture of a fat, naked woman." Rothstein sent this second picture to the gallery.

A short time later Val O'Farrell, a private detective, came to see Rothstein. He had been hired by Henry E. Huntington to locate two pictures Huntington had sent a New York art dealer for some restoration work. O'Farrell said he thought that Rothstein might know where the pictures were. He gave Rothstein photographs of the two pictures.

One of them was the Gainsborough. The second was of the "fat, naked woman," a Rubens.

Rothstein said, "I think I can help you locate the pictures. But Mr. Huntington will have to write me personally asking for my help."

A short time afterward he received a "Dear Mr. Rothstein" letter from Huntington asking his assistance in locating the pictures. "I would be very grateful for any help you can render me in this search."

Rothstein showed the letter to everyone he encountered. "He's one of the biggest men in America," Rothstein told the group at Lindy's, "and he has to ask me for favors."

The letter also stated that there was a substantial reward for recovering the pictures and that Huntington would be most happy to pay Rothstein for any expenses he might incur. However, Rothstein had different ideas.

He wrote Huntington, informing him that he had been able to locate the pictures and was sending them on. He wanted no reward. As a fellow art lover, he did not begrudge the few dollars of expense involved and under no circumstances would accept reimbursement. Someday, he said, he hoped to take a trip to California and would then visit Huntington and view his collection.

There was a postscript to the letter. Taking no chance on anything happening to the pictures, he had insured them quite heavily. If Mr. Huntington cared to continue the insurance, he could send a check to the issuing company. Rothstein's company, of course.

Huntington paid the premium by return mail. He also sent a cordial invitation to Rothstein to visit him when, and if, he came to California.

Rothstein kept the letter prominently displayed in his office.

Even in those busy days there was still time for an occasional crap game or poker game. It had to be a special occasion, one where the stakes were high and the play serious.

Richard Donovan and Hank Greenspun, in a series of articles about Nick the Greek, which appeared in *Collier's* in 1954, tell of one such game.

Rothstein always believed that his superior bankroll gave him an edge in any game he played with Nick the Greek. This particular poker game bore him out. In the early stages Nick ran his winnings over the half-million mark, according to his biographers. Then his luck turned. He was still a big winner, however, when what they call the biggest pot "in the biggest poker game ever recorded" occurred.

The game was five-card stud, table stakes. Nick was dealt a pair of kings, back to back. Rothstein had the king of diamonds showing. The other players dropped out. Nick, closer to the dealer, bet

$10,000. Rothstein raised him $30,000, and was called. On the next card, Nick drew a four and Rothstein the nine of diamonds.

It was Rothstein's bet and he pushed $60,000 into the center of the table. Again Nick called.

The third open card was a six for Nick, the seven of diamonds for Rothstein. Rothstein bet $70,000. Nick tapped himself out, calling Rothstein's bet and raising him $142,500. Rothstein called the bet. There being no more bets possible since Nick was tapped out, Rothstein flipped over his hole card as did Nick. Rothstein's was the ace of diamonds!

That meant Rothstein would have to buy either a diamond on his last card, for a flush, or match his ace or his king. One pair would not help, however, if Nick should improve his hand.

The dealer gave Nick his last card, a useless one. And then he dealt Rothstein a fifth diamond.

Rothstein raked in the pot and Nick reached for his coat.

Again according to his biographers, Nick remarked that Rothstein was a "queer, cold man at the table."

There is no question but that this was a big poker game, possibly as big as Donovan and Greenspun maintain. Rothstein would not play in any other kind and Nick knew only one way to gamble, to "go for broke."

And each time he gambled against Rothstein he went broke.

This game, whatever the stakes involved, was the last in which Rothstein made a big winning. The only other game in which he participated, about which anything is known, cost him a sheaf of markers.

And his life.

Chapter 23 *Things Are Quiet Here*

The more times changed, the more Arnold Rothstein remained the same. His ideas, his ambitions and his concepts might alter in degree, but never in kind.

Life, to him, was a balance sheet. His mind was a computing machine. Addition for him and subtraction for others. He had always wanted money and he still wanted money. He just wanted more of it in 1928 than he had wanted in 1908 or 1918.

He never questioned himself, never had moments of introspection or self-examination. He had periods of depression, but did not seek to find their cause. He took his periods of elation as matter-of-factly. He wore both as unconcernedly as he wore his neat, well-fitting blue suit.

He had always been acquisitive. He remained so. Once he gained possession of something he would not let go. Letting go would mean that he had lost, and he was a bad loser. He had no respect for good losers. Long ago he had told Nicky Arnstein, "Good losers make losing a habit." He did not want to be a victim of that habit.

This need to hang on—to clutch even with slipping fingers—caused him to forget one of the primary rules of gambling. Hitting a streak of hard luck, he did not play safe. Instead, he began to press, to double up, in the hope of recouping.

This began late in 1927. It started at five o'clock one morning when he returned, at the end of an uneventful day, to the apartment at 912 Fifth Avenue. He opened the door softly, closed it quietly behind him. Then he started to walk pussyfooted to his room.

Carolyn called to him from the darkness, "Arnold! I've been waiting for you."

He switched on a light, turned a worried face quickly toward the sound of her voice. "Are you all right? Is there anything wrong? Do you want me to call a doctor?"

"I'm feeling fine," she said. "I want to talk with you."

"You had me worried," he said. "What's happened?"

She took a deep breath. "I want a divorce, Arnold."

"Why? What have I done?" His lone sign of emotion was a slight tremolo in his voice.

"Nothing special," she said. "It just came to me today that we're not really married. We're just two people who've lived in the same house a long time and like and are used to each other. But we're not really married."

He stared hard at her, trying to read her face as though she had just pushed a big bet into the center of a table. "I love you, Carolyn," he said. "You're the one thing I can be sure of every minute of every day. You're part of me."

"Do you believe that?"

"I do. I've never lied to you. I'm not lying now."

"Not to me," she said. "To yourself. If I'm part of you, it's in the same way that anything else you own is. How many times have you written to me while I was away?"

"I'm no letter writer. I hate to put things on paper."

"Answer me. How many times?"

"Not often," he admitted.

"Not once," she said. "Not a single line."

"Is that so?" He was not doubting her, just expressing wonder.

"Yes, it's so." She smiled bitterly. "It's been weeks since we've spent an evening together. I can't remember the last time we had dinner together. If I disappeared, you wouldn't know it unless someone told you."

He buried his head in his hands and then looked up at her. "I wish I could tell you what you mean to me." He searched for words.

Then haltingly he said, "What it is, is that as long as you're here, I'm not really alone. If you go away—if you divorce me—I will be alone. Does that make sense?"

"I'm alone now, Arnold. Maybe I'm selfish. Maybe I'm just thinking about myself. But I have to, Arnold. I'm beginning to dry up, to grow bitter. I'm beginning to feel sorry for myself. I look in a mirror and wonder what's wrong with me. It's no good for you to go on needing me, but having me feel that you don't want me."

"Want you?" He walked to her, took one of her hands in both of his. "Of course, I want you."

A bitter smile crossed her face. "We've been in this apartment four years, Arnold. I waited for you here instead of in my bedroom because I wasn't sure you knew your way there. You've never been in it."

He turned away from her, dropping her hand. His back to her, he said, "Does it have to be right away?"

"No. It's been so long, a little more time won't matter."

It was a few days later that he came to her and said, "Carolyn, maybe we can work this out. There's a doctor—a psychologist— someone told me about. I've had a talk with him. He'd like to talk with you." He gave her a card. "He's famous," Rothstein said. "Everybody's talking about him." It was the fame that counted with Rothstein.

The card was that of John B. Watson, whose work *Behaviorism* was one of the most discussed books of the day.

"I'll go see him," she said. She dropped a hand on Rothstein's sleeve. "I'm not like you," she said. "I still bet on long shots."

When she went to see Watson, he said, "Mr. Rothstein described you very well. The color of your hair and eyes and the erect way you walk. He told me I could tell you what he said to me. He said he loved you very much."

"He told me that too. I suppose he thinks it's true."

"Do you?"

"He loves money, gambling, me. The same kind of love, I think."

Then Watson told her how Rothstein had described his feelings about her, his reactions to her. The beautiful doll in a glass case, bearing the sign "Look. Don't touch."

"I'm a woman, not a doll."

"Not to him. It isn't that he doesn't want you to be a woman. It's just that he's unable to think of you that way. It's all in his conditioning. It might be possible to change him, Mrs. Rothstein, but it would take a long time. I've told him that."

"What did he say?"

"Very little. I think he believed I could give him a pill or give you one and then everything would be all right."

"There aren't any such pills, are there?"

"No, Mrs. Rothstein."

"Thank you for talking to me."

Rothstein did not again mention Watson to her.

In the spring of 1928 Carolyn prepared to go to Europe. "When I come back," she said, "I'll see a lawyer."

"I guess that's it," he said. "I've been thinking about money. Would two thousand a month suit you?"

"Whatever you think is fair."

"Let's say two thousand a month unless you remarry. If you remarry, I'll give you fifteen thousand a year. If you get a divorce or become a widow, I'll go back to two thousand a month. That all right?"

"You don't have to pay me off, Arnold."

"I'm not paying you off. I'm just paying a debt." His lips relaxed into a tight smile. "As long as you live, Carolyn, you're going to be my wife. That's the way I feel about it and it's the way the world will think of you. I'm not offering more than you deserve for that."

When she sailed, he filled her stateroom with flowers. While she was in Europe, he even wrote her once.

> Dear Carolyn,
> Things are quiet here. Have a good time.
>   Love.
>   Arnold

Broadway was quickly aware that the Rothsteins had separated.

It knew because Rothstein was being seen publicly, by the middle of the summer, with Inez Norton, a blond actress. She was a tall, slender woman who bore a likeness to Carolyn.

This was the first time Rothstein had permitted his attentions to a woman to become public knowledge. It was his way of letting the town know that he wasn't cheating, but free-lancing.

There was a lot of talk about Rothstein that summer. Most of it had to do with his finances. It became common knowledge that he had a considerable amount of "paper" floating about. He had always been "slow pay," a man who tried to keep you on the hook until he won back his losses, but now he was even slower.

The talk began on Memorial Day, 1928, when Rothstein went to Belmont Park, his first appearance at the track in many seasons. It was a bad day for him. At its end he had given markers for $130,000. Not much for Rothstein, of course, but still a lot of money.

June passed, and then July. And Rothstein had not picked up any of his markers. People began to wonder and to whisper.

Sid Stajer told him about this. "What are they worrying about?" Rothstein said. "They know I'm good for the money. Besides, it's a kind of insurance for me. As long as the markers are out, I won't make any more bets."

The fact was that Rothstein had overextended himself. The drain on him was great. Each week there were the bills for the Juniper Park project. Each week he had to meet payments on the country club property and improvements. There were mortgage payments on his real estate empire.

But the biggest drain came from his biggest gamble. It was the money he was laying out for drugs, for organizing his drug empire. This was a cash business and he couldn't give markers in Europe or in Asia for the "white stuff" he was buying.

In addition, he had hundreds of thousands of dollars out on loans. He could not ask Magistrate Vitale or Jimmy Hines or Frank Costello to repay him the money he had "loaned." These loans were bribes in two instances, whether ever called such, and insurance in the third. A new kind of insurance that Rothstein had never had to practice before. No one—not even Rothstein—could press Frank Costello in 1928.

He was, of course, far from broke. His equities in the various properties he owned were in the millions. But he could only realize on these if he sold the properties. And he did not want to. He refused an offer that would have brought him almost $800,000 for the Juniper Park tract. He turned down two offers for the golf course.

His midtown property in New York was going up in value—as all such realty was in those days—and he could have bailed himself out by putting one parcel or another on the market. But he believed that the value would increase and he did not want to sell out except at the top of the market.

He was sure that he held an ace and a couple of jokers in the hole. The ace, of course, was the immense profit he visualized when he unloaded his supply of drugs. The jokers stemmed from the election of 1928.

Al Smith was the Democratic nominee against Herbert Hoover for the Presidency. Rothstein liked Smith, admired him. But he was not one to permit sentiment to overrule judgment when it came to gambling. By September 1 Rothstein had placed more than $400,000 on Hoover.

Franklin D. Roosevelt had been named as the Democratic candidate for governor of New York, to oppose Albert Ottinger. Rothstein had bets of more than $200,000 placed on Roosevelt.

He was to continue to place bets on both Hoover and Roosevelt until the night of November 4. On that night he would place his last bet, $60,000 on Hoover to beat Smith, with Meyer Boston, a betting commissioner, in Lindy's. There was a great irony in this. At the moment, Boston held some of Rothstein's paper from the poker game in Jimmy Meehan's place on the corner of Seventh Avenue and Fifty-fourth Street.

That game began on the night of September 8 and continued well into the morning of September 10, 1928. It was a big game. Not as big as some in which Rothstein had participated over the years, but one in which gains or losses could go into six figures. And did.

The players were a motley group. They included Nate Raymond, a West Coast gambler in New York on his honeymoon; Alvin C. ("Titanic") Thompson, also from out of town, who liked to bet high on anything, including golf, which he played as well as most professionals; Meyer Boston, who, with his brother, Sam, used a Wall Street address as a front for his gambling and stock market activities; Joe Bernstein, a New York gambler; Martin Bowe, a bookmaker; and George McManus, bookmaker and gambler, who was well connected in New York, with one brother in the church and another in the police department.

These, with Rothstein, made up the list of players.

While the game was being held in Meehan's apartment, it was McManus' game. He operated a casual "floating" game and this was one such. It is part of the code of gambling that, in a game such as this, the operator is technically the "host." He guarantees that the game will be on the level and that all obligations will be met.

It was hardly likely that McManus felt he had to assure the strangers about Rothstein. It was more probable that he gave Rothstein assurance about the strangers.

It was, by any standards, an unusual poker game. The bets, which started in the hundreds, rose rapidly to the thousands. Small fortunes were at stake in many of the pots, yet rarely was there any cash in the center of the table. This was because of Rothstein.

From the start he began to use markers. And from the start he was a loser. In a short time the green felt was littered with small white chits, bearing varied numbers, and all signed with a scrawled "A.R."

What cash had been used at the start of the game gradually disappeared from sight. Rothstein, the big loser, played like an amateur. He bucked the percentage and, of course, lost. Long after the others would have been happy to quit—Raymond kept talking about and telephoning to his bride—Rothstein insisted that the game keep going.

Finally the players had reached the limit of their physical endurance. Rothstein, in one last attempt to recoup, offered to cut

Raymond high card for $40,000. Raymond, holding a handful of Rothstein's confetti, took him up.

They cut and Raymond won. He had another piece of confetti.

Now came the moment of settling up. McManus was a loser. He maintained he dropped $51,000 in cash. Bowe lost $5,700. All the others were winners. Raymond was ahead $219,000 on paper. Bernstein's winnings were $73,000. Thompson's amounted to $30,000. All these winnings were potential, not actual. They were represented by Rothstein's I.O.U.'s.

Rothstein collected his markers from the other players, totaled them, called out the amount and then tore them up. His word was all that the "winners" now had. In addition, during the course of play, some $19,000 in cash had gone into Rothstein's pockets. He was that much ahead in hard money.

At least two of the gamblers who remained in the apartment were baffled and irritated. Raymond said bitterly, "Not even a scratch." He meant he did not even have Rothstein's scrawled initials on a piece of paper. Thompson, more philosophic, asked, "Is this the way he always does business?"

"That's A.R.," McManus said. "Hell, he's good for it."

The New York gamblers—Bernstein, Bowe and Boston—all voiced agreement. Bernstein, laughing, said, "You fellows want to sell your paper? I'll buy it at a discount."

Neither Raymond nor Thompson took Bernstein up. While they did not know Rothstein as these others did, they knew his reputation.

McManus said, "He'll be calling you in a couple of days."

That was normal procedure with such an obligation as that which Rothstein had incurred. Raymond and Thompson knew this.

But they were not called. Not in a day or two. Not even after a week had passed. And then a rumor spread about town that Rothstein was going to ignore the money he owed, that he was not going to pay off. His reason: he claimed the game had been crooked.

Rothstein told Nicky Arnstein, "A couple of people told me the game was rigged."

Arnstein, thinking of the marked cards, the holdouts, the quick—

and crooked—shuffles from which Rothstein had profited through the years, said, "Arnold, rigged or not, you have to pay off. Even if it was crooked, no point to your advertising you were a sucker."

The word got to Damon Runyon (he told about it in the obituary he wrote a little later) and he taxed Rothstein with welching. "I never welch," Rothstein said. "I'm just making them sweat a little."

That was more like it. Rothstein could be looking for a chance to buy back his I.O.U.'s at cut rate.

His tactics, if these were his tactics, were effective. Sid Stajer brought Rothstein a message from Raymond. "Raymond says he'll do business. He wants to go home."

"The longer he waits the more he'll want to go home."

Finally Jimmy Hines came to Rothstein as an emissary from McManus. It was a peculiar position for Hines, whose notes and I.O.U.'s were in Rothstein's safe, long overdue. But Hines was McManus' "shammus," his protector, his link with Tammany Hall. "You've got to pay off, Arnold," he said. "You've put George in a bind."

"They'll get their money," Rothstein snapped. "But when I want to give it to them and not a minute before."

This was all the answer Hines could bring back to McManus. It wasn't enough to satisfy.

McManus was being pressed from two directions. As host of the evening he had an obligation to the players who had taken part in the game. True, Rothstein owed the money, but Raymond and Thompson had a right to look to him to collect for them. Bad as this was, he probably could have handled the situation. What struck even deeper was the charge that a game he had arranged was a crooked game. To a gambler "a good name is better than precious ointment."

Angered, worried, McManus, always a heavy drinker, now began to drink even more. And, half drunk, he threatened dire things to Rothstein if the debts were not paid and McManus' reputation cleared. Among those to whom he said such things was Willie McCabe.

McCabe was a hard-talking hoodlum and a dope addict. He had

adopted the sobriquet "Tough Willie," and did his best to live up to it. He carried a gun and had been involved in a number of hold-ups and hijackings. Not quite a punk, he was a long way from being a big shot. He was still looking to make a name for himself.

Now McCabe saw an opportunity to establish himself. He would force Rothstein to pay off. Like the clichés in the Western stories, McCabe, the embryonic killer, would take on the man with the notches on his gun. Normally, McManus would have laughed off the suggestion. But McManus was not normal. Worry and whisky had unbalanced him. He gave the go-ahead to McCabe and told him he would give him ten per cent of the money he collected.

McCabe—he must have been "high" on dope—chose the corner of Forty-ninth Street and Broadway to make his attempt.

Rothstein was talking with Abe Stein, one of his drug salesmen, Damon Runyon and Leo Spitz were standing a yard away. (Spitz was the attorney who had been approached to act for Rothstein before the Chicago Grand Jury which had heard testimony about the 1919 Series.)

McCabe, ignoring passers-by, pushed Stein aside and said to Rothstein, "You, Rothstein. I want that money you owe McManus and I want it quick."

Rothstein looked at McCabe a long instant. He took in the glazed eyes, the stony face. He saw McCabe's right hand was in his pocket, a big bulge showing. Then, his voice larded with contempt, he said, "McCabe, I've taken care of harder men than you for years and I can take care of you. If you ever come near me again, I'll spit in your eye and run you out of town. Now, beat it."

McCabe's jaw dropped. He stared at Rothstein, unable to believe what he had heard. He gaped even more as Rothstein turned his back on him and resumed his conversation with Stein. After a long minute McCabe shook his head, turned and hurried across the street.

Runyon and Spitz, who had moved out of a direct line, now joined Rothstein. Telling of this encounter, Spitz said, "Rothstein never even raised a sweat. If we hadn't heard McCabe's words, we might have believed he had just stopped Rothstein to say 'hello.' "

On October 16 Carolyn came home from Europe. She returned to the Fifth Avenue apartment. Just as her stateroom had been filled with flowers when she departed, so now the apartment was filled for her return.

Rothstein came to see her that evening. His first words were "Have you changed your mind?"

"No," she answered. "I think a divorce would be best for us." She could not resist throwing a barb. "From what I've heard, I thought you had reached the same decision." This was, of course, a reference to Inez Norton, and he understood it immediately.

"She's a nice woman," he said. "I like her very much. But she isn't you. If you wanted it over, I could end it in two minutes." It was hardly a chivalrous remark.

She said, "I just want you to be happy, Arnold."

Then, for the first time in many years, he started to talk about his affairs. And not even in those long-ago days had he been as revealing as he now became. He told her of his deep involvement in the Juniper Park deal, of many calls on him for cash. And then he added, "I dropped a lot of money in a card game. I haven't paid it and I'm being hounded. I won't tap myself out to pay off. They can wait. God knows I've done a lot of waiting in my time."

"Are you in trouble, Arnold?"

He regained his self-control. His pale face resumed its normal blandness. "No," he said. "No trouble. I guess just seeing you has upset me."

In the next two weeks he made no further reference to any money troubles. He had moved from the apartment, but he talked to her regularly.

On November 2 the Rothsteins went to the office of John Glynn, Mrs. Rothstein's attorney. They chatted there for a few moments. Glynn was drawing up the papers for their divorce settlement.

Carolyn said, "If you'd like to make the monthly payments less, Arnold, I'll understand."

He flashed her a quick smile, patted her hand. "If you're thinking about what I said the other day, forget it. Even the Treasury runs short once in a while. I'd say I'm good for a million a year, Carolyn. Does that sound like I have to worry about a couple of thousand?"

"No," she said, "it doesn't."

They left Glynn's office together. He put her in a taxicab. As she looked through the rear window she saw Fats Walsh join him and the pair walked off.

The next time she saw him was in a hospital room.

Chapter **24** *His Usual, Normal Self*

If anything extraordinary marked Sunday, November 4, 1928, for Arnold Rothstein, it was the ordinary way he lived it from the time he arose until 10:47 that evening, when he was found on the service stairway of the Park Central Hotel, a bullet wound in his body.

There are some who would ascribe this to fatalism. Rothstein was part of a violent world and this made violence the norm for him. He was a gambler, a man who awaited the turn of the next card knowing he could not change it.

Russel Crouse, in *Murder Won't Out*, wrote: "The death of Arnold Rothstein was simple enough. Everyone in the world in which he moved knew that somewhere there was a bullet 'with his name on it.' Eventually it reached him. That was all."

Perhaps many did believe this, but Arnold Rothstein was not one of the many.

The gangster world was a world of murder and quick death. But Rothstein felt himself removed from this world. One step removed.

The people with whom he dealt made a business of wholesaling death. His partners and associates—Luciano, Yale, Marlow, Lepke, Anastasia, Madden and Duffy—filled the morgue with erstwhile competition. They made fair-trade laws with shotgun and machine gun.

He dealt with killers, had long lived among them. But he was not one of them. His was another, a higher, stratum.

He might have feared for his life if, like Beansy Rosenthal, he had broken the first commandment of the underworld: Thou shalt not squeal. But he held this commandment in reverence.

No, he did not think he was marked for death. Certainly not for failing to pick up his markers. Actually, that was a form of security. Nate Raymond bitterly pointed this out when he told the police, who questioned him after Rothstein's death, "Why should I have killed him? You can't collect from a corpse."

No, it was not fatalism, not the acceptance of anything the day might bring to him, that caused Rothstein to act on November 4 as he had acted on so many other Sundays in his life. It was his belief that nothing would happen—that nothing could happen—on this ordinary Sunday.

Leaving the hotel where he was living, now that he and Carolyn were separated, he went to his office. Freda Rosenberg was not there, but Sam Brown was waiting for him. The two went over ledgers, made up balance sheets. They recorded Rothstein's wagers on the elections, now just two days away.

This was complex, time-consuming. Rothstein had started betting early in September. His bets were scattered all over the country. The odds varied, from bet to bet, for Rothstein had shopped for the best price.

In addition, Rothstein had taken much lay-off money from bookies and betting commissioners throughout the country, money bet on both Hoover and Smith, on both Roosevelt and Ottinger.

Of course, he had bet "his opinion." That meant he had not merely brokered bets, but had gambled on the result himself. He had given odds of 3 to 1 on Hoover, had placed many bets at even money on the New York gubernatorial race. If Hoover and Roosevelt won, Rothstein stood to profit by approximately $570,000. If both should lose, his losses would be more than $1,250,000.

If Hoover won and Roosevelt lost, he would be a winner by $300,000. If Smith won and Ottinger lost, his losses would be almost $900,000. He had gone heavily down the line on Hoover, certain that this was as close to a sure bet as any election bet ever was.

His wagers had been made with bookmakers in Philadelphia, Boston, Chicago, Kansas City, St. Louis, Baltimore, and many local

New York bookmakers. They had been made orally, without Rothstein posting a dollar. His word had been enough for those with whom he had bet.

This, certainly, is overwhelming evidence that the underworld, so sensitive to such things, did not believe there was a bullet "with his name on it" in some anonymous, or known, gun. In the underworld there are few secrets. If Rothstein had been "no price," his bets would have found no takers.

To clinch this, Rothstein was to make at least one more bet that Sunday. To make it with Boston, who had participated in the poker game.

When Rothstein finished listing his election bets, he turned to office detail. He signed some checks, wrote a memorandum. He was preparing to leave—it was almost seven—when the phone rang. It was Unger, calling from the North Sheridan Hotel in Chicago. The police would find a record of this call when they made their narcotics raid in the hotel some weeks later.

After Rothstein talked with Unger, he left for the Fairfield Hotel to pick up Miss Norton for dinner. He did not have Walsh with him this evening, another sign that he was not filled with either fear or foreboding. He would see Walsh later, also at Lindy's.

He then met Miss Norton, went to the Colony, where they had dinner and where, as she told the police, he was his "usual, normal self."

After dining, he went to Lindy's, remained there until the call from room 349 in the Park Central. He had his short talk with Meehan and gave Meehan the gun. A gun for which he had a permit.

No sign, here, that he feared that bullet.

It was a few minutes later that the night ceased to be ordinary.

There had been nothing in his plans that called for him to be on the emergency operating table in Polyclinic Hospital before midnight of that ordinary Sunday.

And, while the surgeons worked on Rothstein, the police were searching for George McManus, alias "George Richards," who had been identified by many persons as the occupant of room 349. They did not find him. They did not know where to look. They could only have known had someone followed George McManus out of the hotel.

While the police were still getting the first fragmentary reports of the shooting, McManus was in a phone booth at the corner of Fifty-seventh Street and Eighth Avenue. He was calling Jimmy Hines.

After that phone call McManus went into the street, walked quickly uptown to the corner of Fifty-ninth Street. He waited, as Hines had told him to wait, on the northeast corner. That wait was about fifteen minutes.

A Buick sedan pulled up at the corner, a door opened, and someone called, "Get in." McManus got in.

The driver, the lone occupant of the car, was Abraham ("Bo") Weinberg, at that time Dutch Schultz's closest associate. Later Weinberg would be one of Schultz's victims. His would be a perfect murder, for he would be encased in cement up to his waist and dropped into the Hudson River.

Weinberg drove McManus to the Bronx. He told McManus that he had orders to hide him out. Schultz, Weinberg and the gang had an apartment on Mosholu Parkway. That was where Weinberg took McManus. That was the apartment in which McManus stayed for twenty-four days while police were "searching" for him "all over the United States."

After Rothstein was operated upon, and the bullet removed from his insides, he was placed in a private room. A uniformed policeman stood at the door, guarding it. A detective and a police stenographer were inside the room with the unconscious Rothstein.

The first bulletin, a medical bulletin, was given the horde of newspapermen who had rushed to the hospital. The bullet had entered Rothstein's body just above the groin, pursued a downward course as it ripped through several more or less vital organs, and severed an artery on its way. There had been much internal bleeding.

Rothstein's condition was given as "critical." Preparations were being made for transfusions. He had slight chance of recovery.

More police arrived, headed by Inspector John Coughlin, in charge of the Manhattan detective division. He was accompanied by Captain Edmund Meade, commander of the West Forty-seventh Street precinct, the precinct in which the shooting had taken place. A number of detectives, from the precinct squad and from the Broadway squad also were present, among them Detective Patrick Flood, of the Broadway squad.

Assistant District Attorney P. Francis Marro also appeared at the hospital. He had been having a late dinner on Broadway, seen the arrival of police cars and ambulances at the hotel, and had decided to check on what had happened. Now he asked the doctors in charge if he could interview Rothstein. He was told that Rothstein was in a coma.

Word of the shooting quickly reached Lindy's. A contingent of Rothstein's intimates, among them Cantor, Wellman, Stajer, Brown and Walsh hurried to the hospital. Cantor immediately took charge. He telephoned Jack Rothstein, who hurried to the hospital accompanied by the third brother, Edgar.

It was Walsh who notified Carolyn. He called her at home, told her, "Mr. Rothstein has been in an accident."

"Where is he?"

Walsh told her and said, "I'll call for you right away." He was driving Rothstein's car.

When she reached the hospital she was met by her two brothers-in-law and Dr. Philip Graussman, who had long been the Rothstein family physician. Jack Rothstein had summoned him.

At that moment Rothstein was being given a blood transfusion.

The police arranged for her to wait in an unoccupied room. Dr. Graussman joined her after a time and told her that Rothstein, after the transfusion, again had fallen unconscious. He had been given morphine to quiet the pain, serve as a sedative. (Those who live by the sword . . .)

Dr. Graussman suggested that she return to the apartment and wait there for a call from him. In that way she would be saved the importunities of the reporters and photographers. She agreed, was taken through a side door to the street, and went back home.

Not receiving a call by 4:30 in the morning, unable to rest, she went downstairs, found a taxi and returned to the hospital.

A few minutes later she was told, "Mr. Rothstein is asking for you."

His eyes were on the door as she came in. A slight amount of life came into them. He tried to raise himself from his pillow, but could not. As she reached him, he said, "I knew you'd be here."

"Of course," she answered. "Haven't I always been there when you needed me?"

He smiled at her. Then he asked, "Are they going to operate on me?"

She realized that he had no knowledge of the past hours. "Dr. Graussman doesn't think so."

"Well, if I don't need an operation, then I think I'll tell them I want to go home."

"Not yet," she said.

"You won't divorce me now, will you?"

"No. Not ever."

"When I'm well," he said, his voice weakening so it was hardly audible, "we'll go away somewhere. I've got plenty of money. All we'll ever need." Even now his thoughts were of money.

"Don't talk any more." She placed a cool hand on his hot, moist forehead.

"That feels good. I want to go home." His head dropped and he was once more in coma. A doctor and nurse bent over him. The doctor shook his head.

When Carolyn Rothstein left the room she was surrounded by police, reporters, photographers, relatives. "What did he say?" "Did he tell you who shot him?" "Who did it?" No one asked how he was. No one appeared to be concerned.

Maurice Cantor ranged alongside her. "Mrs. Rothstein has no statement to make."

She was taken to a vacant room, was joined there by Jack and Edgar Rothstein. A doctor came in, some time later. "He's unconscious. It looks like we'll have to give him more transfusions."

At noon, so tired she could hardly keep awake, she went home. At five o'clock that afternoon she returned to the hospital.

Some time during her absence Rothstein had a number of visitors. And during that period Rothstein signed a will, prepared by his attorney, Cantor, which named Cantor, Sid Stajer, and Inez Norton as beneficiaries along with Rothstein's family and Carolyn Rothstein.

One of the witnesses to the will was a nurse, Elizabeth F. Love, who testified concerning it at a hearing before Surrogate O'Brien. She was asked by Daniel J. Madigan, attorney for Cantor, who was seeking probate of the will:

"Did you see Mr. Rothstein make that mark [the X on the will] or was it made before you saw it?"

She answered, "Mr. Cantor put the pen in Mr. Rothstein's left hand and it stayed there until Mr. Cantor took the hand and wiggled it and made the mark."

"What did Mr. Rothstein do?"

"He didn't do anything."

"Did Mr. Cantor state that this was the last will and testament of Arnold Rothstein when he asked you to sign it?"

"He said, 'Arnold, this is your will, your will.' Rothstein's eyes were closed at this time, and after [Cantor] explaining over and over again to Mr. Rothstein, Rothstein said in a weak voice, 'Will.' Then Cantor said, 'This is your will, Arnold. I made it this morning, just as you asked me.'"

"In your opinion," Madigan then asked, "was Mr. Rothstein of sound mind when the will was executed?"

"He was irrational most of the time."

"How about the rest of the time?"

"He seldom spoke a thing that had any sense to it."

When Carolyn returned to the hospital she was told nothing of the will. She would learn about it when it was filed for probate. Then there would be a series of hearings as a result of a contest, like the one at which Miss Love testified, and, finally, a compromise which would void the deathbed will.

Carolyn was permitted to see Rothstein again, to speak to him again. She sat beside his bed in a room that was in semidarkness, as though a prelude to the complete darkness of death. She held his hand.

"I want to go home," he whispered. "All I do is sleep here. I can sleep home."

"You're not well enough to go home."

"I feel fine. Besides, I've got to." He made a movement to raise himself, but it was too much for him. "Don't go away," he said. "I need you."

"Not as long as you need me."

"I don't want to be alone. I can't stand being alone."

She pressed his hand.

Again he tried to raise himself. "I've got to go home." The words and the effort were too much for him.

The doctor and nurse rushed to the bed. The doctor gave Rothstein a hypodermic. But he was unconscious. He would not again be conscious.

The doctor said, "You better leave, Mrs. Rothstein."

Carolyn leaned over, kissed Rothstein. Then she left the room. It was the last time she saw him alive.

She was standing in the bare hospital room, staring out at the street, empty because the day was a holiday—Election Day—when Dr. Graussman came in and uttered the words she had been expecting. "Arnold is dead."

The tears came and ceased and came again.

The funeral was the next day. Rothstein was buried in the faith to which he had been born. He looked quite strange in his coffin, a white skullcap on his head, a purple-striped prayer shawl over the muslin shroud.

The coffin was closed.

It was fitting that Rothstein's last ride should be down Broadway.

The rabbi spoke a prayer for the soul of the dead man, "*Arkum, ben Avrahum.*"

His family stood by the grave. A few, only a few, of the people whom he had known, with whom he had lived, were at the services. They included all the beneficiaries of that last will except Inez Norton. Nate Raymond was there, as though taking a last look at a departed fortune.

A dozen detectives wandered among the spectators. There were some curious strangers who, not having known Rothstein in life, wanted to meet him now that he had departed it. The detectives thought they might find a clue to his killer among the curious.

It did not take long. A half hour and the mourners, the curious and the police were gone. Only the echo of the *Kaddish—"Yisgadal, Ve Yiskadash"*—hovered about the untidy brown mound of earth, Gone, too, was Arnold Rothstein. But he had left a heritage.

And a touch of irony.

The same newspapers that were filled with stories about his death reported that Hoover and Roosevelt had won the election. Rothstein's last bets were good bets. But they were uncollectible.

Carolyn Rothstein returned to the apartment. For days she would have visitors from the police, from the District Attorney's office. Her grief was an entry on the police blotter.

In the home of Abraham Rothstein the mirrors were again covered. The male members of the family walked without shoes. Their clothes were rent.

Maurice Cantor moved to have the will—that last will—filed for probate.

In the hideout, on Mosholu Parkway, George McManus sweated. Some miles away politicians and hoodlums were gathered to decide his fate.

In widely scattered locations throughout the world men waited for the word that would tell them what Rothstein's death meant to them. Drug buyers in Europe and Asia. Bankers in Switzerland. Convicts and indicted men, who were free on bail which Rothstein had either provided or guaranteed.

The police announced they were looking for McManus and for his flunky, collector and agent, Hyman ("Gillie") Biller. It came out that Biller had walked into the hands of the police while they were investigating in room 349. He had been told to stop bothering men hard at work. He had taken that directive literally.

The police did pick up three men and hold them temporarily. They were Fats Walsh, "Rothstein's bodyguard," George Uffner, "one of Rothstein's associates," and Charles Lucania, "a waiter." Notoriety had not yet come to Lucky Luciano.

The trio had come to Rothstein's office on Election Day and were charged with being "suspicious characters." They were all released later. The police did not know that their visit had been to check the whereabouts of the different caches of narcotics in this country, the supplies awaiting shipment from foreign countries, and any unfilled orders that ought to be met without delay. Business was business.

It was on Election Day, 1928, that Luciano became one of the two top men in the narcotics trade. Lepke Buchalter, more sensitive, waited until the period of mourning—and the heat—ended before he staked his claim.

Police Commissioner Joseph Warren and District Attorney Joab Banton issued regular bulletins. Inspector Coughlin, in charge of the investigation, said the newspapers were blowing up Rothstein's importance far out of proportion to reality. He denied categorically that Rothstein had any influence with the police or with politicians. He said Rothstein had long ago severed any gambling connections he might have had and that there was no evidence that he was linked with the narcotics racket.

"Our investigation reveals," he said, "that Rothstein was just a businessman who dealt in various forms of insurance."

As Rothstein would have remarked, had he heard this, Coughlin was "one hundred and ten per cent right."

Rothstein had even insured against the conviction of the man who had killed him.

Chapter **25** *The "Fix" Is In*

It took just three days for the rumors circulating in the city to be put into print.

On November 9, the New York *Daily News* said editorially:

"There has been a strange lassitude hampering the activities of detectives seeking to solve this crime, the most sensational Broadway murder since the killing of Herman Rosenthal in 1912. The wise ones along Broadway wagged their heads yesterday. They think the 'fix'—underworld argot for the use of influence restraining the police—is in."

Broadway—those "wise ones"—was right. The fix was in.

It was not lassitude, but fear and the instinct of self-preservation that marked the investigation of Rothstein's killing.

Only in one sense was there any real similarity between Rothstein's murder and that of Rosenthal. Both were gamblers who had been involved in politics. But Rosenthal had been a puny figure and Rothstein a massive one. Even more important, Rosenthal's death had been in 1912 and Rothstein's sixteen years later.

The world of 1912 was as dead as both gamblers. In that long-ago era Rosenthal, the four killers—even Becker—had been expendable. The politicians—Murphy, Foley, Sullivan—were the bosses.

In 1928 a Jack Zelig had been replaced by a Joe Masseria. Luciano, Costello, Lepke and Anastasia were not punks like Lefty Louie and his three accomplices. And the man who had taken over Becker's functions was the man who had been killed.

336

No. The politicians could not find expendables in 1928—unless they chose to make Hines and Marinelli and Olvany and Flynn expendable. That would be hara-kiri and the politicians were not interested in self-immolation.

There was, of course, the continuing pretense of action. Jimmy Walker, himself a victim of the politician-gangster relationship, called on the police department to find the killer.

The police announced they were looking for McManus, Biller and two persons whom they refused to name. They admitted that they had no real clues. No policeman called Jimmy Hines or Ed Flynn, in the Bronx. They could have helped the department.

Three weeks after the murder Walker publicly announced his dissatisfaction with the conduct of the police. He told a press conference in City Hall, "The police did not handle this [Rothstein] case properly." He gave his police commissioner, ailing, naïve Joseph Warren, "four days to solve the Rothstein case or resign."

Apparently there was one expendable. Warren.

Warren, already a dying man, was caught in forces beyond his understanding. He did the only thing he could do, he passed the buck to Coughlin. He ordered Coughlin to find the killer before the four-day deadline expired.

Coughlin, straight-faced, told reporters he would meet the deadline. His men were closing in on McManus.

But the four days passed.

The newspapers would not let the story die. They printed details of the slipshod police investigation. Why had there been no attempt by the police to question Rothstein while he was in the hospital?

But they had questioned Rothstein. Detective Flood had asked Rothstein who had killed him and had been told, "I'll take care of it myself." Further questioning had been precluded by Rothstein's condition. It had been forbidden by the doctors on the ground that any strain probably would kill Rothstein.

The newspapers pointed out that Rothstein's condition had not prevented his seeing hosts of others. It had not prevented the writing and signing of a last will and testament while Rothstein had purportedly been "of sound mind and body."

A list of those who had gone in and out of Rothstein's hospital room appeared in the newspapers. It included a dozen names—but that of only one policeman, Flood.

The police department had no comment.

District Attorney Joab H. Banton and his staff also were under attack. Banton announced he was doing his duty as he saw it. It was not "the function of this office to investigate, but to prosecute on the basis of evidence gathered by the police. When we get such evidence, we will act."

But Banton's hand was forced as early as November 9. On that day, William H. Hyman, an attorney retained by the Rothstein family, asked Banton to take immediate charge of all Rothstein's "books, records, ledgers and any papers having to do with Arnold Rothstein's business and financial affairs."

Then Hyman added solemnly, "If these papers are ever made public, there are going to be a lot of suicides in high places."

Banton said it had always been his intention to take over the papers, but that in order to protect the value of the estate and "the interest of the heirs" he was waiting until Rothstein's employees and associates could check these papers. "Many of them are necessary to the conduct of Rothstein's business."

They certainly were. So necessary that Luciano, Uffner and Walsh had hurried to them before Rothstein's body was cold. So necessary that a dozen others had gone through them before Banton, with the news photographers watching, took possession of them.

"There are more than 40,000 papers," Banton said, "but we believe that some of Rothstein's records might be missing."

One hundred and ten per cent right. They were.

United States Attorney Tuttle, as reported earlier, also wanted to see the records. Banton told him that he would make any evidence that came within the jurisdiction of federal authorities available to Tuttle just as soon as he found it.

Not content with this, Tuttle got a court order for the papers of the Rothmere Corporation, with the results already noted.

On November 14 Banton said that his search of the papers had yielded a "goldmine of pertinent information." He gave no details.

However, the New York *Post* printed that it had learned "checks made out to a prominent politician have been found. These total $75,000. Notes and I.O.U.'s from many persons important in political and official circles have already been discovered. Included among these is a note signed by a city Magistrate."

Banton refused to comment on the story.

His next action was to make a public plea for information concerning the crime. He offered immunity to anyone, except the actual killer, who would give him such evidence.

That same night Will Rogers, appearing in a Broadway show, asked the killer, if he was in the audience, to stand and take a bow. It became part of Rogers' nightly act.

Next Banton announced that he knew the names of all the persons who had been in room 349 on the night of the murder. "We know the killer of Rothstein," he said. "We do not know the motive but have had a half-dozen explanations from different sources."

Rogers decided this was too funny to burlesque.

On November 21 Banton announced that press of other duties was forcing him to assign the search of the Rothstein papers to two of his assistants and a police lieutenant, Richard Oliver. Oliver had been one of the detectives involved in the Dominic Henry case. The three, Banton said, would give him daily reports on anything of importance they might find.

Banton threw a bombshell the very next day. He rescinded his previous order. He said that the search promised little, that it was a "dreary and onerous task" which would take "many, many weeks" and he could not spare his two assistants from their regular tasks for that length of time. As to the papers—he was releasing them to attorneys who represented the different claimants to the Rothstein estate. He had been assured that, if they discovered anything that merited his attention, they would immediately inform him.

One of the attorneys was Nathan Burkan, a Tammany district leader!

Tuttle, who already had the Rothmere papers, protested this action. He got a court order permitting him to assign two men to go through the documents. However, his men could find no papers.

Burkan informed the court that they had, somehow, disappeared. They were, he swore, either lost or stolen. Filing case, ledgers, books —all gone!

A bitter chorus of protests rose. In addition to those of Tuttle, there were protests from Joseph K. Guerin, counsel for the trustee in Nicky Arnstein's bankruptcy, and from the Fidelity and Surety Company, major victim of the bond thefts of a decade earlier.

Guerin charged that the papers "undoubtedly would lead" to the recovery of millions in Liberty Bonds. "We have information that convinces us this is the case."

The Fidelity and Surety Company filed a sworn affidavit which declared that Rothstein was the "fountainhead" of a bond theft conspiracy and that at the time of his death he "had in his possession $4,000,000 of the missing securities or the proceeds, or had invested the proceeds in real estate or other fields and securities, so as to destroy, if possible, all means of identification."

Burkan then announced that a considerable portion of the papers had been found. Somehow a whole carload of documents had been mislaid, but they were being recovered slowly. All interested parties could examine them as they turned up.

Tuttle, Guerin and investigators for the casualty company grabbed these papers. They found nothing in them that, as far as the record shows, substantiated their charges. Guerin did say, however, that "one path leads straight to banks in Switzerland and Belgium." No one ever followed that path to the end.

On November 26 Nate Raymond, Jimmy Meehan, Alvin Thompson, Martin Bowe and Sid Stajer were arrested and charged with being material witnesses. All were held in bail of $100,000. No one had yet moved in to take Rothstein's place in the bail bond business, so they stayed in jail.

That same night Detective John Cordes received a phone call in which he was told that, if he wanted McManus, he would find him in a barbershop at 242nd Street and Broadway at seven o'clock the next morning. Cordes notified his superiors and the District Attorney's office of the call. He was ordered to go to the barbershop and, if McManus did appear, to bring him immediately to Banton's office.

Cordes kept his appointment. When he reached the barbershop, he found McManus being shaved. Cordes waited for the barber to finish. When McManus was powdered and perfumed, he greeted Cordes and the pair went downtown to the District Attorney's office.

McManus was placed under arrest, charged with murdering Rothstein. He refused to say anything about the killing, his whereabouts for three weeks, or his relations with Rothstein. He referred all questions to his attorney, brilliant, sardonic, James D. C. Murray.

On December 4, McManus, the missing Biller, John Doe and Richard Roe were indicted on murder charges.

A few days later Raymond, Thompson, Bowe and Meehan had their bail reduced to $10,000. This was provided quickly and they were free. Stajer, however, had to remain jailed for some time longer. It was not until January that his bail was cut and he was able to leave the Tombs.

At about the same time Walker removed Warren and appointed Grover Whalen in his place. In his autobiography, *Mr. New York,* Whalen told the circumstances behind his appointment. He said Walker visited him at his office in the old John Wanamaker store on Astor Place and said, "Grover, I've got to make a change of police commissioners. This Rothstein murder has raised hell."

Over his repeated objections, Whalen found himself the new commissioner. When he took office, there were two persons in jail because of the Rothstein murder. One was McManus and the other was Bridget Farry, the hotel maid who had been so vocal on the night of November 4 and had identified McManus. Both were being held without bail, McManus on a murder indictment and Mrs. Farry as a material witness.

In March, 1929, Murray obtained McManus' release on $50,000 bail. The courts had ordered Banton either to bring McManus to trial or permit him freedom on bail.

But no court came to the aid of Mrs. Farry.

The months passed.

New charges and sensations became daily occurrences. Soon after the fanfare concerning Rothstein's narcotics trade faded the New York *Sun* reported that Banton had evidence proving Rothstein had operated a most profitable "insurance racket" in connection with his legitimate business.

The paper said that Rothstein had been an accredited agent for some British and Canadian insurance companies. All issued health and accident policies.

As agent, Rothstein had insured such prominent Broadway personages as Marilyn Miller, Jeanne Eagels, Fannie Brice, Ethel Barrymore and Bea Palmer, the inventor of the "shimmy," who later became the highest paid singer in vaudeville and night clubs in the United States. However, it appeared that none of these persons, nor many others who were "insured," were aware of it.

The applications for the policies had been forged. So, too, had been reports of injuries and illnesses, doctors' certificates and numerous affidavits which had been presented to the three companies.

"At least one prominent actress," the *Sun* reported, "was insured . . . and a claim for an accident was paid although at the time she was appearing in New York and had no accident. It is charged her name was forged to the affidavit, and that the name of a doctor who does not exist was signed to the physician's certificate which accompanied a claim for $20,000."

Banton admitted that he was conducting an inquiry. However, his office reported some months later, that it had been dropped at the request of the insurance companies involved.

Rothstein's name remained in the headlines as three different groups contested for his estate. A compromise was reached which gave all the contestants something. The preliminary value set on the estate was $2,510,497. Later this was revised upward to $3,200,000.

The *New York Times* reported that Rothstein was the owner of realty and other property with a gross value of some $23,000,000 and his equity in these properties was more than $3,000,000.

The executors of the estate announced they were seeking repayment of loans amounting to more than a million dollars. They filed various suits, among them one against Frank Costello. Costello pleaded the statute of limitations, but was ordered to pay the estate $40,000 plus interest.

Others listed in the suits included speakeasy owners, restaurant operators, theater owners, bookmakers, attorneys, actors, private detectives, clothing manufacturers, and gamblers. Ironically, among the gamblers was Alvin Thompson, against whom a judgment for $12,700 was obtained.

There was something peculiar, still not explained, about how Thompson came to borrow money from Rothstein on October 22, 1928, and November 1, 1928. At that time Thompson was holding— or was supposed to be holding—Rothstein's I.O.U. for considerably more than that sum. This was the money Thompson had won in the McManus-Meehan poker game.

Thompson never explained the loan. But, then, he never satisfied the judgment either.

In July, 1929, Fats Walsh was murdered in Florida. The Rothstein story was back in the headlines. The police said that Walsh's murder had nothing to do with that of Rothstein. Walsh, they said, had told them he had quit Rothstein's employ back in May, 1928. They quoted Walsh as saying Rothstein was "too cheap and tight with his dough."

The police did not bother to explain how Walsh happened to have been at Lindy's the night Rothstein was killed, how he happened to be driving Rothstein's car, how he happened to have called Carolyn Rothstein.

By July, 1929, the police seemingly had run out of explanations or had decided there was no use in making them.

A municipal election was held in 1929. Fiorello LaGuardia, then a Congressman, was named by the Republicans to run against Walker. He made an issue of the Rothstein case, but not as big a one as he was to make of it four years later.

Banton, speaking for the administration, though not a candidate for re-election, said he would try McManus as soon as he located

Biller. He had "sufficient evidence to convict McManus and Biller together, but not enough to try McManus alone."

Murray said he would move for dismissal of the indictment unless McManus was brought to trial.

Reluctantly—and shortly before the election in which Walker soundly defeated LaGuardia—Banton permitted the case to be set for trial immediately after the election, a year after Rothstein's death. It was to be the last case Banton would try as district attorney.

The case which Banton finally presented was pathetically weak. He had little evidence, no witnesses. Bridget Farry, at last freed from jail, was a prosecution witness nominally, but a defense witness actually. Made forgetful by her long stay in jail, she looked at McManus and swore that McManus was not the man she had seen in room 349 on the night that Rothstein was shot.

The players at the poker game gave no useful evidence. And all of them had ironclad alibis for November 4, 1928.

When the prosecution completed its "case," the defense asked for a directed verdict of acquittal. Judge Charles C. Nott granted the request and McManus was adjudged innocent.

Surrounded by his family, his counsel and his friends, McManus left the courtroom wearing the Chesterfield overcoat which had, only a few minutes earlier, been marked as a prosecution exhibit.

Commenting on the trial in his autobiography, Whalen wrote:

"The failure to present incontrovertible evidence sufficient for a conviction was due entirely to the laxity of the police who had been assigned to the case originally, and to the commanding officers of the detective and uniformed forces at the time of the murder."

Some three weeks later Thomas C. T. Crain succeeded Banton as district attorney of Manhattan. Asked about the murder and subsequent trial, Crain replied, "I don't know anything about the Rothstein case at the present time, but I think it should be solved."

It was a pious wish. It remains a pious wish today, a generation later. Legally the case remains unsolved. No one has ever been found guilty of firing the bullet which killed Rothstein. The case is marked "open" in the records of the New York City police department.

To quote Whalen again: "The case has never been fully explained, and, as the laws of our country provide, every man must be considered innocent until proven guilty. McManus died a natural death in Sea Girt, New Jersey, in 1940."

The truth is buried with McManus, with Hines, with Edward J. Flynn, with Dutch Schultz, with Bo Weinberg, and, of course, with Arnold Rothstein.

The story the underworld has long believed, and which it still repeats, is this:

Rothstein entered room 349 to be confronted by a man half crazed by drink and frustration. This man pulled a gun on Rothstein and held it on him. Rothstein, never a coward, tried to take the gun away from him, or push it aside. In the scuffle the gun was discharged and a bullet entered Rothstein's body.

Suddenly sober, the killer fled. And Rothstein gathered his strength and walked down the two long flights of stairs to where Vince Kelly found him.

Legally the killing was not murder but manslaughter. It might even have been considered "involuntary manslaughter." But the killer was not fleeing possible electrocution. He was fleeing from all the other effects the shooting could have.

Only the sheerest accident—the most outrageous fluke—could have resulted in the solution of the killing. Too many politicians, too many gangsters, too much money, too many reputations joined in covering up the facts.

The police knew this. The District Attorney knew it. Pressure came from both the Hines and Marinelli factions in Tammany, who wanted secrecy, not exposure. Secrecy concerning the killing and even more secrecy about Rothstein's records and papers. These latter were more frightening to them than anything else. They knew the killer; they did not know what Rothstein might have put—or received—in writing.

Banton went through a series of futile, panicky maneuvers, not knowing from one day to another what orders he would be getting from the politicians to whom he owed so much. He permitted himself to be made a fool, a buffoon.

Whatever case he might have had against McManus was dissipated during the year between shooting and trial. He antagonized his best witness, Bridget Farry. He allowed other witnesses to disappear. When he did go to trial, it was an empty gesture.

The police department also was immobilized. It did not matter that Whalen replaced Warren. Whalen was honest, sincere, well-intentioned. But he was an amateur in politics. The department knew that commissioners came and went, but Tammany's influence went on forever.

When Whalen called on his men to solve the murder, they knew—if he did not—that they were being asked to reveal the inner workings of the politician-underworld relationship. Some police did not care to do this and others did not dare to.

So Whalen became the unwitting and unwilling victim of The System, 1929 model.

Consider the cover-up, the forces fighting to hide the facts. Remember how little—how small a portion—of the truth was ever made known. And against these weigh the overwhelming effects of that murder. Examine the results of Rothstein's death. The political results.

LaGuardia was the first to profit from it. The *Times* commented editorially on October 6, 1929, that the Rothstein murder had "wrecked one police administration, vexes another, and has become one of the most important topics of the current municipal election campaign."

Ernest Cuneo, LaGuardia's former law clerk, wrote in *Life with Fiorello:*

"[In 1929] LaGuardia's immediate future was to be shaped by a seemingly unrelated series of events . . . begun with a gambling game and a pistol shot. . . .

"The gentleman on the receiving end of the bullet was, of course, Arnold Rothstein, Banker to the Underworld, one of the most verminous characters ever to infest New York City.

"If Rothstein alive had been an unsavory article, Rothstein dead was a calamity. His activities had not been limited to the dregs of society; on the contrary, certain of his dealings had involved some very eminent citizens indeed. . . ."

One of these citizens, LaGuardia revealed in his 1929 campaign, was Magistrate Albert H. Vitale.

Recall that during the period when authorities, Rothstein's associates, his heirs, and others were playing "button, button, who's got the button?" with the Rothstein papers, all admitted that some of the papers had disappeared. Many hoped that they had disappeared forever.

At least one had not. That was a promissory note given Rothstein by Vitale in the amount of $19,400. Somehow it had come into LaGuardia's possession. And LaGuardia used it, albeit not successfully, in 1929. However, it started a chain reaction—this one paper out of some forty thousand.

Vitale was removed from office in 1930 for borrowing the money. He said it had been for "speculative purposes." The Appellate Division of the Supreme Court also investigated a charge that Vitale had been influenced by Rothstein to dismiss robbery charges against Charles Fawcett. It found him "guilty of gross carelessness, inattention, ignorance and incompetency" in the case. But it did not find him criminally liable, declaring, "a public official should not be removed from office for a single act of carelessness."

However, that was academic. The court had already agreed to remove Vitale for making the loan.

Because of the Vitale case, an investigation of the Magistrates' Courts of New York was begun. It resulted in a number of removals and resignations, revealed the close ties between the minor judiciary and Tammany.

This brought on the Seabury investigation.

To be followed by the appointment of Thomas E. Dewey as special prosecutor.

Next came numerous prosecutions, including the jailing of Lucky Luciano. (Luciano was freed a number of years later by the same Dewey, then governor of New York, who has never made public his reasons for the action.)

A further result of these inquiries was Walker's resignation as mayor, after a series of hearings before Governor Roosevelt, which took the Tammany curse off Roosevelt and put him in the lead for the Democratic presidential nomination in 1932.

It enabled William Randolph Hearst to pay back his old Tammany enemies, and their descendants, for the slights of a generation earlier.

As for Tammany itself, the results of Rothstein's death were cumulative.

First came the resignation of Olvany as leader. He was succeeded by mousy, white-mustached John F. Curry, an Irish district leader who got the job because he was supported by Marinelli and his gangster associates.

Hines, forced out of a position of power within Tammany, joined with Dutch Schultz's other good friend, Edward J. Flynn, and the two held control of federal and state patronage. Their feud with Tammany made it possible for LaGuardia to win, in 1933, the mayoralty that had escaped him in 1929.

With Rothstein's death, the balance within Tammany was upset for good. The gangsters gained ascendancy over the politicians, and the Italian gangsters ascendancy over the Irish. The hoodlums were now the senior partners in the conspiracy against decent government.

No wonder Cuneo wrote: "The trail of blood left by the dying Rothstein led straight to the paths of corruption within the city machine."

Corruption that had been shaped, taught, and for so long administered by Arnold Rothstein.

Chapter 26 No One . . . Resembles Him

Skip a decade.

On March 1, 1938, Jack Rothstone, executor of the estate of his late brother, Arnold Rothstein, filed an accounting of the estate with the Surrogate of New York County. He listed no assets.

Jack Rothstone asked the Surrogate to declare the estate bankrupt.

What had happened to the millions?

The first accountings filed with the Surrogate in 1928, in 1929, had shown assets that aggregated as much as $3,000,000, none less than $2,510,947. But that had been before the depression.

While Rothstein's assorted sets of heirs, named in his numerous wills, fought each other, realty values collapsed. Equities in various properties became deficiencies. The Juniper Park tract, none of its houses ever rented, all of them finally condemned and destroyed, was sold to satisfy a tax judgment. The golf course went the way of Juniper Park.

First the Fairfield Hotel, then other Manhattan realty, was foreclosed by mortgage holders and sold at auction.

And what of those who had owed Rothstein money?

No one ever paid a dead man. Some, like Fats Walsh and Larry Fay, had been gunned to death. Others, like Sid Stajer and Jimmy Meehan, were in jail. More had disappeared, were out of the jurisdiction of the court, beyond the reach of process servers.

From all this, the New York *Herald Tribune* drew a moral: It said editorially:

"Thus the descent from glory. . . .

"Rothstein was a unique figure in the life of this city. No one has arisen since his death who resembles him very closely, which is probably all for the best. . . .

"No one need be much surprised that the fruits of his life and works turned out to be no more substantial than a structure he might have built out of a deck of his own well riffled cards."

The *Herald Tribune* was taking editorial license.

True, there was none in 1938 who resembled Rothstein very closely. Ten years had passed, a new era had been born. But it owed so much to the old. As what era does not owe to the past?

There were no more dinosaurs after the Mesozoic era. And the mastodon disappeared with the end of the Pleistocene epoch. But then came the elephant, heir to the latter, better adapted to the world in which he lived.

In 1938 there was no Rothstein. But there were Frank Costello, Lepke Buchalter, Albert Anastasia, Joe Adonis, Frank Erickson. Elephants all, in New York. They occupied the main room of the structure Rothstein had erected. The politicians sat in the anteroom.

Jimmy Hines was drawing his weekly pay from the policy racket. But not for much longer. And it would be he, not the gangsters, who would go to jail.

Magistrate Aurelio, nominated by both Republican and Democratic parties, knew who had really nominated him. He called Frank Costello to express his gratitude, to pledge that gratitude. He knew to whom it belonged.

Murder, Inc., Albert Anastasia, president and chairman of the board, operated from its Brooklyn headquarters. Abe Reles, high on its table of organization, decided to squeal, to name names. He was held under 24-hours-a-day surveillance, policemen always with him. Yet he managed to "commit suicide." That was what the police, straight-faced, called it.

These may not have been dinosaurs or mastodons, but they stomped hard.

So Jack Rothstone asked the court to adjudge his brother's estate bankrupt. He listed a number of uncollectible assets. And some, of course, he excluded.

The tribute workers paid to hoodlums who controlled their unions. The workers were still getting the "protection" for which they had paid Rothstein. Their employers were involved with hoodlums, as they had been with Rothstein, partners and victims at the same time.

The dope traffic flourished, greater, more profitable than ever. Yasha Katzenberg was roving the world, buying supplies. George Uffner was making deals. No longer with Rothstein, of course, but with Costello, Luciano, Buchalter. (Unlisted heirs, who had found the estate solvent, very solvent indeed.)

Frank Erickson was now king of the lay-off men. His profit from gambling was great. Rothstein had shown him how to wholesale gambling.

The System remained. Different from that long-ago era when Lincoln Steffens first described and named it. Different from what it had been when Herbert Bayard Swope wrote about it in 1912. Different, indeed, from what it had been when Rothstein died in 1928.

But the difference stemmed from Rothstein, traced to him.

He had led crime into the business era. He had shaped it so it could survive in this new age. That had been the historical function he had performed.

His death accelerated some of the changes for which he was responsible. The changes, certainly, were inevitable, would surely have come with the repeal of prohibition.

Rothstein's age was dying at the time he was dying. A few more years of life might have made him an atavism.

It is probable that, gambler that he was, player of hunches, he was aware of this. The evidence is there. His last, desperate gambles. His pouring so much of his fortune into that one, big bet on narcotics. His delay in paying debts he knew he must pay.

Look at him in those last days. He must have known his power—still great—rested in his political importance. And even that was

lessening as Tammany canted, ever more, toward Marinelli, toward
Masseria, toward Costello.

Above all else, Rothstein knew the power of the bankroll. And
he knew that the gangsters—the owners of mass crime—had the
biggest. They could buy whatever they wanted—including politicians.

He could take rueful credit for having taught so well. He had
led them, but they were getting ready to knock him down in the
rush.

Where he had found a few legitimate fields in which to invest
his illegitimate gains, they had found many, would find more. They
would invest in distilleries and savings banks, hotels and oil wells,
race tracks and finance companies, breweries and dress factories.

He had shown the gangsters how to work with politicians, how,
in so many instances, to make the politicians work for them. But
Frank Costello, who replaced him, did not have to work with politicians. He was the boss.

Alas, poor Tammany!

And where Rothstein had been limited by the boundaries of New
York City, Costello knew no boundaries.

In May, 1929, he called a meeting at which were present all the
important gang leaders of the Atlantic seacoast. There that part of
Rothstein's estate which never was listed in any will was divided.
The "hidden" assets.

Dope to Lucky and Lepke.

Bookmaking to Erickson.

The garment center—what Rothstein still had of it—to Lepke.

A general agreement that Costello would run the political empire.

A few years later the lesson learned in New York, the lessons
taught by Rothstein, would be detailed at a meeting of gang bosses
from all over the country.

Kastel and Meyer Lansky could have New Orleans.

Buggsy Siegel could have Las Vegas and Southern California.

Longy Zwillman was given New Jersey.

Willie Moretti was allotted Florida.

And what did they share? The sources of income that Rothstein had first developed.

And the *Herald Tribune* reported: "the fruits of his life and works turned out to be no more substantial than a structure he might have built out of a deck of his own well riffled cards."

No, Rothstein left a most substantial legacy indeed.

He died, victim of a bullet wound inflicted in room 349 of the Park Central Hotel in 1928. Albert Anastasia, one of his heirs, was murdered in a barbershop of that same hotel in 1957 because he was seeking to take over control of the domain Rothstein had created.

The premise of this book—the reason it was written—was that Arnold Rothstein exerted a major influence on today's society, that he helped shape it. That it bears his mark.

The bullets that killed Anastasia provide a bitter emphasis to proof of that premise.

BIBLIOGRAPHY

ALLEN, FREDERICK LEWIS. *The Big Change.*
———. *Lords of Creation.*
———. *Only Yesterday.*
ANSLINGER, H. J., and WILLIAM F. TOMPKINS. *The Traffic in Narcotics.*
ASBURY, HERBERT. *Gangs of New York.*
———. *Great Illusion,* an informal history of Prohibition.
———. *Sucker's Progress,* an informal history of gambling in the United States, from the colonies to Canfield.
BEARD, CHARLES and MARY. *Rise of American Civilization.*
BERGER, MEYER. *The Eight Million.*
———. *The Story of the New York Times.*
BRADLEY, HUGH. *Such Was Saratoga.*
BROWN, HENRY COLLINS. *Brownstone Fronts and Saratoga Trunks.*
———. (ed.). *Valentine's Manuals.*
CLARKE, DONALD HENDERSON. *In the Reign of Rothstein.*
———. *Man of the World.*
Collier's. "Nick the Greek," series by Richard Donovan and Hank Greenspun. April 2-30, 1954.
CRANE, MILTON (ed.). *Sins of New York.*
CROUSE, RUSSEL. *It Seems Like Yesterday.*
———. *Murder Won't Out.*
CROWELL, CHESTER T. *Liquor, Loot and Ladies.*
CUNEO, ERNEST. *Life with Fiorello.*
DAVIS, CLYDE BRION. *Something for Nothing.*
DE CASSERES, BENJAMIN. *Mirrors of New York.*
FEDER, SID, and JOACHIM JOESTEN. *The Luciano Story.*
FERBER, NAT. *I Found Out.*
FITZGERALD, F. SCOTT. *The Great Gatsby.*
FLOYD, WILLIAM. *People Versus Wall Street.*
Forum. "Honesty in Politics" by Richard F. Warner. April, 1931.
FOWLER, GENE. *Beau James.*
———. *The Great Mouthpiece.*
GILPATRIC, GUY. *Brownstone Front.*
HARLOW, ALVIN F. *Old Bowery Days.*
HILL, JOHN, JR. *Gold Bricks of Speculation.*
HOLBROOK, STEWART H. *Age of the Moguls.*
JOHNSON, GERALD. *Incredible Tale.*
JOSEPHSON, MATTHEW. *Robber Barons.*
KATKOV, NORMAN. *Fabulous Fanny.*

KEFAUVER, ESTES. *Crime in America.*

LAMB, MRS. MARTHA J., and MRS. BURTON HARRISON. *History of the City of New York* (3 vols.).

LEFEVRE, EDWIN. *Making of a Stockbroker.*

————. *Reminiscences of a Stockbroker.*

LEVINSON, EDWARD. *Labor on the March.*

LEWIS, ALFRED HENRY. *Apaches of New York.*

LYNCH, DENNIS TILDEN. *Boss Tweed.*

MERZ, CHARLES. *The Dry Decade.*

MINNIGERODE, MEADE. *Certain Rich Men.*

MORELL, PARKER. *Diamond Jim.*

————. *Lillian Russell.*

MORRIS, LLOYD. *Postscript to Yesterday.*

MOSS, FRANK. *The American Metropolis* (3 vols.).

MOTTRAM, R. H. *History of Financial Speculation.*

New Republic. "Racketeer," by Louis Adamic. January 7, 1931.

NICOLSON, HAROLD. *Dwight Morrow.*

PARKHURST, REV. CHARLES H., D.D. *Our Fight with Tammany.*

PEEL, ROY V. *The Political Clubs of New York City.*

PETTEY, GEORGE E. *The Narcotics Drug Diseases and Allied Ailments.*

PRALL, ROBERT H., and NORTON MOCKRIDGE. *This Is Costello.*

Reader's Digest. "Gangsters in the Dress Business," by Lester Velie. July, 1955.

REYNOLDS, QUENTIN. *The Fiction Factory.*

RICE, GEORGE GRAHAM. *My Adventures with Your Money.*

RINGEL, FRED J. (ed.). *America as Americans See It.*

ROTHSTEIN (BEHAR), CAROLYN. *Now I'll Tell.*

SEIDMAN, HAROLD. *The Labor Czars.*

SEIDMAN, JOEL. *The Needle Trades.*

SIEGFRIED, ANDRE. *America Comes of Age.*

STEFFENS, LINCOLN. *Autobiography.*

STODDARD, WILLIAM LEAVITT. *Financial Racketeering and How to Stop It.*

SULLIVAN, EDWARD DEAN. *Chicago Surrenders.*

————. *The Labor Union Racket.*

SULLIVAN, MARK. *Our Times* (6 vols.).

TERRETT, COURTENAY. *Only Saps Work.*

THOMPSON, CRAIG. *Gang Rule in New York.*

TURKUS, BURTON B., and SID FEDER. *Murder, Inc.*

VAN DEVANDER, CHARLES. *The Big Bosses.*

VAN EVERY, EDWARD. *Sins of America.*

————. *Sins of New York.*

VAN WYCK, FREDERICK. *Recollections of an Old New Yorker.*

WALKER, STANLEY. *Mrs. Astor's Horse.*

————. *Night Club Era.*

WALL, E. BERRY. *Neither Pest nor Puritan.*

WASHBURN, WATSON, and EDMUND DeLONG. *High and Low Financiers.*

WERNER, M. R. *Tammany Hall.*

WESTON, PAUL B. (ed.). *Narcotics U.S.A.*

WHALEN, GROVER. *Mr. New York.*

WILEY, HARVEY W. *History of the Crime Against the Food Law.*

WINKLER, JOHN K. *Morgan the Magnificent.*

WYCKOFF, RICHARD D. *Wall Street Ventures and Adventures.*

Yale Review. "When Politics Seasons Justice," by Raymond Moley. Spring, 1932.

Index

Printed in the United States
40818LVS00003B/127